T0323810

THE OPIOID EPIDEMIC

The Opioid Epidemic

Origins, Current State and Potential Solutions

ETHAN O. BRYSON
Icahn School of Medicine at Mount Sinai, New York

CHRISTINE E. BOXHORN
Medical College of Wisconsin, Milwaukee

CAMBRIDGE
UNIVERSITY PRESS

CAMBRIDGE
UNIVERSITY PRESS

Shaftesbury Road, Cambridge CB2 8EA, United Kingdom

One Liberty Plaza, 20th Floor, New York, NY 10006, USA

477 Williamstown Road, Port Melbourne, VIC 3207, Australia

314–321, 3rd Floor, Plot 3, Splendor Forum, Jasola District Centre,
New Delhi – 110025, India

103 Penang Road, #05–06/07, Visioncrest Commercial, Singapore 238467

Cambridge University Press is part of Cambridge University Press & Assessment,
a department of the University of Cambridge.

We share the University's mission to contribute to society through the pursuit of
education, learning and research at the highest international levels of excellence.

www.cambridge.org
Information on this title: www.cambridge.org/9781009256575

DOI: 10.1017/9781009256551

First published 2023

A catalogue record for this publication is available from the British Library.

A Cataloging-in-Publication data record for this book is available from the Library of Congress.

ISBN 978-1-009-25657-5 Paperback

CONTENTS

FOREWORD

Persons with substance use disorders have been noted since antiquity. Explanations regarding the cause of these disorders have changed over time. For centuries, these disorders were viewed as moral weaknesses falling under the purview of religious leaders. In the eighteenth century, economic incentives enticed the British to export opium to China. The adverse health effects of opium lead the Chinese and others to take legal actions to suppress this trade. By the late nineteenth century, persons with substance use disorders were frequently regarded as criminals. In the early twentieth century, restrictive laws formally criminalizing the nonmedical use of many psychoactive substances were enacted. Even the United States Constitution was amended to prohibit "the manufacture, sale, or transporting of intoxicating liquors" within the United States. By the mid-twentieth century the amendment to the constitution had been repealed and persons with substance use disorders were thought to have a "spiritual malady" by some (e.g., Alcoholics Anonymous). Others viewed substance use disorders as a behavioral problem or a mental illness. The 130-page first edition of the American Psychiatric Association's *Diagnostic and Statistical Manual*, published in 1952, listed "alcoholism," "drug addiction," "alcoholic intoxication (simple drunkenness)," and three chronic brain syndrome disorders associated with intoxication among its list of 106 mental disorders.

Treatment of these disorders consisted of patient participation in self-help programs, professional counseling, or a combination of both. However, positive treatment outcomes were limited. Most recently, a "medical model" has guided treatment of substance use disorders. The current thinking is that substance use disorders are "brain diseases" amenable to pharmaceutical treatments. In the United States, acamprosate, disulfiram, and naltrexone are approved for the treatment of alcohol use disorder; whereas, buprenorphine, methadone, and naltrexone are approved for the treatment of opioid use disorder. Research has focused on finding new medications that can be used for the treatment of other substance use disorders. Meanwhile, many medications have been used "off label" for the treatment of substance use disorders. Addiction medicine is a newly recognized medical subspecialty in the United States that focuses on the prevention, diagnosis, treatment, and long-term care of patients with substance use disorders, and physicians in this new specialty are poised to help advance our understanding and treatment of these disorders.

It is the brain that produces behavior. One common explanation about addiction involves dopamine, dubbed the "feel-good neurotransmitter" that is part of the brain's reward system designed to help with survival. In this version of the medical model, the use of certain substances triggers dopamine release or a so-called "dopamine rush." These dopamine rewards might even be produced by activities that do not involve drugs and are said to explain the compulsive behaviors of other "addictions" such as habitual gambling or excessive sexual activity. Yet, this concept is all too simplistic. The brain's microanatomy is extremely complex, plastic, and not well defined. Brain physiology is also extraordinarily complex and involves the convoluted interplay of neurotransmitters, receptors, reuptake proteins, ligand-gated ion channels, protein phosphorylation, single nucleotide polymorphisms, gene expression, epigenetic regulation, messenger RNA synthesis, and protein synthesis. How exactly does a neurological system designed to support survival become corrupted to produce the compulsive use of alcohol or drugs despite negative consequences? How do environmental factors such as socioeconomic status, cultural elements, or community norms influence the expression of genetic predispositions? The future will shed more light on exactly how the brain works to produce the behaviors associated with substance use disorders.

Objective tests such as laboratory analyses or medical imaging assist physicians with the clinical diagnosis of many medical and surgical conditions. These tests are based on an understanding of the underlying pathophysiology or the principle anatomical abnormalities of medical or surgical maladies. This is not true of mental illnesses since the underlying pathological processes are not known. As such, the diagnosis of a substance use disorder is based solely on the patient's symptoms and the subjective observation of behaviors. With an improved understanding about how the brain works, the diagnosis of mental illness will finally be based on chemical analyses, medical imaging, or other objective data.

It is difficult to accurately imagine the future of addiction medicine. Could sixteenth-century physicians even begin to imagine that antibiotics would someday be developed to treat and cure "consumption" given that it was not even known that bacteria existed until Antoine Van Leeuwenhoek observed them in mid-century? Undoubtedly, newer and more effective treatments will also emerge based on an improved understanding of the pathophysiology of substance use disorders along with testing methods that will identify specific etiologies. In the not too distant future, genetic testing could be available and used to identify those at risk for a specific substance use disorder, perhaps even in neonates. Subsequently, preventive measures could be aimed at preventing the onset of the disorder. It could also become possible for testing to identify the specific genetic cause of a substance use disorder in a given patient so that a specific targeted treatment could be delivered. Before moving forward, it is important to understand where we are and how we got here. Even though the substance use disorders are common and are associated with tremendous biopsychosocial consequences, there exists a vacuum of information for medical practitioners concerned with the management of the substance use disorders leaving them ill-prepared to manage those who suffer the repercussions of these disorders.

This book provides more background information about opioid use disorder and the opioid epidemic: a historical perspective, the epidemiology, the contribution of biological and socioeconomic factors, the role of governmental drug policies, related criminal activity, the use of "drug courts," medical problems secondary to opioid use, and the economic burdens placed on society. The current state of the diagnosis, harm reduction, treatment, and prevention of these disorders are each detailed within. Treatment issues that are addressed include the management of acute opioid withdrawal symptoms (AKA "detoxification"), outpatient and inpatient treatment programs, long-term care, and the maintenance of abstinence to stop the cycle of relapse and remission. Also reviewed are "harm-reduction" strategies when abstinence is not feasible. Examples of harm reduction include: syringe exchange programs, safe injection centers, the distribution of naloxone rescue kits, and urine drug testing strips for patient use.

Much has been written about substance use disorders from the perspectives of philosophy, psychology, and psychiatry. Who better to write a book for clinicians and the general public with a different perspective than two anesthesiologists? Anesthesiologists specialize in the administration of medications that alter brain function. Dr. Bryson's extensive research experience includes the study of addiction among anesthesiologists in the United States. Despite advances in treatment, addiction still remains a major issue in the anesthesia workplace, and outcomes of current treatment have not appreciatively improved over the years. Dr. Boxhorn is among the first physicians to complete a formal one-year fellowship in the new specialty of addiction medicine. These two authors provide a synopsis of what is known today about opioid use disorder and the opioid epidemic, which will serve as a foundation for what is to come in the future.

Richard D. Blondell, MD
Professor Emeritus of Family Medicine
Jacobs School of Medicine and Biomedical Sciences at the
University at Buffalo

PREFACE

Despite substantial advances in our understanding and treatment of opioid use disorders, the disease of addiction remains as a major human problem. When it comes to opioids, we are now dealing with a worldwide epidemic, one whose major public health and economic implications will likely affect us all for generations to come. The effects of opioid addiction are ubiquitous and, like the coronavirus pandemic, have the potential to impact everyone, even those who don't even misuse opioids themselves. If we do not become addicted to opioids ourselves, chances are high that someone we love will. There is also a strong possibility that most of us will know someone who is in recovery from an opioid addiction.

For those who have not yet experienced opioid addiction and recovery personally, it can be hard to accept and understand, and it can be easy to dismiss the actions of others as poor choices based on moral failings. People addicted to opioids are often seen as weak and responsible for their own situations, but the truth is based in human biology and therefore much more complicated. If we are truly going to come up with an effective solution to this shared problem, we will first need to understand the origins of addiction, the biology and psychology of opioid misuse and addiction, and the degree to which this epidemic has spread across the globe.

The Opioid Epidemic presents for you an overview of the historical origins of opioid addiction, a summary of the current state of the worldwide epidemic, and an examination of the likelihood of success for current and proposed solutions. It is written both for the lay person who may not possess a deep understanding of the minute and somewhat technical issues involved with the causes, identification, and treatment of opioid addiction, as well as for the medical professional who possesses this intimate knowledge. The scope of the material covered in this book is broad enough to serve as an introduction to the topic for the casual reader, an ancillary text for college-level courses on psychology, human behavior and related fields, and as a reference for the medical professionals who are increasingly encountering patients with opioid addiction in their practices. While not intended to be a fully comprehensive text on the topic of addiction, we provide, in one source, both the answers to commonly asked questions and directions to external resources via online content for more in-depth information.

Our book is organized into four sections which follow a parallel path similar to what happens when an individual becomes addicted to opioids, from the origins of their addiction to recognizing that they have a problem, through treatment, and then into recovery. In this case though, instead of an individual, the person we are discussing is the entire population of the planet. Throughout the text we have included links to external content that we hope our readers will find informative and helpful and, at the end, in the appendix, links to resources for those who want to find help for themselves or other people in their lives who are suffering as a result of the opioid epidemic.

In Part I, *The Origins of Addiction*, we find out how humans from very different backgrounds around the world can and have become addicted to the same basic substance. We examine the culture-specific agents which tend to cause problems for some users (but not others) and the biological basis for why that is. Social factors affecting opioid addiction, including culture, religion, policy and regulations are examined here as we look into the origins of opioid misuse and how we got to where we are now.

In Part II, *Recognizing That a Problem Exists*, we look closely at the current state of the opioid epidemic. We take a deep dive into the raw data and statistics which describe the immensity of the problem we are faced with and begin to break these numbers down into easier to digest and understand chunks. We discover what is currently driving the opioid epidemic and why this is such a difficult problem to address. We examine the costs to society and the impact on our healthcare system this epidemic is having and take a closer look at for-profit recovery programs more focused on the bottom line than actually helping patients.

In Part III, *The Treatment Plan*, we closely examine the current state of opioid addiction treatment. We look into the success and failures of the many different currently available treatment modalities and find out what is working, and what is not. We examine the financial costs of addiction on the individual level, why the cycle of addiction keeps people not only dependent on drugs but also on government and social assistance programs, and then focus on the legal implications of addiction.

In Part IV, *Recovery*, we review with a critical eye changes to policy which will need to be made if we are ever going to achieve any meaningful success. Key to ending this epidemic will be stopping the cycle of relapse, changing antiquated drug laws, implementing proactive measures to prevent addiction in susceptible populations, rethinking how we educate people about opioids and the potential for addiction, and strategies which improve the quality of illicit drugs.

The history of our relationship with opioids has been marked by periods in which our use has increased due to technological innovations allowing for greater potency, intensity of experience, and greater availability. Opium, not nearly as potent as the morphine and other drugs eventually derived from it, was our first introduction to opioids. For centuries it was used as an effective medicine, a painkiller, a sleep aid, and for recreation. Originally taken orally as a tea or fortified drink, the discovery that it could be smoked increased the intensity of the experience for the user, leading to greater rates of addiction and reducing the time it took for someone to become addicted. The isolation of morphine from opium and the invention of the hypodermic needle allowed for opioids to be administered intravenously, further increasing the intensity of the experience for the user, and further reducing the time from first use to addiction. Heroin is now produced and distributed in a form that is so potent the user can get the high formerly only available to those willing to inject the drug by simply insufflating (snorting) the powder. This, combined with advances in the ability to manufacture opioids in several different forms over the past 200 years, has dramatically increased the availability of these drugs and rapidly increased the rate at which opioid addiction is growing worldwide. The number of people addicted to opioids has now reached epidemic proportions and is continuing to increase at an alarming rate. It is our hope that by closely examining the past and the present state of the opioid epidemic we will be able to discover how we can change the course of this epidemic.

PART I

The Origins of Addiction

PART I

1 A BRIEF HISTORY OF OPIOID MISUSE AND ADDICTION

What Is Opium?

Opium, manufactured from the sap of the opium poppy *(Papaver somniferum)*, has been cultivated by humans for centuries. It has been used, in one form or another, for medicinal as well as recreational purposes, and is the precursor to all modern-day opiate pharmaceutical agents. The term opioid refers broadly to all compounds related to opium and these drugs are classified as either naturally occurring, semi-synthetic, or fully synthetic, depending on their origin. Opiates are drugs specifically derived from opium, and include the naturally occurring products morphine, codeine, and thebaine and the semi-synthetic congeners derived from them, which include medications such as heroin and buprenorphine. These semi-synthetic drugs were developed by chemically modifying the naturally occurring psychoactive components present in the opium poppy to take advantage of specific properties inherent to the different compounds present in the plant. In some cases the intent was to increase potency by reducing the volume required to create a similar effect, in other cases attempts were made to adjust the duration of action or reduce the incidence of unwanted side effects. When these desired effects could not be achieved by modifying these naturally occurring compounds, scientists worked to create fully synthetic versions. The fully synthetic opioids include medications such as methadone and fentanyl, which have been synthesized to act in a similar manner as the natural occurring opioids but are not directly made from the natural occurring compounds.

Morphine, the active ingredient in opium, derives its name from Morpheus, the Greek god of dreams, son of Hypnos, the god of sleep. In its pure form it is 10 times more potent than unrefined opium. Originally isolated from opium by German scientist Friedrich Sertürner in 1803, morphine very quickly became widely used as strong painkiller, alleviating much of the pain related to battlefield injuries suffered by soldiers on both sides during the United States

Civil War (April 12, 1861 to May 9, 1865). Sadly, as a result of this widespread use, it is estimated that roughly 400,000 of these soldiers became addicted to the drug, continuing to suffer in a different way long after the war was over.

Several attempts were made during the last half of the nineteenth century to create a safer and less addictive alternative to morphine, and in 1874 heroin was synthesized from morphine by English chemist Alder Wright. In the 1890s, heroin was produced by the German pharmaceutical company Bayer and marketed as a morphine substitute. In addition to its properties as a potent painkiller (heroin is actually metabolized into morphine once it enters the body), heroin is also a potent cough suppressant and Bayer declared heroin a safer alternative for children suffering from coughs and colds. Unfortunately, despite their best efforts at finding a safer alternative, heroin did not turn out to be less addictive than morphine. By the early 1900s, heroin addiction in the United States and Western Europe had become even more of a problem than morphine addiction.

In 1924, the US Congress passed the Anti-Heroin Act, making it illegal to manufacture, import, or sell heroin in the United States. By that time, however, people had already developed a strong taste for the drug and the trade in illegally produced heroin rapidly increased. So-called "black tar heroin," named for its dark orange or brown color and tar-like consistency, is a form of heroin that is generally manufactured in Mexico and imported to the Western and Midwestern United States, while "white powder heroin" is more often manufactured in Columbia and imported into the Eastern United States. As we will see in the chapters that follow, regardless of where the heroin comes from, it is generally manufactured with few quality control measures and contains (sometimes dangerous) adulterants designed to increase profits.

Origins of Opium

Though it is likely that humans have maintained a somewhat complicated relationship with *Papaver somniferum* for some time longer than this, the earliest known reference to the cultivation of these poppies for the opium they contain is from Mesopotamia around 3000 BCE.[1] In the southernmost region of the area, in what is now modern-day Iraq and Kuwait, the ancient Sumerians grew, harvested, and processed this plant to produce medicine and, as is suggested by reference to the bright red poppy flowers as *hul gil*, "the joy plant," for recreational use.[2]

---

[1] Anslinger and Tompkins (1953).   [2] Terry and Pellens (1928), p. 54.

From Mesopotamia, knowledge of the opium poppy spread along trade routes eastward to Persia and westward to Egypt, where records describe opium use during the reign of King Tutankhamen (1333–1324 BCE) as a pain-reliever and a narcotic,[3] and to Greece, where references to opium's powers are chronicled in the ancient literature. In the late eighth century BCE, Homer referred to opium's healing powers in the *Odyssey*,[4] and the *Iliad*,[5] Hippocrates (460–377 or 355 BCE) mentions the poppy as being used in medicinal preparations, and Aristotle (384–322 BCE) describes opium as a hypnotic drug. Opium was frequently used in these ancient societies as a narcotic to induce sleep, an analgesic to relieve pain, and most likely also as a recreational drug.

Opium Comes to China

From the fertile crescent, via trade along the Silk Road, opium traveled east through a region where most of the world's opium poppies are still grown today. From Afghanistan and Pakistan eastward into India, Myanmar, and Thailand, into central Asia, and eventually China where, by the seventh century CE, opium had arrived.

By the 1700s, China had developed a taste for opium and, as demand increased, so did the profitability of importation. Fueled by increased supply, primarily from poppy-growing regions of India under the control of the British Empire, rates of opium addiction increased dramatically in China. In 1796, the Jiaqing emperor (Qing dynasty, 1644–1912) outlawed opium importation and cultivation in an attempt to stem the increasingly problematic issue of opium addiction. Outlawing opium, however, just drove the trade underground and illegal importation, primarily from the regions of India controlled by Great Britain, continued. The British openly smuggled opium into China through the East India Company, in defiance of the Emperor's decree, as this was a considerably lucrative trade, eventually leading to an attempt by China to prevent the British from flooding their homeland with opium. The result: two armed conflicts referred to as the "Opium Wars."

The First Opium War (1839–1842) lasted three years and ended with the Treaty of Nanking. As a result of the treaty China was forced to cede Hong Kong to the British Empire and to keep the ports in Shanghai,

---

[3] Gabra (1956), p. 40.
[4] "Presently she cast a drug into the wine whereof they drank, a drug to lull all pain and anger, and bring forgetfulness of every sorrow … "
[5] "And as a poppy which in the garden is weighed down by fruit and vernal showers, droops its head on one side."

Canton, and other ports open to trade. In 1856, a short 14 years after the Treaty of Nanking, the Second Opium War (1856–1860) began. This time the British and the French fought the Chinese and after four years the Emperor was forced to make the opium trade legal once again in China. As a result of what many consider an inappropriate and immoral use of military power by the British Empire, rates of opium addiction in China continued to dramatically increase.

Opium Comes to the United States

Before the Second Opium War had even begun, thousands of Chinese began to leave China, seeking work in America, primarily as laborers building the trans-continental railroad and mining in the gold fields of California. These immigrants brought with them their culture and traditions, which included for some, at the time anyway, the smoking of opium. Opium dens, businesses which allowed for the purchase and use of opium in a single location, much like a bar or public house provides both alcohol for sale and a place to drink it, were established primarily by and for the immigrant population. Initially located in areas of high Chinese populations in cities in the Western United States, frequently called "Chinatowns," opium dens soon began appearing outside these areas and attracting non-Chinese clientele. By the 1870s, the rates of opium addiction in America began to skyrocket as it had in China, and in 1875, San Francisco became the first city in the United States to attempt to outlaw opium. The initial ordinance approved by the city supervisors was ostensibly race neutral and simply made it a misdemeanor to maintain a business or to patronize any such business where opium was smoked. The use of opium by private citizens whether in public or in their own homes was not targeted, only the public houses. The specific wording in the statute specified that "no *person* shall keep or visit an opium den," but in practice this law was only enforced when it came to dens in the White areas of the city. The concern, clearly, was not that people were smoking and becoming addicted to opium but that White people were smoking and becoming addicted to opium. According to an 1875 article in the *San Francisco Chronicle*, the city's Board of Supervisors enacted this legislation only after learning of "opium-smoking establishments kept by Chinese, for the exclusive use of white men and women" that were attracting "young men and women of respectable parentage." Apparently, America's first law banning any nonalcoholic drug was enacted only when drug misuse and addiction began to become a problem in the White community, a theme that continues to this day and one which we explore further in subsequent chapters.

Laudanum

Laudanum, a mixture of opium suspended in alcohol (opium tincture), was first developed in the seventeenth century by the English physician, Thomas Sydenham (1624–1689). By the eighteenth century the combination had become very well known to the medical community and the general public and was widely used to treat a variety of maladies. Laudanum was touted as "one of the best known and most extensively used household remedies," ostensibly a "cure-all" for multiple ailments including, among other things, yellow fever, cardiac disease, colds, dysentery, and excessive secretions. It was used as a pain reliever for adults and children, and even to soothe fussy babies. Available over the counter without a prescription, laudanum was also commonly used as a "pick-me-up" by middle-class women (more than any other social group in the late-nineteenth century), occasionally leading to addiction. A newspaper article in the *Auckland Star* (July 25, 1890, p. 3)[6] describes the fate of one such woman who had become addicted to the mixture: "A respectable looking woman named Walker was charged today at the police court with a series of petty thefts. She pleaded "Guilty," but for the defense her son gave evidence to the effect that his mother was a laudanum and opium consumer, and not responsible for her actions."

Harrison Narcotics Tax Act

The American "war on drugs" unofficially began in 1914 with the signing of the Harrison Narcotics Tax Act. The act did not outright make opium illegal but imposed a tax on the manufacture and importation of opium and its derivatives (as well as coca leaves) and placed restrictions on their sale and distribution. This strategy of taxing what you want less of and subsidizing what you want more of that we are all familiar with is not a new strategy, and when the US government recognized that a problem with opium existed over a century ago, their initial response was to tax and regulate.

By 1908, opium use in the United States had increased to the point where it was difficult to find someone not either directly or indirectly affected by the problem. In response to demands by the people that something be done, President Theodore Roosevelt appointed Dr. Hamilton Wright (1867–1917), an American physician and pathologist, as the Opium Commissioner of the

---

[6] Phillips (2013).

United States. Despite his apparent enthusiasm for the post, Dr. Wright was unable to stem the tide of the last opium epidemic. Based primarily on conversations with leaders in the south and central Pacific Asian nations, who had far more experience dealing with the management of the opium problem, his commission recommended against outright prohibition and instead proposed a gradual abolition of the trade through taxation and regulation. The degree to which opium addiction had become a problem is outlined in a *New York Times* article from 1911 in which Wright is quoted as saying, "Of all the nations of the world, the United States consumes the most habit-forming drugs per capita. Opium, the most pernicious drug known to humanity, is surrounded, in this country, with far fewer safeguards than any other nation in Europe fences it with. China now guards it with much greater care than we do; Japan preserves her people from it far more intelligently than we do ours, who can buy it, in almost any form, in every tenth one of our drug stores." Heroin was one such form of opium sold by druggists throughout the United States until being banned (see Figure 1.1).

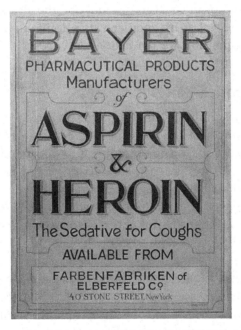

Figure 1.1 Drug store sign for products heroin and aspirin before the US heroin ban 1924 (from Wikimedia Commons). Now illegal in the United States, heroin began as an opioid with legitimate medical use. It is still available by prescription in the United Kingdom and used for acute and chronic pain, especially pain related to a terminal illness, and is used as maintenance therapy for individuals addicted to heroin.

How We Got Here

Over a century ago the world recognized that opioid addiction was a significant problem that needed to be addressed, and yet today, in 2023, we are faced with an escalating epidemic of opioid misuse and addiction, a world in which few, if any of us, have remained unscathed. While this section focuses on the specific factors which have led to the exponential increase in opioid misuse in the United States, the stories are similar, if not exactly the same, around the world as we will see in the chapters that follow.

By the time the Harrison Narcotics Tax Act was passed in 1914, the US government was well aware of the scope of the problem as well as the efforts being made by other countries to stem the rising tide of the epidemic. Canada, Germany, Russia, France, and England had already passed laws regulating or banning outright the opium trade. Even the Crown Colony of Hong Kong, despite its earlier role in the Opium Wars as a central location of the opium trade, had also already passed a strict anti-opium law. Despite this, however, opium refined and ready to smoke continued to be imported into the country, packaged and ready for sale. According to Dr. Wright, "not less than 20,000 pounds per annum have been smuggled into the United States across our northern boundary" and while less was known about the importation of opium across the southern border the government was "sure that large amounts of opium prepared for smoking are imported into Mexico, and that most of it is not consumed there." It is reasonable to assume, then, that what was not consumed in Mexico was also imported into the United States. The country was, quite literally, a primed tinderbox waiting for a spark.

To understand this analogy, one has to consider the "Triad of Fire." For those unfamiliar with the concept, the idea is that for fire to exist three components must come together at the same time under ideal conditions. First, you have to have fuel. If there is nothing to burn, there will be no fire. Second, you have to have an ignition source, the spark that starts the combustion. Third, and this is the most important element, you have to have an oxidizing agent, an atmosphere that supports combustion. In outer space, fire is not supported because there is no oxygen and on Earth a fire can be suppressed by removing its access to the oxidizing agent. In our example the fire is the epidemic, sparked by opioids, consuming lives (fuel) and supported by the sometimes well-intentioned but mostly ineffectual policies (oxidizing agent) designed to combat the opioid epidemic.

The Perfect Storm

By the 1980s, the heroin trade in the United States had become well established. Mexican "black tar" heroin dominated the trade in Los Angeles, San Francisco, and other major cities along the West Coast while Columbian "white powder" heroin dominated the trade east of the Mississippi. Though the product looked different, it behaved the same way, and during this time, it was all about location. In the east, the Columbian cartels had access to ports in the southern United States and well-established distribution networks, stretching from Miami to New York City. If you were a heroin addict on the Eastern Seaboard you were, statistically speaking, more likely to be using a Columbian product. In the west, the distribution routes favored the Mexican cartels, and most users were purchasing the Mexican-produced heroin product. From a business standpoint it seemed like a stable market, with two different manufacturers supplying two separate regions with basically the same product, but all of that was about to change.

In the early 1990s, the Mexican cartels began to expand eastward into the territory historically controlled by the Colombian cartels. The Mexican cartels had basically the same product as the Columbians and were selling it at the same price point, but they held two advantages, which ultimately allowed them to gain territory. First, they were closer to the customer, which allowed for lower distribution expenses; and second, they had developed an innovative marketing strategy. In their attempts to encroach onto their rival distributors' territory they began to offer door-to-door service, increased marketing with free samples, and provided reliable service, something the Columbians had not been able to do.

Simultaneously, in the medical world, things were changing as well. In 1986, Foley and Portenoy published a case series in the journal *Pain*, in which they detailed their experience of treating 38 patients with nonmalignant pain using chronic opioid analgesics and determined that "opioid maintenance therapy can be a safe, salutary and more humane alternative to the options of surgery or no treatment in those patients with intractable nonmalignant pain and no history of drug abuse." The idea that opioids are safe to use for both acute and chronic pain was revolutionary, and only a decade later pain became the "fifth vital sign." The so-called "vital signs," traditionally your heart rate, blood pressure, respiratory rate, and body temperature, are essential for identifying disease processes and guiding response to treatment. Add pain as the "fifth vital sign" and response to treatment includes being free from pain. In 1996, Purdue Pharma released and marketed a new opioid, designed to have less abuse potential. OxyContin came onto the market and, if you are in pain, the establishment proclaimed, it should be treated. In 1998, the Veterans Administration and the Joint Commission on Accreditation of Healthcare Organizations adopted pain as the "fifth vital sign" and it wasn't long afterward that reports of physicians being sued for inadequate treatment of pain began making headlines.

Subsequently, since the 1990s the United States has experienced three waves in the rise of opioid overdose deaths, generally used as a marker for increased opioid misuse activity. In 1999, a rise in opioid overdose deaths was identified as specifically related to a rise in prescription opioid deaths, primarily related to OxyContin misuse. In 2010, likely due to increased enforcement of anti-diversion laws resulting in higher prices for gray-or black-market prescription pharmaceuticals, a significant rise in heroin overdose deaths occurred. In 2013, we began to see a rise in opioid overdose deaths related to synthetic opioids, specifically fentanyl. Today, in some areas, synthetic opioids are more prevalent than heroin. Fentanyl is easier and less expensive to manufacture than heroin. It does not require an agriculture infrastructure and can be completely synthesized in any location. Because it is so much more potent than heroin, it can be transported for the same cost but generate a hundredfold more profit, and because the half-life is so much shorter, customers come down from their high and start to feel withdrawal symptoms more frequently, ensuring that they will return to purchase more product, so long as they don't unintentionally overdose. As we will see in the following chapters, recent statistics suggest that we may actually now be living through what will eventually be called the fourth wave of opioid overdose deaths related to the coronavirus pandemic, though only time will tell.

References and Further Reading

Anslinger HJ, Tompkins WF (1953). *The Traffic in Narcotics*. New York: Funk & Wagnalls.

Aristotle, *Physica Minora*, 456B, 30; *Historia Animalium* I, 6276, 18.

Littré E (1840–1849). On internal diseases. In *Œuvres complètes d' Hippocrate*. Paris: J. B. Baillière, chapter 12.

Gabra S (1956). Papaver species and opium through the ages. *Bulletin de l'Institut d'Egypte* 37(1): 39–46.

Hall HR (1928). The statues of Sennemut and Menkheperr 'Senb in the British Museum. *Journal of Egyptian Archaeology* 14(1): 1–2.

Phillips J (2013). Drugs: Colonial drug-taking. *Te Ara – the Encyclopedia of New Zealand*. December 5. https://teara.govt.nz/en/drugs/page-1

Terry CE, Pellens M (1928). *The Opium Problem*. New York: Committee on Drug Addictions, Bureau of Social Hygiene.

2 WHY DO SOME PEOPLE BECOME ADDICTED TO OPIOIDS WHILE OTHERS DON'T?

What Is Opioid Addiction?

According to the *Diagnostic and Statistical Manual of Mental Disorders*, 5th Edition (DSM-5), opioid use disorder is "a problematic pattern of opioid use leading to problems or distress,"[1] characterized by two or more of the following occurring within a 12-month period:

1. Taking larger amounts or taking drugs over a longer period than intended
2. Persistent desire or unsuccessful efforts to cut down or control opioid use
3. Spending a great deal of time obtaining or using the opioid or recovering from its effects
4. Craving, or a strong desire or urge to use opioids
5. Problems fulfilling obligations at work, school, or home
6. Continued opioid use despite having recurring social or interpersonal problems
7. Giving up or reducing activities because of opioid use
8. Using opioids in physically hazardous situations
9. Continued opioid use despite ongoing physical or psychological problems, likely to have been caused or worsened by opioids
10. Tolerance (i.e., need for increased amounts or diminished effect with continued use of the same amount)
11. Experiencing withdrawal (opioid withdrawal syndrome) or taking opioids (or a closely related substance) to relieve or avoid withdrawal symptoms.

Opioid use disorder is viewed as a chronic disease, characterized by the drug-seeking behaviors and compulsive use patterns specified above. While not everyone who meets the criteria for a diagnosis of opioid use disorder will

---

[1] American Psychiatric Association (2013).

exhibit all of these behaviors, remember that it only takes two criteria to establish the diagnosis. In general, these behaviors are compulsive, difficult to control, and occur despite harmful consequences to the user. In order to fully understand what is going on when someone becomes addicted to opioids it is helpful to go through each of the above criteria and examine what exactly is going on in each situation.

The opioid addict is frequently observed to be *taking larger amounts* of opioids in a single dose *or taking opioids over a longer period than intended.* Because of the addictive nature of these drugs, tolerance develops quickly. Tolerance is when the body becomes resistant to the effects of a drug and a higher dose is required to achieve the desired effect. This phenomenon is not restricted to drugs with misuse potential such as opioids and in fact is commonly seen with medications that do not have psychoactive effects, such as drugs designed to regulate blood pressure or glucose levels. Often when tolerance develops with an antihypertensive, for example, a "drug holiday" is indicated. This is when the antihypertensive that the body has become tolerant to is swapped out for a different medication in a different class that works a different way, which allows the body's tolerance to the initial medication to wain while still maintaining safe and appropriate blood pressure control with the new medication. The same process occurs with opioids, but in the case of the person with opioid use disorder, the desired effect cannot be achieved by switching to a different drug that works in a different way, and more of the opioid is required to achieve the same level of euphoria. In addition to consuming greater and greater amounts of opioids, the affected individual will consume opioids over a longer period of time, often continuing to take opioids that were initially prescribed for a specific indication, long after the pain from the inciting event is gone.[2]

Once occasional use has become chronic, the individual finds themselves trapped in a cycle characterized by a *persistent desire* to curb use or stop using altogether. Often these attempts are *unsuccessful* and *efforts to cut down or control opioid use* result in short periods of withdrawal, ultimately followed by efforts to obtain and use opioids again. Typical behavior of the addict caught in this cycle of opioid misuse includes *spending a great deal of time obtaining or using the opioid or recovering from its effects,* driven by intense *craving,* or *a strong desire or urge to use opioids.* It can be very difficult for those who have not personally experienced addiction to understand why humans have such

---

[2] To diagnose opioid use disorder, you just need two criteria; but if the two criteria are tolerance and withdrawal, which are an expected part of treatment with opioids and other medications, this alone is not enough to be diagnosed with the disorder.

differing relationships with psychoactive substances. Some people have never, and will never, use opioids. Other people have, or will, experiment with opioids and not become addicted. Some of these people who are exposed to opioids will become addicted and eventually recover while, sadly, some will be completely unable to break the cycle of addiction and relapse, ultimately dying due to the direct or indirect effects of opioid use disorder.

Because drug addiction in general, and opioid addiction specifically, is poorly understood by the majority of the population, it is easy to ascribe behavioral changes to moral failings or a lack of willpower. The reality, however, is much more complex. Opioids and other drugs of abuse physically change the chemistry in the brain of the user. Existing connections between different areas of the brain, the so-called "reward pathways," which allow us to associate one behavior with a positive outcome and reinforce it, are physically disrupted by exposure to opioids and other pathways are created, which reward the user for obtaining and using the drug. This resulting reward is so strong that the drive to obtain and use opioids quickly supersedes the drive to meet the basic requirements for survival. Opioid use becomes more important than food, water, or sex.

The individual with opioid use disorder will often exhibit *problems fulfilling obligations at work, school, or home.* As the desire for the reward that comes with opioid use rapidly eclipses the desire to maintain social obligations, behavior changes from actions that are expected and socially acceptable to actions that allow the individual access to *continued opioid use.* Decreased performance at work or school, withdrawal from social activities, and ignoring interpersonal and family relationships commonly herald the onset of opioid use disorder, as the individual instead focuses on obtaining and using opioids *despite* the significant *social or interpersonal problems* that result. *Giving up or reducing activities because of opioid use* is a significant sign that an individual has become addicted.

Recreational opioid use is hazardous to your health, and as we will see in subsequent chapters, the chances that anyone who uses opioids in this way will die from any cause have increased exponentially over the past 40 years. It may seem surprising then that one of the criteria for the diagnosis of opioid use disorder is *using opioids in physically hazardous situations,* especially when any use at all seems to carry with it so much risk of harm, but all drugs with misuse potential can be used in different situations and with different levels of risk. While alcohol can be used in socially acceptable and safer situations, such as drinking at a public house or a restaurant, the social inhibition and decreased motor reflexes that occur even after a small volume of this drug do increase the risk for harm. If the decision is made to drive home despite having had a few drinks, the risk for harm increases significantly. Similarly with opioids, use while driving or operating machinery, or while working in a safety-sensitive position, increases the risk for harm to self and others.

The individual suffering from chronic, active opioid use disorder will also put aside self-care and often ignore medical or psychological problems, as addressing these issues is frequently at odds with the drive to obtain and use opioids. *Continued opioid use despite ongoing physical or psychological problems* is a late sign and suggests that the individual has been addicted to opioids for some time. It is often possible that these medical or psychological problems *have been caused or worsened by opioids*. As we will see in the chapters on treatment and relapse prevention, addressing these issues is key in opioid use disorder treatment. Also key is addressing the issue of tolerance (i.e., *need for increased amounts or diminished effect with continued use of the same amount*) and managing or mitigating *withdrawal (opioid withdrawal syndrome)*. Often, individuals later in the disease process, once significant tolerance to opioids has built up, will report *taking opioids (or a closely related substance) to relieve or avoid withdrawal symptoms*. It cannot be overemphasized here that tolerance and withdrawal occur as a natural consequence of chronic opioid use and do not themselves indicate that a person has developed opioid use disorder, rather it is the maladaptive behaviors that are associated with compulsive opioid misuse that characterize the disorder.

While the initial decision to take opioids recreationally is voluntary for most people, many are exposed incidentally due to issues with chronic pain or even an acute incident or accident requiring a short period of pain management. Regardless of the inciting event, repeated opioid use can lead to changes in the brain, which mold their behavior as described above, changes that reduce an addicted person's ability to practice self-control, interfere with their ability to resist intense cravings to obtain and use opioids, and eventually interfere with their ability to function in society.

Why Are Some Affected and Not Others?

Just as the disease of addiction is complex and multifactorial so too is the risk that someone exposed to opioids will subsequently become addicted to them. As of this writing, a single factor has not been identified that can either accurately predict or quantify the risk of a given individual developing opioid use disorder. Like many other diseases, there is a combination of factors at play that can influence the risk for addiction. Factors such as an individual's biology, development, and environment all play a role in increasing, or decreasing, individual risk. The more risk factors a person has, the greater the chance that exposure to opioids will lead to addiction. Conversely, the fewer risk factors an individual has, the less likely that exposure will result in opioid use disorder.

Individual Risk Attributed to Biological Factors

Let's start with biology. According to van Staaden, several studies involving experiments designed to investigate drug reward and reinforcement in non-mammalian organisms suggest that this phenomenon, seen across a broad swath of the animal kingdom, must have a genetic component. Several studies performed by a number of independent researchers have focused on the mechanisms of drug reward and reinforcement in a diverse range of nonmammalian organisms. These studies that van Staaden refers to suggest that the emergence of traits such as the ability to quickly learn to favor areas with higher concentrations of drugs with addictive potential, and repeatedly return to these areas, despite negative consequences, occurred long before mammals existed. Many addictive substances, plant-derived alkaloids especially, are capable of producing consistent psychoactive effects in a number of animal species. Early in the Precambrian era these key drivers of addiction, as we now understand it, became established in creatures as diverse as insects (honey bees, fruit flies, ants), crustaceans (crabs and crayfish), roundworms (*Caenorhabditis elegans*), molluscs (snails), and flatworms (planarians), creatures which all exist today and still exhibit these altered (and aberrant) expressions of motivation and learning. Behaviors such as these eventually evolved in mammals as well, and in humans the genetic component relating to the risk for the development of opioid use disorder is thought to account for roughly 50% of an individual's risk *attributed to biological factors alone*. This does not mean that if one of your parents was diagnosed with opioid use disorder then you have a 50% chance of developing the disease yourself, it simply means that there is at most a 50% chance that you have inherited a genetic predisposition for becoming addicted after exposure. Genes are complicated things and the genes that account for an individual's risk for developing opioid use disorder have not yet been fully elucidated. Some genes that are inherited remain dormant and others are expressed only partially. Genetically determined gender plays a role in risk, with genetically male individuals having a higher risk for developing opioid use disorder. Ethnicity also plays a role, in so much as risk is different in different ethnic populations. However, as we will see, environmental factors, depending on location, can significantly increase or decrease the expression of this genetic risk, making it very difficult to parse out what factors are ultimately responsible for the development of addiction. Lastly, the presence of mental illness contributes greatly to the risk for the development of addiction, both from a genetic predisposition and, once again, from the negative effects these types of illness can have on an affected individual's environment, which can then significantly affect risk in a cycle of positive or negative reinforcement.

Individual Risk Attributed to Environmental Factors

Biology is only the beginning, however, and as stated above, this genetic material we are all born with interacts with environmental factors during critical developmental stages in a person's life to influence the risk for the development of addiction. The term "critical developmental stages" refers to points at which a susceptible individual is at greater risk for developing opioid use disorder after exposure, and this is particularly a problem before the brain has been fully developed. Opioids do cross the placenta and in-utero exposure can not only result in physical dependence in the newborn, exhibited by physiological signs of opioid withdrawal, but may also affect brain development. While exposure to opioids at any age can result in the development of opioid use disorder, opioid use during the teenage years is particularly problematic. The frontal cortex, the part of the brain that acts as the "police officer" and suppresses words or actions, with potentially negative consequences, is not fully developed until the early 20s. As teenagers, this part of the brain, which controls decision making, judgment, and self-control, is still learning how to function and, as such, this population is particularly prone to engage in risk-taking behavior. Such behavior is essential not only for the development of the individual but also deeply ingrained in humans and all other animals alive today. Evolution has favored those with the ability to take risks, to examine the novel and strange, potentially discovering new sources of food or shelter, and it is no surprise that such behaviors persist. Unfortunately, these types of experimentation, when they involve opioid use before the frontal cortex has fully developed, confer a significantly increased risk for addiction when exposed to opioids, which persists into adulthood. In a recent study sponsored by the National Institute on Drug Abuse (NIDA), part of the National Institutes of Health in the United States, people who reported multiple symptoms consistent with severe substance use disorder at age 18 exhibited two or more of these symptoms in adulthood.[3] According to the authors of the report, "these individuals were more likely, as adults, to use and misuse prescription medications, as well as self-treat with opioids, sedatives, or tranquillizers."

The development of opioid addiction in an affected individual results in changes in motivation and specifically influences how a person learns.

---

[3] NIDA (2022).

The capacity to learn has allowed animals of all species to survive long enough to reproduce, it is not uniquely human, and just as insect and flatworm behavior can be influenced by environment, so too can human behavior. A genetically at-risk individual may or may not develop opioid use disorder based entirely on the environment in which they exist. Environmental influences that have the potential to increase or decrease risk include interpersonal relationships, especially between close family members during the developmental period. Parental guidance plays a large role during this period and the behavior patterns established as a child are often difficult to change as an adult. Early exposure to drug use, either personal or observed, increases risk while access to support structures and other resources, including supportive friends, can reduce risk. Many other environmental factors, such as ethnicity, economic status, and physical and sexual abuse, play a significant role in the risk for developing addiction.

Individual Risk Attributed to Social Factors

While biology does play a significant role in the development of addiction, it is the environment in which we grow and develop as children and ultimately exist as adults that determines whether or not an at-risk individual will subsequently develop opioid use disorder. Race, which generally refers to the outward manifestation of someone's genetics, that is, their physical characteristics such as skin, hair, or eye color, has been associated with different degrees of genetic susceptibility to the development of opioid use disorder. This susceptibility, however, is only a small part of the equation and the chances that any one individual will develop opioid use disorder is strongly influenced by ethnicity (cultural factors including nationality, regional culture, ancestry, and language), gender, economic resources, and geography. Early exposure to opioid misuse through family and peer behavior is a strong environmental factor, which can increase someone's risk, and so it follows that, in areas of the world where opioids are not as prevalent, the incidence of opioid use disorder is characteristically lower. Within each community, different cultures have different levels of propensity for developing opioid use disorder, and in areas where there is more mixing of different races and cultures, a person's risk for developing opioid addiction more closely reflects the risk of the community at large and not the genetic risk of the individual. In the past, social factors such as the presence of economic resources and peer or family support were thought to be somewhat protective and that a biologically at-risk individual in this setting would be less likely to develop opioid use disorder, but as we will see, the opioid epidemic has turned out to be the great equalizer. This epidemic now affects people of all ages, all genders, all racial and ethnic groups, and members of all socioeconomic strata.

The effects of social factors on opioid misuse vary considerably by geography, even within different countries and, in many cases, are related to one's ability to access medical care and treatment.[4] In the United States, Whites, Native Americans, and Alaskan Natives have a higher risk in developing an opioid use disorder than Blacks, Hispanics, and Asian Americans. Men, regardless of race, are much more likely than women to develop opioid use disorder, and risk is increased regardless of gender for people who are disabled, widowed, or unemployed. Affluence appears to be somewhat protective, as individuals with higher education (those who have achieved a graduate degree versus only a high school diploma), a mortgage (those who own their home versus renters), health insurance, and greater household income (families with financial resources greater than five times the poverty line versus families living below the line) are at reduced risk for dying from an opioid overdose. Geographically, those living in the South Atlantic and Mountain states are at greater risk than those living in the West North Central states, and rural residents on the whole have less of a risk than those who live in urban or suburban areas. As well, access to regular medical care can have a significant impact on an individual's risk for developing opioid use disorder and their ability to achieve recovery. Discussed in greater detail in the following chapter, these healthcare disparities between poor, middle-class, and affluent individuals have been identified as one of the main drivers of the opioid epidemic.[5]

Social pressures that result from entrenched cultural beliefs can also impact risk. In Latin America,[6] for example, addiction among women and men is treated differently, with both men and women viewing women who develop opioid use disorder much more negatively than men who develop the same disease. According to Ochoa-Mangado, author of "Gender differences in the treatment of opioid dependency," this cultural attitude can lead to diminished social acceptability, increased rejection, and public criticism for women with opioid use disorder, possibly leading some to be less likely to seek help from relatives or friends. She describes this situation as "undoubtedly related to socio-cultural factors, family structures, community networks, and even political conditions."[7] With a prevalence of 0.3% for heroin use, there is one female for

---

[4] Altekruse et al. (2020).   [5] The Partnership for a Drug-Free New Jersey (2021).
[6] The portion of the Americas comprising countries and regions where Romance languages, languages that derived from Latin such as Spanish, Portuguese, and French, are predominantly spoken. Latin America includes the following countries: Argentina, Bolivia, Brazil, Chile, Colombia, Costa Rica, Cuba, the Dominican Republic, Ecuador, El Salvador, Guatemala, Honduras, Mexico, Nicaragua, Panama, Paraguay, Peru, Puerto Rico, Uruguay, and Venezuela.
[7] Ochoa-Manga et al. (2008).

every four to five males in the region addicted to opiates, but only one female for every seven males in treatment for opioid use disorder.

Becoming addicted to opioids is not as simple as taking a pill and discovering you can't live without taking another one; it is the end result of a cascade of events, which began long before the person who develops opioid use disorder swallows an opioid for the first time. As we have learned, the environment in which we have evolved has allowed for opioid addiction to persist within the population for millennia. Opioid use disorder has a genetic component that does not prevent the person who carries the gene from reproducing and passing it along to their offspring, and therefore the disorder persists in the population. It is within this environment that genes favoring risk-taking ultimately persist, conferring an increased risk for addiction but not so much risk that the ability to reproduce is stunted. We cannot yet change our biology, so to combat the opioid epidemic we must address the environmental and social factors which ultimately result in opioid addiction. These factors can work to either increase or decrease the chances that a susceptible individual will develop opioid use disorder, and, since we do not yet know how to accurately identify these at-risk persons, it is essential that we immediately assume that everyone is at risk and work diligently to mitigate this risk. If we are to stem the tide of the opioid epidemic there is a lot of work to be done, but, as we will see in the chapters that follow, there is significant hope for the future.

References and Further Reading

Altekruse SF, Cosgrove CM, Altekruse WC, Jenkins RA, Blanco C (2020). Socioeconomic risk factors for fatal opioid overdoses in the United States: Findings from the Mortality Disparities in American Communities Study (MDAC). *PLoS One* 15(1): e0227966.

American Psychiatric Association (2013). *Diagnostic and Statistical Manual of Mental Disorders*, 5th ed. (DSM-5). Washington, DC: American Psychiatric Association.

Chapman A, Verdery AM, Monnat SM (2021). Opioid misuse and family structure: Changes and continuities in the role of marriage and children over two decades. *Drug and Alcohol Dependence* 222: 108668.

Griffith C, La France B (2018). Socio-economic impact on opioid addiction susceptibility. *Edelweiss Psychiatry Open Access* 2: 1–3. https://edelweisspublications.com/articles/22/220/Socio-Economic-Impact-on-Opioid-Addiction-Susceptibility (accessed December 2, 2022).

Hasin DS, O'Brien CP, Auriacombe M, et al. (2013). DSM-5 criteria for substance use disorders: Recommendations and rationale. *American Journal of Psychiatry* 170 (8): 834–851.

Mateu G, Astals M, Torrens M (2005). Psychiatric comorbidity and opioid dependency disorders: From diagnosis to treatment [in Spanish]. *Adicciones* 17(Suppl. 2): 111–122.

NIDA (2022). Drug use severity in adolescence affects substance use disorder risk in adulthood. Press Release, April 1. https://nida.nih.gov/news-events/news-releases/2022/04/drug-use-severity-in-adolescence-affects-substance-use-disorder-risk-in-adulthood

Ochoa-Mangado E, Madoz-Gúrpide A, Salvador E (2008). Gender differences in the treatment of opioid dependency [in Spanish]. *Drogas & Genero, Actas Españolas de Psiquiatría* 36(4): 197–204. www.drogasgenero.info/documento/ochoa-mangado-enriqueta-et-al-diferencias-genero-tratamiento-la-dependencia-opiaceos

Organization of American States, Inter-American Drug Abuse Control Commission (2015). Report on drug use in the Americas. www.cicad.oas.org/oid/pubs/druguseamericas_eng_web.pdf

Partnership for a Drug-Free New Jersey (2021). The opioid epidemic and the impact of race. https://knockoutday.drugfreenj.org/wp-content/uploads/2021/12/KOOAD_12_9_webinar.pdf

Rico MA, Kraychete DC, Iskandar AJ, et al. (2016). Use of opioids in Latin America: The need of an evidence-based change. *Pain Medicine* 17: 704–716.

Singh GK, Kim IE, Girmay M, et al. (2019). Opioid epidemic in the United States: Empirical trends, and a literature review of social determinants and epidemiological, pain management, and treatment patterns. *International Journal of Maternal and Child Health* 8(2): 89–100.

van Draanen J, Tsang C, Mitra S, Karamouzian M, Richardson L (2020). Socioeconomic marginalization and opioid-related overdose: A systematic review. *Drug and Alcohol Dependence* 214: 108127.

van Staaden MJ, Hall FS, Huber R (2018). The deep evolutionary roots of 'addiction'. *Journal of Mental Health and Clinical Psychology* 2(3): 8–13.

3 HOW CULTURE, RELIGION, AND SOCIETY IMPACT OPIOID ADDICTION

As we learned in Chapter 2, while biology does play a significant role in the development of addiction, it is the environment in which we grow and develop as children and ultimately exist as adults that determines whether or not an at-risk individual will subsequently develop opioid use disorder. Race, which generally refers to the outward manifestation of someone's genetics, that is, their physical characteristics such as skin, hair, or eye color, has been associated with different degrees of genetic susceptibility to the development of opioid use disorder. This susceptibility, however, is only a small part of the equation and the chances that any one individual will develop opioid use disorder is strongly influenced by ethnicity (cultural factors including nationality, regional culture, ancestry, and language), gender, access to economic resources, and geography. Early exposure to opioid misuse through family and peer behavior is a strong environmental factor that can increase someone's risk, and so it follows that in areas of the world where opioids are not as prevalent the incidence of opioid use disorder is characteristically lower. Within each community, different cultures have different levels of propensity for developing opioid use disorder, and in areas where there is more mixing of different races and cultures, a person's risk for developing opioid addiction more closely reflects the risk of the community at large and not the genetic risk of the individual. In the past, social factors such as access to economic resources and peer or family support were thought to be somewhat protective and that a biologically at-risk individual in this setting would be less likely to develop opioid use disorder. But, as we will see, the opioid epidemic has turned out to be the great equalizer. This epidemic now affects people of all ages, all genders, all racial and ethnic groups, and members of all socioeconomic strata.

The effects of social factors on opioid misuse vary considerably by geography, even within different countries, and, in many cases, are related to one's ability to access medical care and treatment.[1] As an example, within the

---

[1] Altekruse et al. (2020).

United States, Whites, Native Americans, and Alaskan Natives have a higher risk for developing opioid use disorder than Blacks, Hispanics, and Asian Americans (though members of these populations tend to suffer to a greater degree when afflicted and are at higher risk for overdose deaths). Men, regardless of race, are much more likely than women to develop opioid use disorder, and risk is increased regardless of gender for people who are disabled, widowed, or unemployed. Affluence appears to be somewhat protective, as individuals with higher education (those who have achieved a graduate degree versus only a high school diploma), a mortgage (those who own their home versus renters), health insurance, and greater household income (families with financial resources greater than five times the poverty line versus families living below the line) are at reduced risk for dying from an opioid overdose. Geographically, those living in the South Atlantic and Mountain states are at greater risk than those living in the West North Central states, and rural residents on the whole have less of a risk than those who live in urban or suburban areas.

Race

As part of a presentation on the opioid epidemic and the impact of race, Dr. Robert L. Johnson, Dean of the Rutgers New Jersey Medical School, points to entrenched disparities in access to healthcare in the United States as one of the main drivers of the opioid epidemic.[2] He describes health disparities as "the differences between groups of people which can affect how frequently a disease affects a group, how many people get sick, or how often the disease causes death." Dr. Johnson points out that these inequities are caused by the uneven distribution of social determinants of health, including education, housing and the neighborhood environment (sidewalks, parks, safe public spaces), access to transportation, employment opportunities, the law and the justice systems, and healthcare in general. These effects are more common in public health systems and are more likely to negatively impact minority members of a community, those whose race, ethnicity, gender, and/or sexual identity is not the same as that of the majority in power.

According to Jayme S. Ganey, the Program Manager of Culture Connections for Family Connections of New Jersey (USA), these health disparities are a result of "old ways of thinking and doing when the culture, education and times have shifted." Ganey stresses that older systems, those that have historically dehumanized instead of humanizing, offer simple "band-aid" solutions to complex problems. These solutions do not take into account the reality

---

[2] Partnership for a Drug-Free New Jersey (2021).

experienced by the diverse stakeholders, which should be involved in the decision-making process. The end result is a population that feels they are not being counted or heard and are, as a result, much less likely to participate in or benefit from any available programs. This is particularly troubling because even though the majority of persons with opioid use disorder in the United States are White, as of 2020 the majority of deaths related to opioid misuse occur in the Black community.

The reasons proposed to explain this dichotomy between Black and White populations in the United States focus primarily on healthcare-related factors, which are the result, at least in part anyway, of the significant historical differences in socioeconomic status between the two groups. According to Friedman et al.,[3] White patients generally have greater access to opioid prescriptions than Black patients in both the emergency room and in the doctor's office setting, resulting in higher exposure to opioids per capita (and a subsequently higher rate for opioid use disorder in the White population). James and Jordan of Yale University[4] suggest that this implicit bias inherent in the medical system, which resulted in racially discriminatory-based prescribing practices, has actually shielded members of the Black community from the brunt of the epidemic due to this physician–patient dynamic.[5] They also point out, however, that this same dynamic is responsible for the increased mortality rate when Black patients do develop opioid use disorder, calling for the development of more "culturally targeted" programs specifically designed to benefit Black communities. These programs, suggest James and Jordan, should include "the use of faith-based organizations to deliver substance use prevention and treatment services, the inclusion of racial impact assessments in the implementation of drug policy proposals, and the formal consideration of Black people's interaction with the criminal justice system in designing treatment options."

Culture and Religion

While the goals of prevention of opioid misuse and other factors that have the potential to interfere with the maintenance of health may be the same across cultures, many cultural differences exist in the perception and recognition of these types of problems, and in the preferred strategies for coping with them.

---

[3] Friedman et al. (2019).
[4] Keturah James is a student at Yale Law School in New Haven, Connecticut. Ayana Jordan, MD, PhD, is an assistant professor, addiction psychiatrist, and attending physician at Yale University School of Medicine.
[5] James and Jordan (2018).

Global differences in opioid use and misuse vary greatly by region, primarily having to do with availability, cultural attitudes towards use, and religious prohibitions or acceptance. Using alcohol as an example, it is easy to see how cultural and religious beliefs can dramatically impact the degree to which a psychoactive substance is used in a particular area. While the majority of the world's population does not use alcohol regularly or at all (reportedly fully 46% of all men and 73% of all women in the world abstain from alcohol),[6] where alcohol is socially acceptable, its use is not evenly distributed. In Europe, for example, over 80% of the population uses alcohol, whereas in regions with a predominantly Islamic faith the vast majority of the population abstains. Different cultures, just like different religions (and in many cases the two are so intertwined as to be one and the same), create shared attitudes and beliefs within a population regarding what is and what is not acceptable behavior, and this can strongly influence someone initiating or attempting to cease opioid misuse.

Treatment strategies for opioid use disorder that focus on, or at the very least, recognize these strong and well-established cultural beliefs are more likely to result in greater retention and lower rates of relapse. As an example of how cultural values can influence behavior, Flores et al. discuss Hispanic culture and the values of *familismo, machismo,* and *personalismo* in "Kickeando las malias" (Kicking the Withdrawals) in "Staying clean": The Impact of Cultural Values on Cessation of Injection Drug Use in Aging Mexican–American Men.[7] *Familismo* (familism), an obligation to the family that de-emphasizes the individual, can provide context for someone in early recovery to understand the need to form an emotional support network. Putting aside the negative connotations associated with *machismo,* positive attributes such as courage emphasize that recovery is extremely difficult and requires considerable strength and resilience. *Personalismo* emphasizes warm and sincere personal interactions with others and can be seen as a culturally appropriate context in which to frame the need to learn how to live a clean and sober life in a world without opioids. According to Unger et al., Hispanic families who have migrated into the United States and away from areas with stronger traditional values show a loss of traditional Hispanic cultural values, which has been shown to increase the risk for substance use behaviors in those with diminished cultural or familial ties.[8]

In regions where the majority of the population is of the Islamic faith and alcoholism rates are low, the same cannot be said for opioid misuse, as opium is not directly forbidden in the Qur'an. Mehran Zarghami[9] proposes that

[6] World Health Organization (2010).   [7] Flores et al. (2014).   [8] Unger et al. (2002).
[9] Professor of psychiatry at the Department of Psychiatry School of Medicine Mazandaran University of Medical Sciences, and Psychiatry and Behavioral Sciences Research Center, Addiction Institute, Mazandaran University of Medical Sciences, Sari, Iran.

a common (positive) traditional attitude towards opium consumption in Iran stems from the thousands of years' relationship between the people of Mesopotamia (modern-day Iraq and Kuwait) and *Papaver somniferum*. In a survey of Iranian literature conducted by Zarghami, several well-known Iranian poets, who have made "a substantial contribution on cultural attitude formation of the Iranian population," have routinely used the phrase "Teriac" (raw opium) to denote a substance that can treat almost every disease. As a result, opium consumption is seen as a positive activity in Persian culture and many routinely use the raw opium as a painkiller as well as a treatment for maladies as diverse as hyperlipidemia (high blood cholesterol), hypertension (high blood pressure), diabetes, and many other chronic diseases.

Things become more complicated, however, in traditional Muslim communities that exist within Western countries where the majority of the population does not follow Islamic law. While the Islamic religion prohibits alcohol and other drugs, substance use remains prevalent in Muslim communities in the United States and other western countries. Sarah Mallik[10] investigated the perspective of Imams (the traditional leaders of mosques) and how they treat Muslim Americans with substance use disorder in her paper "An undercover problem in the Muslim community." According to Mallik, despite religious prohibitions, substance use is prevalent among Muslims living in Muslim-minority countries: "Among Muslim-American undergraduate students, 46% report drinking alcohol (14% of Muslim Americans reported binge drinking) and 25% report illicit drug use." This presents a challenge for treatment of opioid use disorder in Muslim communities that exist within non-Muslim majority countries where Christian faith-based interventions, such as the 12-step program that defines Alcoholics Anonymous, are widely utilized. Mallik suggests that culturally and religiously tailored interventions may ultimately be more successful, and that the development of these targeted programs are necessary to facilitate effective care for Muslims with opioid use disorder.

Despite its long history of involvement in the production of opium, India prohibits the nonmedical use of all intoxicating substances. Even still, opium use is common in many Indian states, including Arunachal Pradesh, where opium has traditional medical and religious uses within the tribal community. It is accepted as a legitimate remedy for insomnia, pain, diarrhea, and physical and mental stress, and is used socially on celebratory occasions such as births, marriages, and festivals. The largest state in Northeast India, Arunachal Pradesh shares long international borders with both China and Myanmar, but according to a 2013 study published in *BMC Public Health*,[11] the close proximity to opium

---

[10] Mallik (2021).   [11] Chaturvedi et al. (2013).

trade routes out of Myanmar alone does not account for the degree of acceptance of this practice within the community. While reported in all of the tribes in Arunachal Pradesh, the degree to which opium is used is not the same across different tribal communities. Buddhist tribes, such as Khamti and Singpho, have the highest usage, and within the majority Tangsa tribal community opium use is higher in those who practice the Indigenous religion. Interestingly, tribal members who practice Christian-based faiths report generally low opium use, further demonstrating the strong effects that religious doctrine can have on reducing opium use, even for members of a community with traditionally high use.

In China, a culture which has traditionally been defined primarily by collectivism, individuals tend to see themselves as interdependent with their groups, usually behaving according to social norms or regulations. Though there exists a long history of opioid misuse in the country, as discussed in Chapter 1, on the whole this behavior is not viewed as acceptable and generally runs contrary to these societal norms. Because people in a collective-type culture are more likely to maintain specific societal roles and status and to exercise restraint in order to avoid shame and maintain public dignity, the power of public perception can play a powerful incentive for individuals to hide their personal opioid misuse. A recent investigation by Liu et al.[12] into the influence of traditional Chinese culture on younger adolescents showed some variations in the degree to which the younger generation has internalized traditional Chinese collectivistic culture. Because collectivistic individuals are incentivized to preserve family values and generally "believe that it is their responsibility, as a family member, to save the family's face and maintain the family's dignity," a strong desire to avoid bringing shame to their family is closely associated with behaviors that enhance their ability to avoid opioid use. Interventions or treatment plans which focus on the traditions of Confucius, Taoism, and Buddhism may be more effective in those who have a historical connection to these religions. Confucianism may be especially influential as these teachings focus on the family as the fundamental unit of society and specifically include interdependent responsibilities and expectations, which contradict the behaviors associated with opioid misuse.

Socioeconomic Status

According to a nationally representative Mortality Disparities in American Community (MDAC) study published in 2020,[13] the risk for fatal opioid overdose in the United States is greater among people in low as compared to high

[12] Liu et al. (2010).   [13] Altekruse et al. (2020).

socioeconomic status. Economic deprivation appears to be a significant risk factor for fatal opioid overdoses in the United States and "contributes to patterns of declining life expectancy that differ from most developed countries." Access to healthcare is strongly correlated with getting into recovery, successfully completing a treatment program, or obtaining medications. According to several studies, in the United States Caucasians are 35 times more likely to visit hospitals for buprenorphine as compared to their African-American counterparts, and generally this is because of difficulty accessing these services and inadequate insurance. If a person does not have adequate insurance or the financial resources to pay for treatment out of pocket, the chances that they will be successful in recovery are significantly reduced. Even with medical insurance, however, accessing care can still be challenging. Private insurance rarely covers more than 50% of the often considerable cost for mental health services, and for those with government insurance (Medicaid or Medicare in the United States), access to programs is limited due to below-market-rate reimbursement for healthcare providers. The end result is that the majority of patients have to pay cash outright or supplement their inadequate insurance, and this reduces available options for people from a lower socioeconomic status.

Gender Disparities

In some countries or regions, addiction among women is seen more negatively than addiction among men. In Latin America specifically, this viewpoint often results in women with opioid use disorder suffering to a greater degree than men with the same disease. Fear of decreased social acceptance and increased rejection by other members of peer and social support groups often lead to hesitancy in these affected women, who are much less likely to ask for help and seek treatment. Public criticism for women with drug addiction can also make it less likely that relatives and friends will advocate for them, further stigmatizing women with opioid use disorder. While the majority of prevalence studies have found males to have a higher percentage of opioid misuse worldwide, the number of females is not insignificant. In Latin America, use of opioids by females older than age 14 years is roughly 0.3% and current estimates are that those with opioid use disorder is about one to three per thousand in this population. According to Ochoa-Mangado et al., "The situation is undoubtedly related to sociocultural factors, family structures, community networks, and even political conditions."[14]

---

[14] Ochoa-Mangado et al. (2008).

In South and South-East Asia, historically anyway, opioid misuse was primarily a male phenomenon. While this is still the case and male opioid users far outnumber females, there has been a rise in the number of females misusing opioids. According to The Association of Southeast Asian Nations (ASEAN)[15] this is due, in part, to increases in female sex work in parts of China and Vietnam. Many of the member nations have substantial populations of female sex workers who live precariously with little or no family support and are increasingly misusing opioids.

In this population:[16]

- Women drug users are likely to have a male sexual partner who injects drugs.
- Women tend to be introduced to drugs by a husband/boyfriend or male member of their family.
- Access to drugs usually occurs through the male sexual partner.
- Women are more likely to share needles and to be injected by someone else.
- Women experience difficulty in avoiding drug use/abstaining/accessing drug treatment if the male partner is an active drug user.

Opioid misuse worldwide is predominantly a male phenomenon, but as more and more people become addicted to opioids, the number of women and girls impacted directly by addiction increases as well. North Cumbria, a relatively isolated area of the United Kingdom, located in the northwest corner of the island, just south of Scotland and directly across from the Isle of Man, is the second most sparsely populated county in England. This rural area encompasses the Lake District National Park and contains some of the most beautiful countryside in the area. Similar to regions in the southern United States, areas of natural beauty are juxtaposed with areas of disadvantage, particularly in towns along the coast. Jennifer Payne of the University of Glasgow investigated what influences resulted in opioid misuse in female members of this population and challenges the traditional assumption of women being coerced into illicit drug use.[17] While Payne acknowledges that "a known individual, usually male, was often present at initiation [into opioid misuse] and [that] this relationship appears pivotal" she points out that a number of complex personal circumstances, including curiosity and trust, are influential in the decision to begin to misuse opioids. In this investigation, circumstances associated with females using opioids included bereavement,

---

[15] The Member States of the Association are Brunei Darussalam, Cambodia, Indonesia, Lao PDR, Malaysia, Myanmar, Philippines, Singapore, Thailand, and Vietnam. The ASEAN Secretariat is based in Jakarta, Indonesia.
[16] ASEAN (2007).   [17] Payne (2007).

depressive illness, victimization, and a desire to be free of the stress associated with having to bear the primary burden of managing a household and caring for children without assistance from a partner. In most cases, opioids were introduced by male friends or romantic partners but in many cases the decision to "give it a go" was one made of circumstance. Availability of opioids and lack of economic opportunity in this region, coupled with a desire to be "peaceful" and uninvolved with the mundane responsibilities of everyday life, as is the case in many economically depressed areas of the world, seems to be a contributing factor for women who, seeing men using opioids, decide to try some for themselves.

Since many women with a history of opioid misuse begin to use early, often during their teenage years and after leaving formal schooling prior to completion, efforts aimed at preventing opioid misuse in the female population should focus specifically on factors that encourage self-esteem and self-efficiency and empower young women with the opportunity to make choices that do not involve opioid misuse. Completion of available basic education programs inevitably results in increased economic opportunities. Reducing the incidence of unwanted pregnancies, which necessarily prevent many females in economically depressed areas from participation in life outside the home, can do the same, and the creation of support systems directed at combating the domestic abuse that, in many cases, is a strong influencer for women who ultimately end up misusing opioids, can potentially reduce the number of females directly affected by the opioid epidemic. Given that the overwhelming number of females with opioid use disorder is initiated into opioid misuse by a trusted male friend or sexual partner, a focus on female-only support networks for at-risk young women may have a greater impact than co-ed peer groups.

In summary, race, culture, religion, geography, and socioeconomic factors all influence an individual's potential to both develop and recover from opioid use disorder, but the extent to which these factors have influence varies greatly across the globe. Changing economic conditions worldwide, including the economic transition that has resulted from deindustrialization, in the United States and many other developed countries, has resulted in high levels of economic distress experienced by residents in areas with formerly healthy economies. The resulting decay in physical infrastructure, lack of opportunities for both employment and recreational activities as well as, in the case of rural areas, large geographic distances with limited transportation have led to an increase in isolation and contributed to the significant increase in opioid misuse. Social conditions in economically depressed urban and rural settings, where availability of harm-reduction and drug treatment services is limited has led to an amplification of opioid misuse fed by a lack of opportunity and an abundance of misinformation.

Strategies to prevent opioid misuse, if they are to be effective, should be framed in the cultural context of the community these interventions are targeted towards. Just as there are significant global variations in the forms in which the fruit of the opium poppy is consumed, so too are there a myriad of different cultural attitudes associated with opioid use. When it comes to the treatment of opioid use disorder, one size does not fit all.

References and Further Reading

Altekruse SF, Cosgrove CM, Altekruse WC, Jenkins RA, Blanco C (2020). Socioeconomic risk factors for fatal opioid overdoses in the United States: Findings from the Mortality Disparities in American Communities Study (MDAC). *PLoS One* 15(1): e0227966.

ASEAN (2007). Drug use and HIV in Asia: Treatment and care for HIV-positive injecting drug users. http://apps.who.int/iris/bitstream/handle/10665/206034/B1485.pdf?sequence=1

Chapman A, Verdery AM, Monnat SM (2021). Opioid misuse and family structure: Changes and continuities in the role of marriage and children over two decades. *Drug and Alcohol Dependence* 222: 108668.

Chaturvedi HK, Mahanta J, Bajpail RC, Pandey A (2013). Correlates of opium use: Retrospective analysis of a survey of tribal communities in Arunachal Pradesh, India. *BMC Public Health* 13: 325.

Degenhardt L, Grebely J, Stone J, et al. (2019). Global patterns of opioid use and dependence: Harms to populations, interventions, and future action. *Lancet* 394: 1560–1579.

Flores DV, Torres LR, Torres-Vigil I, et al. (2014). From "Kickeando las malias" (kicking the withdrawals) to "Staying clean": The impact of cultural values on cessation of injection drug use in aging Mexican-American men. *Substance Use & Misuse* 49(8): 941–954.

Friedman J, Kim D, Schneberk T, et al. (2019). Assessment of racial/ethnic and income disparities in the prescription of opioids and other controlled medications in California. *JAMA Internal Medicine* 179(4): 469–476.

Griffith C, La France B (2018). Socio-economic impact on opioid addiction susceptibility. *Edelweiss Psychiatry Open Access* 2: 1–3.

James K, Jordan A (2018). The opioid crisis in Black communities. *Journal of Law, Medicine & Ethics* 46(2): 404–421.

Jutkowitz JM, Spielmann H, Koehler U, Lohani J, Pande A (1997). Drug use in Nepal: The view from the street. *Substance Use & Misuse* 32(7–8): 987–1004.

Liu H, Li J, Lu Z, Liu W, Zhang Z (2010). Does Chinese culture influence psycho-social factors for heroin use among young adolescents in China? A cross-sectional study. *BMC Public Health* 10: 563.

Mallik S, Starrelsa JL, Shannon C, Edwards K, Nahvia S (2021). "An undercover problem in the Muslim community": A qualitative study of imams' perspectives on substance use. *Journal of Substance Abuse Treatment* 123: 108224.

Ochoa-Mangado E, Madoz-Gúrpide A, Salvador E (2008). Gender differences in the treatment of opioid dependency [in Spanish]. *Drogas & Genero, Actas Españolas de Psiquiatría* 36(4): 197–204. www.drogasgenero.info/documento/ochoa-mangado-enriqueta-et-al-diferencias-genero-tratamiento-la-dependencia-opiaceos/

Parmar A, Patil V, Sarkar S, Rao R (2018). An observational study of treatment seeking users of natural opiates from India. *Substance Use & Misuse* 53(7): 1139–1145.

Partnership for a Drug-free New Jersey (2021). The opioid epidemic and the impact of race. https://knockoutday.drugfreenj.org/wp-content/uploads/2021/12/KOO AD_12_9_webinar.pdf

Payne J (2007). Women drug users in North Cumbria: What influences initiation into heroin in this non-urban setting? *Sociology of Health & Illness* 29(5): 633–655.

Rajkumar RP (2021). What are the correlates of global variations in the prevalence of opioid use disorders? An analysis of data from the Global Burden of Disease Study, 2019. *Cureus* 13(10): e18758.

Singh GK, Kim IE, Girmay M, et al. (2019). Opioid epidemic in the United States: Empirical trends, and a literature review of social determinants and epidemiological, pain management, and treatment patterns. *International Journal of Maternal and Child Health* 8(2): 89–100.

Unger JB, Ritt-Olson A, Teran L, Huang T, Hoffman BR, Palmer P (2002). Cultural values and substance use in a multiethnic sample of California adolescents. *Addiction Research & Theory* 10(3): 257–279.

van Draanen J, Tsang C, Mitra S, Karamouzian M, Richardson L (2020). Socioeconomic marginalization and opioid-related overdose: A systematic review. *Drug and Alcohol Dependence* 214: 108127.

World Health Organization (2010). ATLAS on substance use: Resources for the prevention and treatment of substance use disorders. www.who.int/publica tions/i/item/9789241500616

Zarghami M (2015). Iranian common attitude toward opium consumption. *Iranian Journal of Psychiatry and Behavioral Sciences* 9(2): e2074.

4 THE EFFECT OF POLICY AND GOVERNMENTAL REGULATIONS ON THE OPIOID EPIDEMIC

On October 26, 2017, the Acting Health and Human Services (HHS) Secretary (United States) issued a statement regarding the opioid epidemic.[1] As requested by then-president Donald Trump, Secretary Eric D. Hargan declared the opioid crisis a nationwide public health emergency:

> *Today's declaration, coupled with the President's direction that executive agencies use all appropriate emergency authorities and other relevant authorities, is another powerful action the Trump Administration is taking in response to America's deadly opioid crisis.*
>
> *President Trump has made this national crisis a top priority since he took office in January, and we are proud to be leading in this effort at HHS. His call to action today brings a new level of urgency to the comprehensive strategy HHS unveiled under President Trump, which empowers the real heroes of this fight: the communities on the frontlines of the epidemic.*

Declaring a public health emergency allowed the Trump administration to take very specific actions to address the epidemic without the bureaucratic "red tape" which so often slows down many governments' ability to respond quickly to a pressing need. Included in this response was the acceleration of temporary appointments of specialized personnel to address the emergency (a process that would otherwise likely require confirmation hearings or other vetting processes), the expansion of access to addiction treatment via telemedicine, and provisions that allowed for changes to existing programs, specifically within programs originally designed to address the HIV/AIDS epidemic, to more directly address the current opioid crisis.

---

[1] U.S. Department of Health and Human Services (2017).

The new five-point "Opioid Strategy" focused on the following priorities:

- improvement of access to prevention, treatment, and recovery support services;
- increasing the availability and distribution of overdose-reversing drugs;
- strengthening public health data reporting and collection;
- increasing support for research on addiction and pain;
- advancing the practice of pain management away from opioids.

When the public health emergency was declared, citizens of the United States were overdosing on opioids, according to the Centers for Disease Control and Prevention (CDC), at the alarming rate of 91 per day. Of the 52,404 Americans who died from drug overdoses in 2015,[2] the overwhelming majority, an estimated 33,000 (63%), died of opioid overdoses. Since then, despite the considerable effort and expense, these numbers keep increasing.[3] By the end of 2019, almost 500,000 people had died from overdoses involving any opioid, including prescription and illicit opioids, over the preceding 20 years of the epidemic.[4] As of the beginning of 2021, in the United States alone, 188 people die each day as a result of an opioid overdose.[5] The effect of individual governmental drug policies and regulations such as this has, in many cases, been the main driving force behind the direction that the opioid epidemic has taken in the United States and many countries around the world. Unfortunately, as we shall see, these differing governmental policies have had dramatically different effects.

The Law of Unintended Consequences

This increase in deaths caused by opioid overdose in the United States has come in three distinct waves, each caused directly by specific policy or regulation changes or as a direct reaction to these changes. In the 1990s, an effort to increase the market for prescription opioid pills, led specifically by OxyContin manufacturer Purdue Pharma, resulted in a significant increase in the number of individual prescriptions for opioids written between 1999 and 2008.[6] Changing policies pressed for by lobbyists allowed for broader use indications for these drugs and campaigns declaring pain as the "fifth vital sign" encouraged doctors to prescribe more opioids, even for moderate pain. Pharmaceutical

---

[2] The most recent year data was available when the public health emergency was declared in 2017.
[3] In fiscal year 2017, the US Department of Health and Human Services invested almost 900 million US dollars in funding specifically targeted at combating the opioid epidemic.
[4] Centers for Disease Control and Prevention (n.d.).
[5] National Institute on Drug Abuse (n.d.).   [6] Paulozzi et al. (2011).

manufacturers ramped up opioid production and, with a much larger patient base, as sales began to increase exponentially so began the first wave of opioid overdose deaths. This wave primarily involved prescription opioids, medications prescribed for legitimate indications, which either resulted in an overdose when taken in combination with other legitimately prescribed medications or due to increased dosing due to increased tolerance, or resulted in an overdose when diverted for recreational use and not used as directed. As opioid deaths began to increase significantly, it became clear that a problem was developing, but the severity was not immediately appreciated and the government's reaction had significant unintended consequences.

As a direct result of the law enforcement crackdown on prescription opioid diversion to the black market, prescription opioids became much more expensive and difficult to obtain illicitly. Around the same time, many providers began limiting the number of opioids they prescribed, primarily in response to a set of guidelines published by the CDC discouraging the use of opioids as a primary treatment for chronic pain. In addition, with the advent of state programs allowing providers to view a patient's history of opioid prescriptions, people addicted to opioids could no longer visit multiple doctors to obtain prescription pills. As a result, those who were addicted to opioids had to turn to the less expensive and more readily available opioid, heroin, and hence, around 2010, the second wave of opioid overdose deaths began.[7] Once only the scourge of addicts willing to inject this drug intravenously, heroin was now available in purity high enough to allow addicts to obtain a satisfactory "high" from simply snorting or smoking the drug, significantly widening the pool of potential users. Heroin manufacturing and sales continued to increase significantly throughout the second wave as more and more people turned to the drug, unable to obtain the increasingly rare opioid pills. In an attempt to reduce the importation of heroin manufactured elsewhere into the country, the United States began to crack down on shipments at border crossings and target manufacturing facilities in other countries. With demand for the product at an all-time high, and a need to reduce the size of each shipment to avoid detection, manufacturers turned away from heroin and towards the production of synthetic opioids such as fentanyl.

Because fentanyl is produced in a laboratory and does not require poppy fields, manufacturing facilities are easier to hide, and because the drug is 50 times more potent than heroin, the size of a fentanyl shipment of equivalent strength is up to 50 times smaller and much more easily smuggled into the country comparatively. The increased importation of illicitly manufactured fentanyl, which began

---

[7] Rudd et al. (2014).

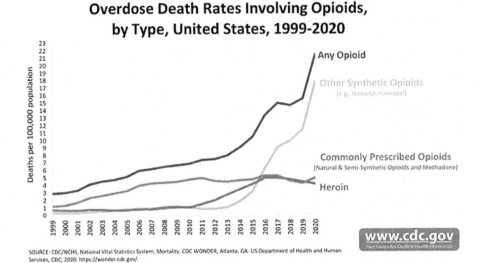

Figure 4.1 Increasing trend in opioid-related overdose deaths showing overall mortality and change in contribution to overdose mortality from heroin, commonly prescribed opioids and synthetic opioids.[8]

in 2013, marked the beginning of the third wave of increases in opioid overdose deaths in the United States, which continues to this day.[9] In addition to illicit fentanyl, opioid traffickers have started to import other fentanyl analogs, including the much more potent analog carfentanil (estimated to be 30–100 times more powerful that fentanyl), further increasing the incidence of opioid-related overdose deaths.[10] Some argue that we are in the midst of a fourth wave, as the ongoing coronavirus pandemic, combined with the increasing trend of misusing opioids with stimulants, has led to even higher rates of overdose-related deaths.

The Effect of Combating Opioid Misuse with Prison

One of the expected effects of the extreme ramping up of anti-drug law enforcement activity has naturally been a sizable increase in the prison population. When the United States began its "war on drugs," the number of individuals held in state and federal prisons for drug-law violations was

---

[8] From the CDC, materials developed by CDC Injury Center, accessed August 31, 2022. Reference to specific commercial products, manufacturers, companies, or trademarks does not constitute its endorsement or recommendation by the US Government, Department of Health and Human Services, or Centers for Disease Control and Prevention.
[9] O'Donnel et al. (2017a).   [10] O'Donnel et al. (2017b).

much lower than it is today. To put this in perspective, in 1980 the total number of persons incarcerated for violating anti-drug laws in the United States was roughly 25,000 people, less than 10% of the total number of individuals who were incarcerated at that time. Forty years later, after over four decades of waging war, the total number of prisoners serving time for violating anti-drug laws has increased to roughly 300,000 and persons now incarcerated for violating these laws now make up over 20% of the prison population.[11] Much of this increase can be attributed to policy changes made during the crack cocaine epidemic of the 1980s, which resulted in more persons charged with drug-related offenses receiving prison time instead of probation and new mandatory minimum sentencing guidelines, which resulted in longer prison terms.[12]

According to a 2018 report from the Pew Charitable Trusts, however, using the prison system to combat the opioid epidemic by locking up those who violate anti-drug laws is not likely to solve the opioid epidemic. This report specifically looked at the drug imprisonment rates for each state in the United States and compared that number to three markers for the severity of drug problems: self-reported drug use, arrests for drug-related offenses, and overdose deaths. Proponents of a "tough-on-crime" policy, in general, argue that an increased likelihood of incarceration for a particular offense associated with longer prison sentences will serve as a deterrent to committing that offense. For drug-related offenses, the thought is that tough crime policies will reduce the amount of drug use, and subsequently also the number of arrests and overdose deaths, in a community with these policies in place. Unfortunately, analysis of these data demonstrated no statistically significant correlation between incarceration rates and these markers, concluding "higher rates of drug imprisonment did not translate into lower rates of drug use, arrests, or overdose deaths."[13]

Global Policy Differences

In 1990, a project supported by a grant from the German Marshall Fund and the Alfred P. Sloan Foundation sought to "illuminate the similarities and differences among European and American drug policies and drug problems." In a 1993 report, based on conferences held in Washington DC (United States) and Bellaigo (Italy) in 1991, authors Peter Reuter, Mathea Falco and Robert MacCoun document the findings of this effort.[14] Their conclusion was that the

---

[11] U.S. Department of Justice (2016).   [12] James (2016).   [13] Pew Charitable Trusts (2018).
[14] RAND Corporation (1993).

problem of illicit drug use was perceived primarily as a crime issue in the United States, whereas Canada and most countries in Western Europe perceived the issue to be primarily one related to public health. It is not surprising, then, that the policies put in place in each country reflect this perception, with the United States becoming increasingly tough on drug-related crimes and financing law enforcement efforts, while Western European nations focused more on decriminalization and harm-reduction strategies, such as increasing access to methadone, needle exchange programs, and even experimenting with heroin maintenance. The end result has been the opioid misuse epidemic, which accelerated much more quickly in the United States due, at least in part anyway, to the policies and regulations described above. Treating the epidemic as a crime problem by focusing on law enforcement and incarceration has not had the desired effect in the United States, but even treating the epidemic as a public health issue as the majority of the Western European countries did in the 1990s was not entirely protective, and these countries now find themselves dealing with widespread opioid misuse today, though to a lesser degree.

Although neither of these policies, either treating opioid misuse as a crime issue or as a public health problem, has worked to stem the tide of the epidemic in the West, have countries in other regions perhaps had better luck? In Asia, a region that includes the majority of opium-producing countries and where opium use was traditionally used for centuries, opioid policies vary from country to country and in some places have changed significantly over the past hundred years. In his 1976 paper entitled "the Pro-heroin effects of anti-opium laws in Asia,"[15] Joseph Westermeyer, MD, PhD describes how a change in policy from one in which traditional opium use was generally accepted to one where existing anti-drug laws were actively enforced created an epidemic of heroin use in three different countries in this region. According to sources cited by Westermeyer, opioid users in China and Hong Kong had overwhelmingly used opium prior to 1945. Before World War II, the British had not enforced anti-opium regulations in the colony of Hong Kong, instead allowing traditional use to continue without interference. After the war, however, they began to enforce existing laws, which resulted in a significant increase, "within months," of heroin misuse. Individuals formerly addicted to opium almost immediately switched to heroin and new addicts started to use heroin without first using opium. A small percentage of individuals who began using opium before heroin became ubiquitous continued to only use opium but in less than a decade they were in the minority. The main reason for this rapid substitution was the availability of heroin in the region and its increased potency, which

---

[15] Westermeyer (1976).

rapidly attracted new and traditional opioid users alike. Heroin, unlike opium, could either be smoked or injected but could not be eaten like traditional opium. The end result was a much stronger and intense "high," which came on much faster that orally ingested opium and to which most very quickly became addicted. By 1959 it was estimated that 83% of all opioid addicts in Hong Kong were now using heroin only and by 1972 the number had risen to over 90%.

Thailand passed their first anti-opium law 14 years after the British began enforcing anti-opium laws in Hong Kong, primarily as a result of international pressure to reduce opium production. Prior to 1959, as a result of centuries of opium use by tribal peoples, the Thai government allowed for the growing, production and sale of opium locally by way of franchises. After passage of the 1959 law, opium production, sale, transport, and use were forbidden and, just as in Hong Kong 14 years earlier, heroin use began to skyrocket. Within less than 14 years, in 1971, it was estimated that 85% of opioid addicts in Thailand were addicted to heroin, a disease which primarily affected members of the ethnic Thai tribal units, who were the people who had been the primary users of opium prior to 1959. Interestingly, while passage of the 1959 law did significantly increase the number and percentage of persons misusing heroin, it did not significantly reduce opium production or transport out of the country. This is, according to Westermeyer, for three reasons: first, "the tribal areas were not liable to effective Thai law enforcement," meaning that while laws passed by the Thai government did apply to tribal peoples they were unable to be enforced; second, "opium is a primary cash crop for tribal people," suggesting that outlawing production without substituting an equally lucrative crop provided no incentive to stop growing opium poppies; and third, "the extensive mountainous boundaries with opium-producing Burma and Laos could not be adequately patrolled." Just as in Hong Kong, the "solution" to opioid misuse, which was, prior to 1959, perceived of and addressed primarily as a public health issue, ultimately resulted in a greater number of people suffering from opioid use disorder. Exacerbating the problem in both cases was a public health infrastructure woefully unprepared to treat the exponential increase in patients with opioid use disorder, resulting from the introduction of intravenously administered heroin in place of opium, which is primarily smoked or eaten.

As in Hong Kong and Thailand, the same story was born out in Laos. In 1971, once again bowing to international pressure primarily from the United States, which was at the time in the early stages of the war on drugs, the government outlawed the production, sale, and use of opium. As enforcement of the law began, two things became apparent. First, as in Thailand, opium production continued at scale. While police and customs agents were able to intercept some of the product being exported from the country, they were unable to significantly reduce production in the remote areas of the country. Second, as was seen in both Hong Kong and Thailand, heroin became the drug of choice for those previously addicted to opium, and the number and percentage of people using heroin began to skyrocket as well.

It seems clear from these examples, as well as the more recent experience in the United States, that treating the opioid epidemic as a problem to be solved by increased criminal penalties and more aggressive law enforcement measures has not worked, but perhaps the problem is that the laws are not enforced well enough and the penalties are not as severe as they should be. Despite a movement away from aggressive suppression of drug production by law enforcement and the criminalization of users by some Western European countries and Latin American states, the Middle East and North Africa (MENA) countries still impose significantly punitive drug policies.[16] Iran and Saudi Arabia still impose the harshest sentences for breaking anti-drug laws, routinely executing individuals convicted of drug trafficking. According to a 2016 article published in the *Guardian*, of the 246 executions publicly recognized by Iranian authorities in 2015, 122 (42%) were people convicted of drug offenses, as were roughly half of the executions performed in Saudi Arabia that same year.[17] But despite this ultraconservative stance on the cultivation, production, and use of opioids and other drugs, the number of people addicted to opioids appears to be increasing in the region. It is difficult to accurately calculate these numbers, however, as most of the MENA governments do not keep these types of records. In these countries opioid use is seen as a social taboo, is viewed as contrary to the teachings of Islam, and has been generally ignored as a public health problem. Despite this, there is evidence that things are changing in the area. Recognizing that these strict anti-drug policies have failed to stem the tide of the opioid epidemic, countries such as Iran and Morocco have adopted some harm-reduction measures including medications for opioid use disorder, needle exchange programs and even the establishment of treatment centers, many of which, especially the ones designed for women only, must operate hidden from view. As of 2020, methadone, buprenorphine, and extended-release naltrexone (the three medications supported by World Health Organization guidelines for the treatment of opioid use disorder) were available as a treatment modality for opioid use disorder in Lebanon,

---

[16] Felbab-Brown V, Trinkunas H, Sultan Barakat S (2016).
[17] www.theguardian.com/news/datablog/2016/jan/04/executions-in-saudi-arabia-iran-numbers-china.

Morocco, Iran, and the Palestinian Territories.[18] Unfortunately, access to these vital medications remains limited, if at all available, in the other 12 countries that make up the region.

Further south in Africa, there is greater variation in policy when it comes to opioids, and in fact there is even considerable variation between member countries that share regional and economic ties. The member countries of the Economic Community of West African States[19] comprise a vast region on the continent between the equator and the Sahara desert. Similar to policies held by the governments of countries in the MENA region to the north and east, these countries have historically focused on hardline, punitive anti-drug policies. The majority of these policies were actually written into law around the time that the 1988 Convention Against Illicit Traffic in Narcotic Drugs and Psychotropic Substances was adopted globally, and as with similar laws worldwide, the primary influence for this strong anti-drug legislation came from the United States and the United Nations Office on Drugs and Crime. Thirty years later, though the majority of West African countries still enforce harsh penalties for drug-related offenses, some are questioning their effectiveness, as the opioid epidemic continues to transform a region historically involved with transportation of drugs into one with an increasingly greater number of local sale and use. Gambia has reduced prison terms for drug possession, Burkina Faso has moved to a more proportionate public health approach to the opioid epidemic, and in Mali, Senegal, and Ghana existing anti-drug laws are in the process of being revised in order to reduce the considerable negative impact they have had on citizens who suffer from drug use disorders. Not all West African countries, however, are revising existing laws in an attempt to reduce harm. The Nigerian government, for example, remains in favor of tightening their anti-drug laws by removing judicial discretion when it comes to sentences for drug-related offenses, a tactic which, as we have seen in the United States, does not work.

When it comes to prison terms for drug-related offenses in these West African countries, the penalty for drug possession, even for personal use, ranges from a minimum of two months in prison (in Senegal) to a maximum of 25 years in prison (in Nigeria), though most countries impose sentences of 1–5 years in prison.[20] Additionally, not all countries mandate prison for drug use offenses, and many are starting to move away from a policy

---

[18] Alawa et al. (2022).
[19] As of 2017 the member nations were Benin, Burkina Faso, Cabo Verde, Cote d'Ivoire, The Gambia, Ghana, Guinea, Guinea-Bissau, Liberia, Mali, Niger, Nigeria, Senegal, Sierra Leone, and Togo.
[20] Bridge and Ane (2017).

of punishment and towards one of offering treatment. In Cabo Verde, Senegal, and Togo, for example, a judge may offer treatment as an alternative to prison and, in Côte D'Ivoire and Mali, medical detoxification may be offered instead of detoxification in prison for individuals with opioid dependence. Interestingly, in Nigeria the courts may impose mandatory treatment, anti-drug education, aftercare, or rehabilitation but this is in addition to the extremely harsh sentences they impose. Sadly, as we will see in a future chapter, these mandatory treatment programs are generally overcrowded and ineffective, more closely resembling prison than actual treatment programs. As we have seen, Africa has traditionally remained a bastion of conservative, prohibitionist drug policies, but even still change seems to be coming. As of 2018, roughly 20% (11) of countries across the continent of Africa have liberalized or are considering the liberalization of their drug control policies, reducing mandatory minimum sentencing guidelines, choosing not to fully enforce existing anti-drug laws, and, in some cases, even implementing harm-reduction strategies in an effort to shift from a law enforcement to a public health model.[21]

As with the majority of countries in Africa, the former communist countries of Eastern Europe and Central Asia (EECA) maintain traditionally held hardline, punitive anti-drug policies. Drug production, distribution, and consumption is criminalized and the incarceration of people convicted of drug-related offenses has, just as in the United States, resulted in a significant increase in prison populations, directly increased the number of HIV infections, and, because law enforcement is such an expensive policy, resulted in a significant shortfall in available funds for prevention and treatment. In fact, the EECA region is the only area of the world that has seen an increase in HIV infections as well as in mortality with those who have been infected with this virus since 2010, an increase directly tied to the opioid epidemic and increased numbers of people who use injection drugs.[22] Despite scientific evidence from countries in Western Europe that harm-reduction policies such as needle exchange programs and medications for opioid use disorder are significantly more effective and cost significantly less than current policies in place in EECA countries, these programs remain mostly unavailable. The use of methadone and buprenorphine as a treatment for opioid use disorder are currently illegal in Russia, and the chances that this will change soon remain slim. According to a 2021 *Economist* report[23] on drug control policies in Eastern

---

[21] Eligh (2019).   [22] AIDSinfo. https://aidsinfo.unaids.org
[23] Drug control policies in Eastern Europe and Central Asia: The economic, health and social impact. https://impact.economist.com/perspectives/sites/default/files/eiu_aph_investin g_hiv_launch.pdf

Europe and Central Asia, much of this refusal to adopt harm-reduction-based anti-drug policies in favor of criminalization results from strongly held ideas ingrained in these societies. The belief that the use of medications for opioid use disorder is simply swapping one opioid for another, which is seen as a reward and not a treatment, is pervasive among those in a position to make policy changes, despite what appears to be increasing popular support for these types of programs. As well, according to Mr. Roman Khabarov, a former police officer in Russia who is now a human rights lawyer, "Russian law enforcement officials on the whole view drug-related crime as a punishable offense, which will not change overnight and requires a lot of public debate before that view comes close to being reversed."

It is clear from our brief tour around the world that governmental policies and regulations have had and have the potential to have a significant impact on the future direction of the opioid epidemic. If the past 50 years have taught us anything about this impact, it is that policies which support the criminalization of opioid production, distribution, and recreational use have had the unintended effect of driving the epidemic forward in every country and region they have been established. Treating opioid misuse as a problem that can be solved by law enforcement, with extended incarceration and mandatory minimum sentences, does not actually reduce the number of individuals with opioid use disorder, is not a deterrent to crime, and negatively impacts low-level opioid distributors and end users, who are often the most vulnerable in our societies, while generating incredible income for the producers, manufacturers, and global distributors in this criminal enterprise. Focusing instead on treating opioid misuse as a public health problem that can be addressed with proven harm-reduction strategies (which we discuss in future chapters) costs less and is more effective. According to Harm Reduction International's *Global State of Harm Reduction*,[24] the availability of harm-reduction services has not increased significantly globally since 2012.

Specific findings from this report include the following:

- In 2021, the total number of countries implementing needle and syringe programmes (NSP) has increased by just one, from 86 to 87. The new country is Uganda.
- Two new countries (Uganda and Mozambique) have begun implementing opioid agonist therapy (OAT) programmes since 2020. The total number of countries implementing OAT in 2021 is 86 (up from 84 in 2020).
- There were no reports of countries ceasing implementation of NSP, OAT, peer-distribution of naloxone or shutting down drug consumption rooms.

[24] Harm Reduction International (2022).

It seems that if we are going to even just begin to reduce the global impact of this epidemic then we must support a significant change in global anti-drug policy, support harm-reduction programs, and reform archaic anti-drug laws that do not work.

In summary, the anti-drug policies promoted by the United States and other countries around the world have led to both positive outcomes and unintended consequences. Historically, many of these policies have addressed drug use as criminal behavior based in the now archaic belief that opioid addiction is reflective of poor moral choices and not a medical condition. In contrast, Canada and much of Europe have treated opioid misuse as a public health issue, rather than a crime to be punished, through the institution of harm reduction strategies. Unfortunately, there are certain countries in Asia, Africa, and the Middle East that continue to use incarceration as their primary solution to the opioid epidemic, although in recent years Uganda and Mozambique now offer medications to treat opioid use disorder. If we are to find a solution to the opioid epidemic, we will have to change the way we think about opioid use disorder, and mental illness in general, and refuse to continue to support the failed policies of the past.

References and Further Reading

Alawa J, Muhammad M, Kazemitabar M, et al. (2022). Medication for opioid use disorder in the Arab World: A systematic review. *International Journal of Drug Policy* 102: 103617.

Bridge J, Ane M-G (2017). Drug laws in West Africa: A review and summary. West Africa Commission on Drugs (WACD) and the International Drug Policy Consortium (IDPC) briefing paper, November 2017. https://idpc.net/publica tions/2017/11/drug-laws-in-west-africa-a-review-and-summary

Carson EA, Anderson E (2016). Prisoners in 2015. U.S. Department of Justice, Bureau of Justice Statistics. https://bjs.ojp.gov/content/pub/pdf/p15.pdf

Centers for Disease Control and Prevention (CDC) (2011). Vital signs: Overdoses of prescription opioid pain relievers – United States, 1999–2008. *Morbidity and Mortality Weekly Report* 60(43): 1487–1492.

Centers for Disease Control and Prevention (CDC) (n.d.). Wide-ranging ONline Data for Epidemiologic Research (WONDER). https://wonder.cdc.gov

Drug Enforcement Administration (2019). National drug threat assessment. Drug Enforcement Administration Strategic Intelligence Section, U.S. Department of Justice. www.dea.gov/sites/default/files/2020-01/2019-NDTA-final-01-14-2020_ Low_Web-DIR-007-20_2019.pdf

Eligh J (2019). The evolution of illicit drug markets and drug policy in Africa. *ENACT Observer*, June 30. https://enactafrica.org/research/continental-reports/the-evolution-of-illicit-drug-markets-and-drug-policy-in-africa

Felbab-Brown V, Trinkunas H, Barakat S (2016). Breaking bad in the Middle East and North Africa: Drugs, militants and human rights. www.brookings.edu/blog/markaz/2016/03/22/breaking-bad-in-the-middle-east-and-north-africa-drugs-militants-and-human-rights

Gladden RM, Martinez P, Seth P (2016). Fentanyl law enforcement submissions and increases in synthetic opioid-involved overdose deaths: 27 states, 2013–2014. *Morbidity and Mortality Weekly Report* 65: 837–843.

Gladden RM, O'Donnell J, Mattson C, Seth P (2019). Changes in opioid-involved overdose deaths by opioid type and presence of benzodiazepines, cocaine, and methamphetamine – 25 states, July–December 2017 to January–June 2018. *Morbidity and Mortality Weekly Report* 68(34): 737–744.

Harm Reduction International (2022). The global state of harm reduction. https://hri.global/flagship-research/the-global-state-of-harm-reduction/the-global-state-of-harm-reduction-2022/

James N (2016). The federal prison population buildup: Options for congress, May 20, 2016. https://sgp.fas.org/crs/misc/R42937.pdf

Kariisa M, Scholl L, Wilson N, Seth P, Hoots B (2019). Drug overdose deaths involving cocaine and psychostimulants with abuse potential: United States, 2003–2017. *Morbidity and Mortality Weekly Report* 68(17): 41–43.

National Institute on Drug Abuse (n.d.). Drug overdose death rates. https://nida.nih.gov/research-topics/trends-statistics/overdose-death-rates (accessed December 2, 2022)

O'Donnell JK, Gladden RM, Seth P (2017a). Trends in deaths involving heroin and synthetic opioids excluding methadone, and law enforcement drug product reports, by census region: United States, 2006–2015.*Morbidity and Mortality Weekly Report* 66: 897–903.

O'Donnell JK, Halpin J, Mattson CL, Goldberger BA, Gladden RM (2017b). Deaths involving fentanyl, fentanyl analogs, and U-47700: 10 states, July–December 2016. *Morbidity and Mortality Weekly Report* 60: 1487–1492.

Paulozzi LJ, Jones CM, Mack KA, Rudd RA (2011).Vital signs: Overdoses of prescription opioid pain relievers: United States, 1999–2008. *Morbidity and Mortality Weekly Report* 66: 1197–1202.

Pew Charitable Trusts (2018). More imprisonment does not reduce state drug problems, a brief from the Pew Charitable Trusts. www.pewtrusts.org/-/media/assets/2018/03/pspp_more_imprisonment_does_not_reduce_state_drug_problems.pdf

RAND Corporation (1993). Comparing Western European and North American drug policies, an international conference report. www.rand.org/pubs/mono graph_reports/MR237.html

Rudd RA, Paulozzi LJ, Bauer MJ, et al. (2014). Increases in heroin overdose deaths: 28 states, 2010 to 2012. *The Morbidity and Mortality Weekly Report* 63(39): 849.

Reuter P, Mathea F, MacCoun R (1993). *Comparing Western European and North American Drug Policies: An International Conference Report.* Santa Monica, CA: RAND Corporation.

Snell TL (1995). Correctional Populations in the United States, 1993, Bureau of Justice Statistics. https://bjs.ojp.gov/library/publications/correctional-populations-united-states-1993

University of Albany, Sourcebook of Criminal Justice Statistics 2003, Table 6.57. www.albany.edu/sourcebook/pdf/t657.pdf

U.S. Department of Health and Human Services (2017). HHS acting secretary declares public health emergency to address national opioid crisis. https://pub lic3.pagefreezer.com/browse/HHS.gov/31-12-2020T08:51/https:/www.hhs.gov/ about/news/2017/10/26/hhs-acting-secretary-declares-public-health-emer gency-address-national-opioid-crisis.html

U.S. Department of Justice (2016). United States Department of Justice report on prisoners in 2015. https://bjs.ojp.gov/content/pub/pdf/p15.pdf

Westermeyer J (1976). The pro-heroin effects of anti-opium laws in Asia. *Archives of General Psychiatry* 33: 1135–1139.

PART II
Recognizing That a Problem Exists

5 CURRENT DATA AND WORLDWIDE OPIOID MISUSE STATISTICS

The amount of people worldwide who regularly used opioids in 2021 is staggering, and if something is not done to change the course of this epidemic, the numbers will continue to increase year over year, just as they have done over the last decade. Roughly 275 million people globally report having used drugs of any kind in the past year, an increase of almost 50 million people over the past 10 years.[1] While some of this increase was due to the 10% rise in global population over the same period, this alone cannot account for the entirety of the 22% rise in global drug use. Healthcare systems around the world are being stretched beyond their capabilities to manage a population this large, and the number of people with opioid use disorder is projected to continue to increase in size over the next decade. The effects of the opioid epidemic on healthcare systems are particularly devastating in poorer and middle-income countries with less robust resources. As of 2019, roughly 36 million people worldwide were thought to meet the criteria for a drug use disorder, and the percentage of that population that meets the criteria for opioid use disorder continues to increase exponentially. Over the past decade, this number has increased by almost nine million, an increase of over 33%, and now affects 0.7% of the current global population.

While the number of people with opioid use disorder has increased, the availability of effective treatment interventions and access to harm-reduction programs has not. As of 2019, only 12.5% of individuals with opioid use disorder were able to access professional help, and the negative consequences of these shortages of services were disproportionately felt in poorer countries. Unfortunately, programs to address opioid misuse and opioid use disorder are already in limited supply in developing countries and access to mental health and addiction health professionals is significantly under-resourced compared to higher-income areas. To put this in perspective, in 2020 there were 14.63 psychiatrists per 100,000 people in the United Kingdom but only 0.01 psychiatrists per 100,000 people in Tanzania.[2]

---

[1] UNDOC (2021).   [2] Kurth et al. (2018).

According to the 2021 United Nations World Drug Report,[3] the total number of people who used drugs in 2018 was about 269 million people. Broken down by region, that was 80 million in Asia, 66 million in North America, 60 million in Africa, 42 million in Europe, 17 million in Latin America and the Caribbean, and 4 million in Oceania. Of these 269 million people who use drugs, 23% (roughly 62 million people) used opioids, but opioid use is not evenly distributed throughout the world. At 3.6%, North America has the highest prevalence of opioid use; with only 0.8%, Europe has the lowest. Sadly, the number of users worldwide has nearly doubled over the past decade, and projections for Africa specifically are dire as the number of drug users is projected to increase by 40% by 2030. About 50,000 people died from opioid overdoses in the United States in 2019, roughly one death every 10 minutes, more than twice the number of overdose deaths less than a decade earlier in 2010. Most of this increase has been attributed to fentanyl and fentanyl analogs and this region has seen a spike in overdose deaths since the beginning of the coronavirus pandemic. The global economic downturn that resulted from the pandemic has also driven an increase in opioid production in less affluent countries where illicit cultivation of drugs is often a significant source of income. An available supply of opioids necessarily increases the number of individuals with opioid use disorder, but demand is spread unevenly throughout the globe. In this chapter we will examine the prevalence of opioid use in different regions of the world and projections for the global opioid epidemic.

Synthetic Opioids

Opium is expensive and labor intensive to produce. Opium poppies must be grown, processed, and transported to the point of sale, necessitating an immense industry, which depends on the availability of large swaths of land that must be protected, the presence of an intact agricultural and processing infrastructure, and a large labor force. Once produced, the refined heroin and other products must be transported. The final product is bulky and must be hidden from authorities to avoid interception. Synthetic opioids, however, are less expensive to produce, require significantly less land and infrastructure, and are much more potent. The volume of an equipotent amount of fentanyl is about 100 times less than refined heroin, and the financial loss from an intercepted shipment is considerably less as well. As governments have increased their efforts to target the illicit opioid trade at the point of entry into their countries, producers have turned to synthetic products and the

---

[3] UNDOC (2021).

amounts of fentanyl and its analogs seized globally have begun to rapidly increase. Seizures in 2019 rose by over 60% compared with a year earlier and more than 2,000% from 2015. In addition to increases in heroin production, illicit pharmaceutical opioids such as oxycodone or hydrocodone continue to be manufactured as well. In 2019, 52% of these pharmaceutical opioids seized were either fentanyl (39%) or fentanyl analogs (13%).

In a March 18, 2021 lecture, Lt. Jason Piotrowski of the New Jersey State (US) Police Drug Monitoring Initiative discussed the rapid increase of fentanyl-laced heroin in the state over the past five years: "in the 4th quarter of 2020, 93% of suspected heroin [analyzed by our lab] contained fentanyl [in addition to heroin]." To put this in perspective, during the fourth quarter of 2020, five years earlier, only 9% contained fentanyl. Conversely, Lt. Piotrowski reports, "the number of suspected heroin [analyzed in our lab] testing positive for heroin, with no other drugs, has steadily declined, from 98% in the 1st quarter of 2015 to 5% in the 4th quarter of 2020."[4] In the United States it is becoming almost impossible to find pure, unadulterated heroin for sale on the street; you have to assume it has fentanyl in it.

Overdose Deaths

According to the World Health Organization, in 2020 roughly 500,000 deaths worldwide were attributable to drug use.[5] Not surprisingly, more than 70% of these deaths were related to opioids. Ten percent of these deaths alone were in the United States as the opioid epidemic continues to evolve. According to Dr. Mark Rosenberg, a member of the United States Health and Human Services Opioid Task Force and the Center for Disease Control (CDC) Opioid Best Practice Task Force, during the 12-month period from October 2019 to October 2020 in the United States there were more than 91,000 overdose deaths, 68,000 of which were related to opioids. This represents the "highest number of deaths in a 12-month period since the CDC started tracking in 1999."[6]

While the number of deaths caused by heroin or the nonmedical use of diverted pharmaceuticals has been decreasing over the past several years, this decline has been overshadowed by the rapid increase in overdose deaths due to fentanyl and fentanyl analogs. As of 2020, fully 50% of heroin overdose deaths resulted from heroin laced with fentanyl, and synthetic opioids are now also being added to other non-opioid drugs such as cocaine, methamphetamine, and ecstasy, contributing to a rise in heretofore unheard of overdose deaths in persons using these drugs as well.

[4] Partnership for a Drug-Free New Jersey (2021).   [5] WHO (2021).   [6] Rosenberg (2021).

Disease Burden

As the number of individuals with opioid use disorder continues to rise, so too does the burden of disease caused by opioid misuse. The greatest harm related to opioid use remains the transmission of disease, due to unsafe injection practices such as sharing needles. Users continue to become infected with HIV and hepatitis C. In some regions, over 50% of the population of injection drug users is currently infected with HIV, though the past decade has seen a decline in the number of deaths related to HIV and AIDS. Hepatitis C related liver cancer, cirrhosis, and chronic liver disease accounts for the majority of the deaths not related to overdose. But it is not just the transmission of infectious disease that puts people who use illicit opioids at risk for death. According to the authors of one recent study published in the *Lancet*, across all major causes of death analyzed, chronic opioid use is associated with many more deaths due to noncommunicable diseases.[7] There is no question that the rate of death from all causes and the burden of chronic disease among people who use illicit opioids are much higher than in the general population. Historically this was due to the increased risk associated with exposure to blood-born infectious disease and the potential for overdose death, suicide, and homicide, but recent data have shown an increasing number of deaths and chronic disease related to chronic opioid use not due to overdose or infectious disease. In the United Kingdom, Australia, and North America, noncommunicable diseases are now responsible for the majority of opioid-related illness and death in older cohorts while still responsible for the minority of the opioid-attributable disease burden in younger cohorts. According to Dan Lewer and his colleagues at the Department of Epidemiology and Public Health at University College London (UK), this reflects "a deprived and marginalized population with multiple determinants of poor health throughout life."

People who chronically misuse opioids generally have more complex health needs, decreased access to regular preventative medical care, and, as a result, an increased risk of death due to noncommunicable diseases. They are more likely to be chronic tobacco smokers and have an increased risk of cancer of all kinds, but specifically lung, breast, gastrointestinal, female genital, and blood cancers. Circulatory diseases such as ischemic heart disease (increased risk for myocardial infarction or "heart attack") and cerebrovascular disease (increased risk for stroke or "brain attack") are more common, as are respiratory diseases such as chronic obstructive pulmonary disease (COPD) and emphysema, influenza, and pneumonia. The incidence of digestive diseases

---

[7] Lewer et al. (2022).

such as gastroesophageal reflux disease (GERD) and non-infectious liver disease are increased in this population, as are morbidity (illness) and mortality (death) related to external causes from accidents as impaired individuals are significantly more likely to experience physical trauma.

Geographical Distribution

As of 2020, the regional distribution of individuals with opioid use disorder continues to parallel the main opioid trafficking routes out of Afghanistan, with increasing use in destination countries. The likelihood that an opioid will be identified as the main psychoactive substance at treatment entry is significantly higher in higher middle-income countries. In the Eastern Mediterranean region, only 20% of countries reported opioids as the main psychoactive substance responsible for entry into treatment but this number increases to 26.5% of countries in the South-East Asia region and 42.9% in the European regions.[8] It remains difficult to obtain an accurate and complete assessment of the actual scope of the opioid epidemic as fewer than 50% of the world's countries have national data collection systems for epidemiological or treatment data. The presence or absence of such data collection systems is strongly affected by income level, with countries in the higher middle-income and high-income groups being more likely (50–76%), than in the low-income and lower middle-income groups (11–31%) to have established programs. For those that do have published data, these often lag behind the rapidly changing present by as much as two to three years. The Americas and Europe have the highest proportion of countries with such data collection systems, but this still includes only 60% of the countries in these areas. Data collection is substantially lower in the regions of the Eastern Mediterranean (20%), South-East Asia (20%), and Africa (7%). Due to this difficulty, current data are presented in "best-estimate" form as the average between the lowest and highest of multiple estimates obtained from region to region, and they may be incomplete for some countries (Table 5.1).

Americas (North America, South America, Central America, Caribbean)

The Americas have a population of approximately one billion people living in what is an ethnically, linguistically, economically, and culturally diverse region composed of 35 different countries. Due to the size of the region, which includes large land masses on both sides of the equator, considerable diversity also exists when it comes to the distribution of opioid misuse, with the

---

[8] WHO (2010).

Table 5.1 Annual prevalence of opioid use by region and globally, 2019[9]

Region	Total number of people who use opioids	Percentage of the population aged 15–64 years
Africa	9,050,000	1.24
Americas	12,580,000	1.86
Asia	35,750,000	1.17
Europe	3,610,000	0.66
Oceania	660,000	2.47
Global	61,650,000	1.22

Subregions: Africa: East Africa, North Africa, Southern Africa, West and Central Africa; Americas: Caribbean, Central America, North America, South America; Asia: Central Asia and Transcaucasia, East and South-East Asia, South-West Asia/ Near and Middle East, South Asia; Europe: Eastern and South-Eastern Europe, Western and Central Europe; Oceania: Australia and New Zealand, Melanesia, Micronesia, Polynesia.

majority concentrated in North America. Opioids, primarily the nonmedical use of prescription medications, are now responsible for more overdose fatalities than all other types of illicit drugs combined in both Canada and in the United States, where more people have reported using controlled prescription drugs than cocaine, heroin, and methamphetamine combined.[10] In the United States, opioids have become the second most common reason (after marijuana) to seek drug treatment, with over 128,000 individuals admitted for treatment to public treatment programs alone in 2014.

In the United States there are now three well-defined opioid-addicted cohorts. The youngest cohort consists of those between the ages of 20 and 40 years old. They are disproportionately White and their opioid addiction began with prescription drug use (addicted after 1995) but is now characterized by significant heroin use. The older disproportionately White cohort also began using mostly prescription opioids around 1995 but this group is made up of individuals 40 years of age and older. The older disproportionately non-White cohort, now aged 50 and above, is composed primarily of heroin users whose opioid addiction began in teen years with heroin use before 1995.

The story in the Americas south of the equator is very different. South America currently produces only 3% of the world's morphine and heroin and

[9] Data from UNODC (2021).
[10] Inter-American Drug Abuse Control Commission (2019).

less than 0.01% of its opium, and the prevalence of its use is uneven. According to the Inter-American Commission on Drug Abuse Control, heroin use remains low in most Latin American countries, even in countries where it is produced. For example, even though Colombia is the region's largest opium producer, Mexico, most likely because of its close proximity to the United States, has the highest incidence of use.[11] After the United States declared the opioid epidemic a national emergency in 2017, opioid manufacturers looked to markets in South America in which to sell these medications, attempting to make up for the significant reduction in profits from US markets. After some strategic company and brand name changes, the pharmaceutical industry is now using the same strategies that were so successful in the United Stated to target Latin America as its potentially strongest market.[12]

Asia Pacific (Central and South Asia, Northeastern Asia, Southeastern Asia, Australia, and Oceania)

Since the majority of the world's opium poppies are grown in this region it is not surprising that the number of individuals with opioid use disorder is high here. Afghanistan is by far the world leader when it comes to opioid production, accounting for 85% of the global total, and production there continues to increase. The country saw a significant 37% increase in the amount of land devoted to growing opium poppies from 2019 to 2020. The remaining 15% of opium production comes primarily from Myanmar, with Mexico and a handful of other countries rounding out the total. According to the World Health Organization,[13] as of 2010 there were over 500,000 people using injection drugs in South-East Asia, and this number has increased significantly over the past decade. Countries in the region with the most use included Bangladesh, India, Indonesia, Maldives, Myanmar, Nepal, and Thailand. Harm-reduction programs in these countries vary, with some offering both needle and syringe exchange programs as well as opioid substitution therapy. Unfortunately, data from this report suggest that these measures have a limited reach and are not of sufficient scale to effectively address the problem as less than one-third of affected persons are able to access a needle and syringe exchange program, even just once a year, and less than 5% receive opioid substitution therapy.

Estimates regarding the number of active drug users in the South-East Asia region vary widely and differ considerably from country to country. The

[11] Inter-American Drug Abuse Control Commission, Secretariat for Multidimensional Security, and the Organization of American States (2015).
[12] HispanTV (2018). [13] WHO (2020)

number of active users who misuse opioids is usually only a small percentage of the population but varies considerably from country to country. India is estimated to have as many as 73 million active drug users (roughly 6% of the 2010 population) but only 2 million (roughly 0.16% of the population) are misusing opioids, and only 500,000 of these people are considered to be opioid dependent. Bangladesh, estimated to have as many as 4.6 million active users in 2010 (roughly 3% of the population at that time) is currently believed to have as many as 7 million as recently as 2020 (4% of the 2020 population). Though opium and cannabis have traditionally been the most popular drugs in this country, according to the United Nations Office on Drugs and Crime (UNODC)[14] heroin has been gaining in popularity since its introduction in the 1980s, and buprenorphine is currently the most misused opioid. There exists a long history of opium use and production in Myanmar and the country is still the second largest producer of opium poppies in the world. Given this, it is no surprise that heroin and other opioids are the most commonly misused drugs here. There are no official estimates of the total number of active drug users in the country, but it has been reported to be between 300,000 and 400,000 (0.6–0.8% of the population). Thailand also has a long history of opioid use. Opium use was legalized in the mid-1800s and by the 1920s there were an estimated 200,000 people dependent on it. When it was banned in the late 1950s, heroin quickly replaced opium as the country's opioid of choice. From current data it is estimated that Thailand has as many as three million active drug users (4% of the 2010 population). The number of total active users in other countries in the South-East Asia region is substantially lower, with just under one million (0.3% of the population) in Indonesia, 8,000 in the Maldive Islands (2%), and an estimated 46,000 (0.2%) in Nepal.

Europe (Northern Europe, Southern Europe, Eastern Europe, Western Europe)

Despite the historical connection between much of Europe and the United States, current data seem to suggest that Europe as a whole is not experiencing the opioid epidemic to the same degree. As in the Americas, prescriptions for opioid medications in most European countries increased from 2004 to 2016 but the levels of use and the increase in prescriptions differed between countries, and some Eastern European countries remain seemingly unaffected by the trend towards increased opioid consumption in the region. With the increase in opioid prescriptions for acute and chronic noncancer pain there has been a parallel increase in some proxies for opioid-related harms in

[14] UNDOC (2005).

France, Finland, and the Netherlands, but not in Germany, Spain, and Norway. In the United Kingdom, opioid overdose deaths, though not opioid prescriptions, increased between 2016 and 2018.[15] Speakers at the 5th European Harm Reduction Conference (November 2021), held in Prague, Czechia, emphasized preparation for the "possible opioid epidemic" by focusing on strengthening already existing harm-reduction measures such as increasing access to naloxone and opioid antagonist treatment, implementing overdose prevention strategies and debating the merits of across-the-board decriminalization as a preemptive strike against what many see as the inevitable increase in opioid misuse in the region.

Though not as high as in North America, the number of opioid overdoses in Europe during 2019 was not insignificant. Deaths related to drug misuse in general are estimated to be 14 deaths per million (among persons aged 15–64 years) but, as in the Americas, there is significant variation between different countries, and higher rates are typically observed in countries in northern Europe.

Middle East/Africa (Middle East, Northern Africa, Southern Africa)

The Middle East North Africa (MENA) region is composed of the following countries: Algeria, Bahrain, Djibouti, Egypt, Iran, Iraq, Israel, Jordan, Kuwait, Lebanon, Libya, Morocco, Oman, Qatar, Saudi Arabia, Syria, Tunisia, the United Arab Emirates (UAE), the West Bank and Gaza, and Yemen. Despite a long history of opioid cultivation, trafficking, and use along trade routes in this area there remain limited data, primarily due to the lack of capacity for collection and analysis by state and regional authorities. Based on the available, though limited, data however, it appears that the trend towards increasing opioid use in the region has continued.

The majority of the countries in the MENA region have historically focused their drug policies on the criminalization of drug possession and use. As a result, state-sponsored harm-reduction programs in this region are not as evolved as in other parts of the world. In what is a clear violation of international human rights law, several countries, including Iran, Libya, Qatar, Saudi Arabia, the UAE, and Yemen, employ judicial corporal punishment, such as state-sanctioned beating, caning, or whipping as punishment for opioid use, purchase, or possession.[16] Additionally, the death penalty for drug offenses exists in Bahrain, Egypt, Iran, Iraq, Kuwait, Libya, Oman, Qatar, Saudi Arabia, Syria, the UAE, Gaza, and Yemen, though Iran and Saudi Arabia are the only states that regularly sentence those convicted of drug offenses to death. In addition to significantly limiting access to proven

[15] Häuser et al. (2021).   [16] UNODC (2016).

treatment and mitigation strategies, strict policies such as these have contributed to the spread of infectious diseases and, according to UNODC, together with South-West Asia, the Near and Middle East now has the highest prevalence of HIV among people who inject drugs worldwide.

In a state-level acknowledgement of the worldwide opioid epidemic, the policies of several countries in this region, including Iran, Israel, Jordan, Lebanon, Morocco, Syria, and Tunisia, have now evolved to allow for the establishment of harm-reduction programs.[17] This government-sanctioned commitment to tackling drug-related harm now includes (limited) access to opioid substitution treatment (Iran, Israel, Lebanon, Morocco, and the UAE) and needle and syringe exchange programs (Egypt, Iran, Israel, Lebanon, Morocco, Oman, Tunisia, and West Bank and Gaza). Iran is currently the only country in the region that provides access to these programs in prison.

Based on estimates published by the United Nations, the number of drug users in Africa as a whole is expected to increase by up to 40% by 2030, simply because of demographic changes. A worldwide increase in the number of people who use drugs is expected but, based solely on the expected rise in population, the increase will be much more pronounced here. This is because the population in Africa is younger (and drug use is higher among young people) and is projected to grow more quickly than in other areas.

In summary, despite overwhelming evidence that it is less expensive to treat an individual with opioid use disorder than it is to deal with the cost of untreated opioid dependence, governments around the world have not committed the financial resources necessary to effectively treat the problem. Along with the increase in the number of people using opioids and suffering from opioid use disorder, the past decade has seen a move away from agriculturally produced opioids and towards the synthetic, more potent, and extremely dangerous fentanyl and fentanyl analogs, further increasing the burden on healthcare infrastructure already, in some areas, stretched past the breaking point.

References and Further Reading

Degenhardt L, Grebely J, Stone J, et al. (2019). Global patterns of opioid use and dependence: Harms to populations, interventions, and future action. *Lancet* 394: 1560–1579.

Family Health International (2002). *National Assessment of Situation and Responses to Opioid/Opiate Use in Bangladesh. What Will Happen to Us? Country Highlights and Recommendations.* Dhaka: CARE.

---

[17] Harm Reduction International (2018).

Harm Reduction International (2018). Regional overview of the Middle East and North Africa. www.hri.global/files/2018/12/10/MiddleEastNorthAfrica-harm-reduc tion.pdf

Häuser W, Buchser E, Finn DP, Dom G, et al. (2021). Is Europe also facing an opioid crisis? A survey of European Pain Federation chapters. *European Journal of Pain* 25(8): 1760–1769.

HispanTV (2018). EEUU apunta a América Latina con la epidemia de opioides [The US points to Latin America with the opiate epidemic]. www.hispantv.com/noti cias/opinion/365152/eeuu-america-latina-epidemia-de-opioides

Inter-American Drug Abuse Control Commission, Secretariat for Multidimensional Security, and the Organization of American States (2015). Report on drug use in the Americas. www.cicad.oas.org/oid/pubs/druguseamericas_eng_web.pdf

Inter-American Drug Abuse Control Commission (2019). Report on drug use in the Americas 2019. http://www.cicad.oas.org/main/pubs/Report%20on%20Drug% 20Use%20in%20the%20Americas%202019.pdf

Kurth AE, Cherutich P, Conover R, Chhun N, Bruce RD, Lambdin BH (2018). The opioid epidemic in Africa and its impact. *Current Addiction Reports* 5(4): 428–453.

Lewer D, Brothers TD, Van Hest N, et al. (2022). Causes of death among people who used illicit opioids in England, 2001–18: A matched cohort study. *Lancet Public Health* 7: e126–e135.

Partnership for a Drug-Free New Jersey (2021). The perfect storm: COVID-19's impact on addiction over the past year. https://knockoutday.drugfreenj.org/wp-content/uploads/2021/03/KOOAD_3_18_webinar.pdf

Rosenberg M (2021). Opioids: Do you think there's a problem? Presentation on Alternatives to Opioids (ALTO). https://knockoutday.drugfreenj.org/wp-content /uploads/2021/05/kooad_5_20_rosenberg.pdf

UNDOC (2004). The extent, pattern and trends of drug abuse in India. www .unodc.org/pdf/india/presentations/india_national_survey_2004.pdf

UNDOC (2005). Report on Bangladesh. www.unodc.org/pdf/india/publications/s outh_Asia_Regional_Profile_Sept_2005/08_bangladesh.pdf

UNODC (2016). Compendium of United Nations standards and norms in crime prevention and criminal justice. www.unodc.org/documents/justice-and-prison-reform/compendium/English_book.pdf

UNDOC (2021). *World Drug Report 2021*. Vienna: United Nations Office on Drugs and Crime. www.unodc.org/res/wdr2021/field/WDR21_Booklet_1.pdf

WHO (2010). ATLAS on substance use (2010): Resources for the prevention and treatment of substance use disorders. https://apps.who.int/iris/bitstream/han dle/10665/44455/9789241500616_eng.pdf?sequence=1

WHO (2020). Report on people who inject drugs in the South-East Asia region. https://apps.who.int/iris/handle/10665/206320?locale-attribute=pt#

WHO (2021). Opioid overdose fact sheet. www.who.int/news-room/fact-sheets/de tail/opioid-overdose (accessed December 5, 2022)

6 CHANGING TRENDS IN OPIOID MISUSE

As the opioid epidemic progresses, the patterns of opioid misuse witnessed in the 1990s and early 2000s have evolved into the trends seen during the modern-day epidemic. These changing trends have been influenced by several factors, including changes in the way opium and synthetic opioids are produced, manufactured, and distributed; the increased availability of pharmaceutical opioids for medical and nonmedical consumption; the increased availability of effective treatments for opioid use disorder such as methadone, buprenorphine, and naloxone; and environmental stressors such as the coronavirus (COVID-19) pandemic.

Opioid Production, Distribution, and Availability

Of the 57 countries known to produce illicit opium (the precursor to opiates such as morphine and heroin), Afghanistan, Myanmar, and Mexico produce 97% of the global supply. Of these three countries, Afghanistan is the largest contributor to the global supply, estimated somewhere around 86%. Though efforts at reducing the number of opium poppy fields have succeeded in significantly shrinking the area of cultivation by 16%, advances in farming and production techniques have increased opium yields by 7% between 2020 and 2021, although this is still less than the peak seen in 2017. In April 2022, authorities banned all cultivation of the opium poppy in Afghanistan. We do not yet know how this will impact opium production; however, as the 2022 harvest was largely exempt from the new laws, cultivation in 2022 has been estimated to be one-third greater than in prior years.[1]

Seizures of opiates increased by 40% in 2020, reaching a record high. In the past 20 years, both opium production and seizures have grown significantly. Although the rate of seizures has increased more than the rate of opium production, based on limited evidence it appears that the quantity of opiates that have not been seized has also grown.

[1] United Nations (2022).

Seizures of pharmaceutical opioids have also risen over the past decade, with rates in 2020 among the highest in recent years. The most frequently seized pharmaceutical opioids by weight include tramadol (54%) and codeine (38%), whereas fentanyl and its analogs only comprised a miniscule amount (3%) in comparison. However, when adjusting these quantities for the potency of the intercepted opioids, fentanyl comprised the majority of all opioids seized in 2020 at 1.4 billion doses. In comparison, the intercepted doses of codeine and tramadol were 32 million and 16 million, respectively. The production and seizure rate of tramadol has declined since 2018, when India imposed national controls that year.

Trends of Opiate and Opioid Use

Over the period from 1999 through 2020, over 564,000 people died from an overdose involving prescription and illicit opioids in the United States alone.[2] Three waves of opioid overdose deaths have been identified, that being overdose deaths related to prescription opioids since the late 1990s, followed by heroin-related overdose deaths beginning around 2010, and finally fentanyl and other synthetic opioid-related deaths, which have been increasing since 2013. According to Dr. Andrew Kolodny,[3] however, to classify these trends as distinct waves is to miss the story told in the details. The three distinct cohorts of opioid-addicted individuals described by Kolodny in Chapter 5 reflects evolving trends in the demographics and types of opioids different groups in the United States were more likely to misuse, and subsequently become addicted to. Since 2013, however, the majority of opioid deaths have been related to fentanyl-adulterated heroin. The cohort hit the hardest is the group using the most heroin, that is, the disproportionately White group of young people in their 20s and 30s.

Dr. Kolodny points out that fentanyl and other synthetic opioids are also responsible for the 100% increase in overdose deaths in teenagers noted since 2013, but to put this dramatic increase in context, this represents only 1% of all overdose deaths during the same period and most likely is the result of experimentation and not opioid addiction. While it is clear that opioid misuse has increased significantly over this period, what is not immediately obvious is that the trends differ significantly in these cohorts, and in some cases the rates of opioid misuse have been declining. In the United States, heroin use among young Black people has been steadily decreasing for the past 40 years but has been

---

[2] Wide-ranging online data for epidemiologic research (WONDER). https://wonder.cdc.gov/ (accessed October 18, 2022)

[3] Medical Director, Opioid Policy Research Collaborative Heller School for Social Policy and Management Brandeis University President, Physicians for Responsible Opioid Prescribing.

increasing in young White people since 1995. Interestingly, this increase in heroin use has not been seen in older Whites, presumably because while their opioid addiction began with prescription opioids just as with the younger cohort of White people, older people in general have greater access to prescription pain medications and can more easily obtain these medications for their chronic conditions. Despite the increased restrictions placed on opioid prescriptions (opioid prescriptions in the United States peaked in 2011 and as of 2020 were at 60% off the high of that year), older people are more likely to have the medical conditions physicians feel comfortable prescribing opioids for and therefore are much less likely to need to switch to heroin when they develop opioid addiction.[4]

In the United States, opioid prescriptions can be tracked over time using the IQVIA tool. This tool estimates the number of opioid and benzodiazepine prescriptions dispensed in the United States at the national, state, and county level, providing data from a sample of retail pharmacies which represents 90% of prescriptions in the United States. The Total Patient Tracker provides data on the total number of unique patients in the retail outpatient setting from United States retail pharmacies. Since the peak of opioid prescriptions in 2011, opioid overdose deaths from prescription opioids have been trending downward.[5] Unfortunately, at the same time, the number of opioid overdose deaths from non-prescription opioids has been increasing at a greater rate, pushing the overall trend upward. There is some encouraging news, however, as the number of overdose deaths did not increase during the first half of 2022, and in some areas the number decreased. According to Dr. Kolodny, however, it is too soon to say if this trend will hold. He emphasizes that in many states across the United States the incidence of neonatal opioid withdrawal syndrome is declining. This, combined with decreasing numbers of overdose deaths, suggests that opioid misuse rates may have leveled off, though it could also suggest increased efficacy of harm-reduction measures put in place over the past several years.

Sadly, some experts believe the United States is at the beginning of the opioid epidemic's fourth wave. Before the COVID-19 pandemic, the opioid epidemic was described as a "triple-wave phenomenon": a wave of prescription opioid-related deaths, followed by heroin-related deaths, and, finally, synthetic-opioid-related deaths. The fourth wave of overdose deaths is less related to opioids and more related to stimulant and polysubstance mortality. From 2017 to 2018, the United States has experienced a threefold increase in cocaine-related deaths and fivefold increase in methamphetamine-related deaths.[6]

---

[4] According to IQVIA™ Total Patient Tracker opioid prescription data from 2018 (United States). www.iqvia.com/solutions/real-world-evidence/real-world-data-and-insights
[5] According to IQVIA™ Xponent data from 2006 to 2018.   [6] Ciccarone (2021).

Adolescent Trends in Opioid Misuse

To understand opioid misuse among adolescents, we can review the results of the annual Monitoring the Future (MTF)[7] survey. The MTF survey, funded by the National Institutes of Health and conducted at the University of Michigan, has measured the rate of substance use among American adolescents since 1975. Since that year, two distinct themes have been noted. The first is referred to as the "1990s drug relapse," in which the United States witnessed a rapid increase in the prevalence of many types of drugs. Researchers have also identified a "cohort effect," in which substance use is influenced by shared attitudes regarding risk of substance misuse, changes in legality of the substance, and the risk of addiction to a substance.

The MTF survey specifically asks about three opioids: heroin, OxyContin, and Vicodin. The prevalence of adolescent heroin use has always remained below 2%, and most recently, in 2022, the estimated annual rate of use was only 0.3%. The rate of heroin use reached its highest levels in the late 1990s, in part due to increased purity of the drug, which allowed individuals to misuse heroin without the need for intravenous injection. This rise in heroin use was counteracted quickly by anti-heroin campaigns and increasing publicity of overdose deaths.

Annual rates of OxyContin and Vicodin misuse have only been tracked since the 2000s. OxyContin reached peak annual use around 2010, where approximately 5.1% of 12th graders misused the drug within that year. Since that time, rates have gradually declined to 1.9% in 2022. Vicodin has followed the same trajectory, reaching peak annual use of 9.7% in 2009–2010 among adolescents in 12th grade, followed by a steady decrease to 1.3% in 2022.[8] This trend of decreasing rates of opioid misuse, especially after a significant increase over the previous years, is encouraging and possibly implies that rates of opioid misuse are no longer skyrocketing.

Regional Trends of Opioid Misuse

Since the United States still holds the dubious distinction of being the country where the opioid epidemic began, and it still exerts significant political and economic pressure on many countries throughout the world, especially when it comes to opioid-control policies, changing trends felt here are likely to indicate changes to come in different regions worldwide. According to the United Nations Office on Drugs and Crime (UNODC), roughly 1.2% of the global

---

[7] Monitoring the Future survey (monitoringthefuture.org). [8] Miech et al. (2023).

population used opioids in 2020 (61 million people), the majority of which reside in either North America or Asia.[9]

Globally, rates of opioid misuse and opioid use disorder have remained steady, representing over 50% of substance use disorders in 2017. However, when dividing the global population by the sociodemographic index (SDI), which accounts for income, education, and fertility, it is the high-SDI regions (namely North America) that have experienced significant increases in the prevalence of opioid use disorder.[10] That being said, North America is not the only region experiencing the devastating effects of opioid misuse. One might argue that there are two separate opioid epidemics, both of which are driven by cheap and abundant opioids. The first is what we are experiencing primarily in North America and is related to the influx of illicit fentanyl. The second impacts North Africa, West Africa, the Near and Middle East and West Asia, where tramadol is the opioid epidemic's driving force.

Africa

Even though Africa has very little access to opioids for the treatment of pain, the illicit use of opioids such as tramadol continues to rise as drug traffickers increasingly utilize African trading routes for the transport of drugs. As a result, Africa has played a significant role in the seizure of opioids over recent years, responsible for approximately 50% of all opioids seized globally between 2016 and 2020.[11]

The northern and western regions of Africa are struggling with illicit use of tramadol, a synthetic opioid about 10 times weaker than morphine, as it is trafficked from India to these regions. Farmers, fishermen, and manual laborers are the primary consumers of tramadol, as it effectively relieves the fatigue and pain associated with long and arduous work. Younger Africans mix tramadol into energy drinks or alcohol at parties, whereas some from West Africa use tramadol to silence the mental anguish associated with years of tragedy and war.

In other parts of the continent, most people who misuse opioids primarily use heroin. As with tramadol, the increasing rate of heroin misuse is, at least in part, a result of drug-trafficking routes through the region. Heroin produced in Afghanistan and South-West Asia enters the continent through East Africa, then crosses into either South or West Africa (the epicenter being Nigeria) before it is transported to markets in Western and Central Europe. Consequently, the increased rates of heroin use are primarily found along the eastern coast of Africa and in South Africa.[12]

---

[9] UNODC (2022).   [10] Pan et al. (2020).   [11] UNODC (2022).   [12] UNODC (2015).

The misuse of codeine, an opioid frequently found in cough syrup, is prevalent across Africa, although most reports come from the areas with the highest concentration of misuse, such as Nigeria and South Africa. More than 20 pharmaceutical companies in Nigeria produce this cough syrup and some will sell multiple bottles directly to drug dealers and consumers for only 0.50 US dollars (US$). Because this cough syrup is cheap and relatively easy to find, it is estimated that around three million bottles of cough syrup are consumed daily by Nigerians.[13]

Middle East and North Africa

Eighteen countries[14] make up the region known as the Middle East and North Africa (MENA) region. These countries are strategically positioned to traffic substances to Western Europe and the Russian federation, including the Balkan route beginning in Afghanistan and traveling through Iran. Countries along the Balkan route have some of the highest rates of opium and heroin consumption, as in Iran where over 80% of Iranians seeking addiction treatment cite opioids as the primary reason for treatment. Opium and shireh, a smokable opium product, are among the most misused opioids in Iran.

Political instability has left this region vulnerable to drug trafficking, especially in the countries of Egypt, Syria, Israel, and Iraq. Egypt has experienced significant political and economic turmoil over recent years, likely contributing to the rise in the misuse of many types of drugs. Tramadol misuse is a significant issue, although heroin use is common as well. Due in part to unsafe injection practices, Egypt reports the highest prevalence of hepatitis C in the world.

Other MENA countries, such as Iraq, Kuwait, Libya, Qatar, Syria, the UAE, and Yemen, have higher rates of tramadol misuse. Intravenous injection of buprenorphine, a medication typically used to treat opioid use disorder, is a fairly common practice in the north African country of Algeria.[15,16]

Asia

Since 2015, the cultivation and production of opium in Myanmar and Laos has decreased due to an ongoing shift towards synthetic drugs, which has been compounded by the COVID-19 pandemic. However, Myanmar remains the major source for opium throughout Southeast and East Asia, as well as Australia, and most of the opium is transported to China.

---

[13] BBC (2018).
[14] Algeria, Bahrain, Egypt, Iran, Iraq, Israel, Jordan, Kuwait, Lebanon, Libya, Morocco, Oman, Qatar, Saudi Arabia, Syria, Tunisia, United Arab Emirates (UAE), and Yemen.
[15] MENAHRA (2021).   [16] International Drug Policy Consortium (2022).

Our understanding of opioid misuse in Asian countries has been extremely limited to date, and data are scarce. These countries tend to be low- or middle-income countries, with punitive approaches to substance use, and they frequently experience political and economic instability, all of which impact a country's ability to collect reliable data.[17] The majority of opioid users globally are in Asia, with India accounting for almost one-third of opioid use worldwide.[18] Since 2010, the prevalence of opioid use in Southeast Asia appears to have remained stable, with heroin and tramadol being the most frequently misused opioids. A significant portion of the opium cultivated in Myanmar is consumed regionally, with over three million heroin users consuming around US$10 billion of the drug each year. It therefore comes as no surprise that almost 90% of individuals in Myanmar seeking treatment for a substance use disorder are opioid users.[19]

Afghanistan has faced an increasing problem of opioid misuse since 2001, as political and economic instability have driven the production and trafficking of opium from Afghanistan throughout West Asia. From the limited data we have from this region, it is estimated that 1.6 million Afghans, primarily male, misuse drugs such as heroin and opium. Afghanistan also has a high prevalence of intravenous drug misuse, driving up transmission rates of hepatitis B and C, and HIV.[20]

Central Asia links Afghanistan to Eastern Europe and the Russian Federation, and high rates of opiate use can be found in urban areas along the trafficking routes, with more than 90% of opioid users in Central Asia using them intravenously.[21] Although Asia, and especially China, produces a significant portion of the world's illicit fentanyl supply, synthetic opioids have not entered the street-drug markets in the Asia-Pacific region to any significant degree, as the supply of heroin continues to meet the region's demand and trafficking routes have been firmly established for years.[22]

Europe
The effects of the worldwide opioid epidemic continue to be felt in Europe; however, the drug markets and epidemiology differ in several significant ways. The number of overdose deaths attributable to opioid misuse is significantly higher in the United States when compared to Europe – for example, in 2017 there were over 70,000 opioid-related deaths in the United States compared with 8,300 in Europe. One reason for this discrepancy is that heroin, not fentanyl, remains as the primary opioid misused in Europe. Fentanyl-associated

---

[17] Peacock et al. (2018).   [18] Taylor et al. (2021).   [19] UNODC (2021a).
[20] MENAHRA (2021).   [21] UNODC (2008).   [22] Taylor et al. (2020).

overdose deaths have been reported; however, for the most part, fentanyl misuse has been primarily localized to Estonia.[23]

All European countries, except for Belgium and France, have reported increased consumption of prescription opioids (both legal and illicit) over the past decade. From 2008 to 2018, increased consumption rates of buprenorphine, fentanyl, morphine, and oxycodone were seen in Austria, Estonia, and the Netherlands, whereas consumption rates in Cyprus, the Czech Republic, German, Ireland, Latvia, Norway, Slovakia, Switzerland, and others increased for at least two of these four opioid types. In fact, the rate of opioid consumption in the United Kingdom, Germany. and Austria surpassed the rate in the United States in 2018. Per recent studies, within the UK, Scotland has the highest proportion of high-risk opioid users (16.2 per 1,000 people versus 1.3–6.3 per 1,000 people on average) and the highest rate of opioid overdoses in Europe. Scotland's overdose death rate increased significantly between 2010 (10.9 deaths per 100,000 people) and 2018 (22.7 deaths per 100,000 people). No other European country has reported a similarly drastic rise of overdose deaths and, in comparison, multiple countries (e.g., Estonia, Northern Ireland, Norway) have experienced a slight decrease in overdose death rates. There was a spike in synthetic opioid poisonings in Northern Ireland between 2011 and 2013; however, this has been declining since. Decreasing rates of synthetic opioid poisonings have also been witnessed in the United Kingdom, whereas rates increased in the Netherlands and Belgium (as of 2018).

The major opioids associated with overdose in Scotland are heroin and methadone, and apart from the opioid-related deaths in Northern Ireland, synthetic opioids have not significantly contributed to opioid-related mortality in Europe. Treatment admissions for opioid use disorder in Scotland have exceeded rates in the rest of Europe, and between 2008 and 2018, heroin was the largest contributor to opioid-related admissions. Methadone was close behind until 2018 when buprenorphine took its place. Tramadol plays a significant role in treatment admissions for Northern Ireland.[24]

It has been estimated that 6% of the Russian population uses opioids on a regular basis, 90% of whom use heroin at least sometimes. Approximately one-third of the heroin produced in Afghanistan travels north into Russia and plays a significant role in the country's economy and political landscape. Russia is also home to other highly dangerous opioids like krokodil (desomorphine, known for its "flesh-eating" effects) and khanka (an opioid produced from poppy straw). Opioid-related deaths have been rising for years in parallel with increasing rates of HIV, which is associated with shared use of drug

---

[23] Krausz (2021).   [24] Pierce et al. (2021).

paraphernalia.[25] Reliable Russian data can be difficult to find; however, per one estimation, overdose deaths rose from 4,569 to 10,043 between 2019 and 2021, certainly influenced by the COVID-19 pandemic and increased accessibility of drugs sold on the dark web.[26]

Oceania

Oceania refers to the thousands of countries, most of which are islands, located in the Pacific Ocean. These are typically divided into four subregions: Australia and New Zealand, Polynesia, Melanesia, and Micronesia. For now, there is a significant lack of data about substance use in Oceania, the exception being Australia and New Zealand. Between 2007–2008 and 2016–2017, the rate of hospitalizations in Australia due to opioid poisoning increased by 25% and the rate of opioid-related deaths increased by 62%. During this same period, the lifetime prevalence of nonmedical opioid use increased from 5.8% to 10.5%, and in some regions the use of fentanyl had doubled. New Zealand has also reported the nonmedical use of fentanyl among its citizens. Interestingly, in 2019 the estimated rate of opioid misuse decreased, likely due to the rescheduling of codeine as a prescription drug (as it was available over the counter beforehand).

It is well known that the indigenous people of Australia and New Zealand are disproportionately affected by substance use. The Māori people are three times more likely to suffer a drug-related death compared to non-Māori people in New Zealand, and Aboriginal and Torres Strait Islander people are four times more likely, compared with non-Indigenous Australians.[27]

North and South America

The epicenter of the opioid epidemic is in North America, not only in the United States but also in Canada. Based on data from 2019, approximately 1% of the adult Canadian population has used opioids for nonmedical purposes in the past year. Of all Canadian adults who have taken opioids in the past year, a larger percentage used them for nonmedical purposes in 2019 when compared to 2017 (6% versus 3%, respectively). When analyzing the content of drugs seized in Canada, the number of samples containing fentanyl has increased from 69% in 2020 to 72% in 2021. There are regional differences in fentanyl availability, however, as hydromorphone is most frequently identified in Quebec, New Brunswick, Nova Scotia, and Prince Edward Island, whereas oxycodone is most often found in samples from Newfoundland and Labrador. Newer opioids, such as nitazenes and brorphine, have been detected

[25] Galeotti (2016).   [26] Kaganskikh (2022).   [27] UNODC (2019).

in drug samples since 2019. Opioid overdose deaths in Canada have been increasing over the past decade, even more so since the start of the COVID-19 pandemic. Thus far, most opioid-related overdose deaths have occurred in the provinces of British Columbia, Ontario, and Alberta.[28]

Rates of illicit and prescription opioid misuse have remained low in Mexico, although there are pockets of increased heroin misuse primarily in the northern regions, near the border between Mexico and the United States.[29] As with Mexico, opioid consumption in the rest of Latin America has remained low, despite Columbia being the largest producer of opium in the area. Based on a 2017 study, only 0.1% of the population in Argentina had used heroin, opium, or morphine in the past, and similarly, a 2013 study estimated that only 1% of Columbians had ever used an opiate during their lifetime. Access to prescription opioids is very limited in Brazil, and low rates of opioid misuse reflect this fact. Puerto Rico is an outlier, with a significantly higher prevalence of opioid misuse.[30] Synthetic opioids such as fentanyl are now being detected in samples of heroin and lysergic acid diethylamide (LSD) in South America, which is not surprising considering that large amounts of illicit fentanyl is being produced by cartels in Mexico.[31]

Harm Reduction and Treatment

During the 2022 "Knock Our Opioid Abuse Day" conference, Jennifer Fearon, New Jersey State Health and Human Services Policy Advisor and John Butler, New Jersey State Criminal Justice Policy Advisor, spoke about harm-reduction measures that have been put in place to combat the opioid epidemic and mitigate the harm caused by opioid misuse in the State of New Jersey.[32] Specific measures aimed at promoting public health through harm reduction include expanding syringe access and other vital support services through harm-reduction centers, increasing access to medications for opioid use disorder (MOUD) such as buprenorphine, expanding access to and training on the use of naloxone, and developing nonpunitive approaches to drug-related crimes, including repealing the criminal offense of possession of syringe and expungement of possession or distribution of hypodermic syringe or needle offenses. This is just one example of what one state is doing in 2022 to address the opioid epidemic through harm reduction and decriminalization of opioid use disorder, but New Jersey is not alone. The trend of shifting away from old,

---

[28] Canadian Centre on Substance Use and Addiction (2022).
[29] Goodman-Meza et al. (2019).   [30] Pacurucu-Castillo et al. (2019).
[31] UNODC (2021b).
[32] Presentation available at www.youtube.com/watch?v=-HnH6PzfykQ.

outdated, punitive measures is being seen throughout the United States and laws authorizing provision of harm-reduction services, including the distribution of sterile syringes and provision of other support services to persons who use drugs intravenously, are being debated in the state legislatures or have already been passed.

Recent trends in harm-reduction expansion have been encouraging. In the past two years, the number of countries offering needle syringe programs increased from 86 to 92, medications for the treatment of opioid use disorder increased from 84 to 87, and legal and operational drug consumption sites from 12 to 16. More countries are now offering "take home naloxone" programs and 104 countries now include references to harm reduction in their national policy documents, which increased from 87 only two years prior. Unfortunately, the availability of harm-reduction measures in prisons has not changed much.

Five of the six countries newly offering needle syringe programs come from Africa. As of 2022, the African countries of Kenya, Mauritius, Mozambique, Seychelles, South Africa, Uganda, and United Republic of Tanzania provide all of the following: one or more treatment programs that use MOUD, one or more needle and syringe programs, and one or more safe drug-consumption rooms.[33] That being said, resources are exceptionally scarce, and a lack of funding limits the availability and expansion of these programs.

In the MENA region, many countries unfortunately continue to employ punitive tactics towards drug users, including corporal punishment and the death penalty. However, Afghanistan, Iran, Lebanon, Oman, and Palestine have adopted various types of harm-reduction strategies in their national plans. Naloxone, which can reverse an opioid overdose, is distributed in Afghan and Iranian communities. MOUD such as methadone and buprenorphine are typically not accessible throughout this region, although four countries do offer methadone or buprenorphine, or both. Despite the limited availability, there are ongoing efforts to increase access to these lifesaving treatments. Since 2016, Lebanon has opened four new locations for MOUD, insurance coverage for MOUD has been expanded in Iran, and Pakistan is advancing towards the registration of methadone and buprenorphine as MOUD.[34] Afghanistan banned the cultivation of the poppy in the spring of 2022, and although it is too early to tell what the effects will ultimately be, the implications for the world market will likely be significant.

Many Asian countries continue to incarcerate opioid users in specialized facilities called compulsory drug detention centers, although some countries in

---

[33] Harm Reduction International (2022).   [34] MENAHRA (2021).

the region have shifted their policies more towards harm-reduction strategies like needle exchange programs and MOUD. In Malaysia, some compulsory treatment centers have been converted into voluntary methadone clinics. However, only six Asian countries have made MOUD accessible to those in criminal justice settings, and therefore the majority of people sentenced to compulsory drug detention centers receive no medication at all.[35] Not all countries in Asia offer medications such as buprenorphine, methadone, or naltrexone for the treatment of opioid use disorder to the general public either. Once again, data are significantly lacking for this region of the world; however, cost seems to be a significant barrier, especially for buprenorphine, which can be eight times more expensive than methadone.[36] However, China and Malaysia have both made significant progress in increasing the accessibility of MOUD to their respective populations.

Access to harm-reduction programs, treatment and MOUD in Europe varies by country. Approximately 28% of individuals entering drug treatment in Europe report opioid misuse as the primary reason for doing so; however, Bulgaria (72.6%), Lithuania (82.2%), and Slovenia (75.8%) are far above the European average.[37] Countries such as Estonia and Lithuania offer methadone and buprenorphine only, whereas the Netherlands and Switzerland offer methadone, buprenorphine, diacetylmorphine (heroin), and extended-release morphine among others.[38] Despite the devastation caused by drug use in Russia, medications such as methadone and buprenorphine cannot be obtained in the country. Viewing opioid use disorder as a moral failing, rather than an addiction, the Russian government continues to treat those with addiction in a punitive manner.

According to the 2022 publication, *The Global State of Harm Reduction*,[39] both Australia and New Zealand offer MOUD, have at least one needle exchange program in the country, and distribute naloxone throughout the community. In addition, both countries have expanded the distribution of safer injecting equipment and naloxone, using mail services. Unfortunately, the data about substance use and treatment in the Pacific Islands Countries and Territories of Micronesia, Fiji, Kiribati, Marshall Islands, Papua New Guinea, Samoa, Solomon Islands, Timor Leste, the Kingdom of Tonga, and Vanuatu are poor; however, there is no indication that any harm-reduction programs exist in these countries.

Harm reduction and MOUD are not found in most of Latin America, with a few exceptions. Mexico, Colombia, and Puerto Rico offer both MOUD and

---

[35] Wegman et al. (2017).   [36] Reid et al. (2014).   [37] EMCDDA (2022).
[38] Krausz et al. (2021).   [39] Harm Reduction International (2022).

needle syringe programs, whereas the Dominican Republic has only needle syringe programs, and Argentina only has MOUD. Mexico is the only country in the region with a safe drug-consumption room, and this is reserved for women who inject drugs. In North America, needle syringe programs, safe consumption sites, and treatment with MOUD are available in the United States and Canada. However, there are significant regional variations in accessibility. For example, both needle syringe programs and MOUD are offered to prisoners in Canada, whereas only MOUD is offered to prisoners in the United States. For the general population in the United States, the only state with licensed drug-consumption rooms is New York; six states still do not have needle and syringe programs. However, all have at least one licensed opioid treatment program.[40]

The Impact of COVID-19

The COVID-19 pandemic has impacted the opioid epidemic in numerous ways, from altering drug production and trafficking to increasing the rates of opioid misuse and overdose deaths. Measurements employed by countries to limit the spread of the virus, such as shutting down borders, forces drug traffickers to look for other ways to bring their product across state lines. And with a reduction in legal trade, the drugs that can be smuggled in legal imports are also reduced. Because fentanyl has extremely high potency, and is therefore less bulky than heroin, it is easier to transport this opioid undetected. In addition, the COVID-19 pandemic negatively impacted the job market, creating the incentive for unemployed workers to enter the drug trade out of necessity.[41]

Since the onset of the COVID-19 pandemic, the number of opioid-related overdoses in the United States has soared. In the first 12 months of the pandemic, more than 93,000 individuals died from drug overdoses, almost 30% higher than the previous year. Canada has experienced a similar rise in overdose deaths, citing a 91% increase during the first two years of the pandemic. The exact reason for this dramatic increase is not completely apparent. However, we currently believe that disruptions in treatment, reduced access to harm-reduction services, the impact of isolation on stress levels and mental health, and the unpredictability of drug purity and composition have all played a major role. The COVID-19 pandemic has exacerbated preexisting health inequalities; racial and ethnic minorities have been disproportionately

[40] Harm Reduction International (2022).   [41] UNODC (2020).

affected, with a greater proportion of overdose deaths occurring in Black and Hispanic communities.[42]

Although Europe has seen an increase in the number of opioid prescriptions during the pandemic, experts do not believe this indicates an oncoming crisis as in North America, for several reasons. In Europe, drugs are prescribed in a much more controlled manner, there are more resources for the treatment of addiction, and the influences of pharmaceutical companies are nowhere near what they have been in the United States. However, there is always a possibility that an opioid epidemic in Europe could occur. As researcher Remy Sounier states, "We shouldn't think that because we have prescriptions in Europe, this problem doesn't affect us ... We can have an opioid crisis in Europe too."[43]

In response to the pandemic, the utilization of telehealth to provide addiction treatment has expanded rapidly. Prior to the pandemic, numerous restrictions in the United States prevented providers from offering addiction treatment virtually. However, once these restrictions were lifted, medications such as buprenorphine could be prescribed via telehealth without an initial in-person evaluation. Based on limited research, it appears that patient satisfaction with telemedicine is high and many prefer telehealth to in-person visits.[44] It is not yet apparent how telemedicine has impacted retention rates and treatment success for those with an opioid use disorder, although certainly this will be of significant interest to researchers in the field.

Predicted Trends for the Future

This epidemic's impact on children cannot be ignored. In 2017, approximately 2.2 million children were impacted in some way by the opioid epidemic. Assuming current trends, the number of affected children will almost double to 4.3 million by 2030. The total societal cost is enormous, when considering the costs associated with higher likelihoods of incarceration, mental illness, substance use, and obesity, totaling upward of US$400 billion in 2030.[45]

Therefore, we cannot allow the epidemic to continue its current course. As awareness and concern about opioid-related harms increases and more resources are directed towards harm-reduction programs and preventive efforts, the hope is we can "turn the tide." The role of big data[46] and computer modeling continues to grow in accuracy and utility. In 2017, the National Academies of

---

[42] Ghose et al. (2022).   [43] Bauer-Babef (2021).   [44] Edinoff et al. (2022).
[45] United Hospital Fund (2019).
[46] Per the Oxford Dictionary, big data refers to "extremely large data sets that may be analyzed computationally to reveal patterns, trends, and associations, especially relating to human behavior and interactions."

Sciences, Engineering, and Medicine helped develop a model known as SOURCE[47] to help scientists understand the epidemic's evolution and offer information to guide future policies. SOURCE has been found to accurately replicate the opioid crisis from 1999 to 2020, and so its predictions for the future could be plausible. Using SOURCE, researchers have estimated several trajectories between 2020 and 2032. For example, SOURCE estimates that the penetration of fentanyl in the drug market will be higher in 2032 (80.7%) versus 2020 (56.2%). At the same time, the availability of MOUD (buprenorphine, methadone, naltrexone) and distribution of naloxone kits will significantly increase. If SOURCE is correct, opioid-overdose deaths will continue to rise for several years but then begin to fall (another source[48] estimates the death rate will peak around 2025), with an estimated 543,000 to 842,000 lives lost between 2020 and 2032.[49] Of course, we cannot take this information as absolute truth, as there are many influences (both future and present) that are unaccounted for in this model. However, it certainly is a great starting point to guide policy and advocate for additional resources.

References and Further Reading

Bauer-Babef C (2021). Opioid use: 'more controlled' in Europe than in the US. *Euractiv*, 20 October. www.euractiv.com/section/health-consumers/news/opioid-use-more-controlled-in-europe-than-in-the-us/

BBC (2018). Nigeria's deadly codeine cough syrup epidemic. 30 April 2018. BBC [Online Video]. www.bbc.co.uk/news/av/world-africa-43944309

Canadian Centre on Substance Use and Addiction (2022). Canadian drug summary: Opioids. www.ccsa.ca/sites/default/files/2022-11/CCSA-Canadian-Drug-Summary-Opioids-2022-en.pdf

Centers for Disease Control and Prevention (2019). Annual surveillance report of drug-related risks and outcomes: *United States*. www.cdc.gov/drugoverdose/pdf/pubs/2019-cdc-drug-surveillance-report.pdf

Ciccarone D (2021). The rise of illicit fentanyls, stimulants and the fourth wave of the opioid overdose crisis. *Current Opinion in Psychiatry* 34(4): 344–350.

Edinoff AN, Kaufman SE, Chauncy TM, et al. (2022). Addiction and COVID: Issues, challenges, and new telehealth approaches. *Psychiatry International* 3: 169–180.

EMCDDA (2022). *European Drug Report 2022: Trends and Developments*. Luxembourg: Publications Office of the European Union.

---

[47] Simulation of Opioid Use, Response, Consequences, and Effects (https://github.com/FDA/SOURCE).
[48] Sumetsky et al. (2021).   [49] Lim et al. (2022).

Friedman J, Godvin M, Shover CL, et al. (2022). Trends in drug overdose deaths among US adolescents, January 2010 to June 2021. *JAMA* 327(14): 1398–1400.

Galeotti M (2016). Narcotics and nationalism: Russian drug policies and futures. In *Improving Global Drug Policy: Comparative Perspectives and UNGASS 2016.* New York: New York University Center for Global Affairs.

Ghose R, Forati AM, Mantsch JR (2022). Impact of the COVID-19 pandemic on opioid overdose deaths: A spatiotemporal analysis. *Journal of Urban Health* 99: 316–327.

Goodman-Meza D, Medina-Mora ME, Magis-Rodriguez C, et al. (2019). Where is the opioid use epidemic in Mexico? A cautionary tale for policymakers south of the US–Mexico border. *American Journal of Public Health* 109(1): 73–82.

Harm Reduction International (2022). The global state of harm reduction. https://hri.global/flagship-research/the-global-state-of-harm-reduction/the-global-state-of-harm-reduction-2022/

International Drug Policy Consortium (2022). Middle East/North Africa. https://idpc.net/regions/middle-east-north-africa

Kaganskikh A (2022). "If only we had the political will." Why Russia's rise in drug overdose deaths is unlikely to end soon. *Meduza* 21 July. https://meduza.io/en/feature/2022/07/21/if-only-we-had-the-political-will

Kiang M, Basu S, Chen J, Alexander MJ (2019). Assessment of changes in the geographical distribution of opioid-related mortality across the United States by opioid type, 1999–2016. *JAMA Network Open* 2(2): e190040.

Krausz RM, Westenberg JN, Ziafat K (2021). The opioid overdose crisis as a global health challenge. *Current Opinion in Psychiatry* 34: 405–412.

Lim TY, Stringfellow EJ, Stafford CA, et al. (2022). Modeling the evolution of the US opioid crisis for national policy development. *Proceedings of the National Academy of Sciences of the United States of America* 119(23): e2115714119.

MENAHRA (2021). *Assessment of Situation and Response of Drug Use and Its Harms in the Middle East and North Africa.* Sin El Fil, Lebanon: Middle East and North Africa Harm Reduction Association.

Miech RA, Johnston LD, O'Malley PM, et al. (2023). *Monitoring the Future National Survey Results on Drug Use, 1975–2022, Volume I.* Ann Arbor, MI: Institute for Social Research, University of Michigan.

Pacurucu-Castillo SF, Ordonez-Mancheno JM, Hernandez-Cruz A, Alarcon RD (2019). World opioid and substance use epidemic: A Latin American perspective. *Psychiatric Research and Clinical Practice* 1(1): 32–38.

Pan Z, Zhang J, Cheng H, et al. (2020). Trends of the incidence of drug use disorders from 1990 to 2017: An analysis based on the Global Burden of Disease 2017 data. *Epidemiology and Psychiatric Sciences* 29: e148.

Peacock A, Leung J, Larney S, et al. (2018). Global statistics on alcohol, tobacco and illicit drug use: 2017 status report. *Addiction* 113: 1905–1926.

Pierce M, van Amsterdam J, Kalkman GA, Schellekens A, van den Brink W (2021). Is Europe facing an opioid crisis like the United States? An analysis of opioid use and related adverse effects in 19 European countries between 2010 and 2018. *European Psychiatry* 64(1): e47.

Reid G, Sharma M, Higgs P (2014). The long-winding road of opioid substitution therapy implemented in South-East Asia: Challenges to scale up. *Journal of Public Health Research* 3(1): 204.

Sumetsky N, Mair C, Wheeler-Martin K, et al. (2021). Predicting the future course of opioid overdose mortality: An example from two US states. *Epidemiology* 32(1): 61–69.

Taylor J, Pardo B, Hulme S, et al. (2021). Illicit synthetic opioid consumption in Asia and the Pacific: Assessing the risks of a potential outbreak. *Drug and Alcohol Dependence* 220: 108500.

United Hospital Fund (2019). The ripple effect: National and state estimates of the US opioid epidemic's impact on children. https://uhfnyc.org/media/filer_public/6e/80/6e80760f-d579-46a3-998d-1aa816ab06f6/uhf_ripple_effect_national_and_state_estimates_chartbook.pdf

United Nations (2022). Afghanistan: Opium cultivation up nearly a third, warns UNODC. *United Nations News*, November 2022. https://news.un.org/en/story/2022/11/1130057

UNODC (2008). *Illicit Drug Trends in Central Asia*. Tashkent, Republic of Uzbekistan: UNODC ROCA.

UNODC (2012). *Methadone Maintenance Treatment: Intervention Toolkit*. Bangkok: United Nations Office on Drugs and Crime, Regional Office for South Asia.

UNODC (2015). *Afghan Opiate Trafficking through the Southern Route*. Vienna: United Nations Office on Drugs and Crime.

UNODC (2019). *Global Smart Update: Understanding the Global Opioid Crisis*. Vienna: United Nations Office on Drugs and Crime.

UNODC (2020). *COVID-19 and the Drug Supply Chain: From Production and Trafficking to Use*. Vienna: United Nations Office on Drugs and Crime.

UNODC (2021a). Opium production drops again in Myanmar as the synthetic drug market expands. www.unodc.org/roseap/2021/02/myanmar-opium-survey-report-launch/story.html

UNODC (2021b). *Synthetic Drugs and New Psychoactive Substances in Latin America and the Caribbean 2021*. Vienna: United Nations Office on Drugs and Crime.

UNODC (2022). *World Drug Report 2022*. Vienna: United Nations Office on Drugs and Crime. www.unodc.org/unodc/data-and-analysis/world-drug-report-2022.html

Wegman MP, Altice FL, Kaur S, et al. (2017). Relapse to opioid use in opioid-dependent individuals released from compulsory drug detention centres compared with those from voluntary methadone treatment centres in Malaysia: A two-arm, prospective observational study. *Lancet Global Health* 5: e198–e207.

7 THE ACTUAL COST OF THE OPIOID EPIDEMIC

Simply stated, the economic costs of the opioid epidemic can be broken down into direct and indirect costs. The direct costs to society are more easily quantifiable as these are the funds that must be allocated for purchase of any and all goods and services above that which we would normally allocate for these items, were there no opioid epidemic. This includes the increased financial burden on the criminal justice system for items such as law enforcement, the judiciary, corrections, probation services, and parole, as well as increased treatment-related costs such as inpatient and outpatient addiction treatment, medication-assisted treatment with methadone or buprenorphine, and the purchase of naloxone. Indirect costs are less easily quantifiable as these costs represent the funds we don't have due to the opioid epidemic, and these calculations must, in some cases, rely on estimates. Costs arising from the need to treat health complications related to opioid misuse are in some cases easy to identify, as in the case of an opioid overdose, but may not be readily apparent in all cases. Imagine a physical injury which occurs while an individual is under the influence of opioids but is not recognized or documented as related to opioid misuse in the medical record. Less quantifiable costs to society include other indirect costs, sometimes called the "hidden costs" of the opioid epidemic, and include loss of productivity and the negative impact on the children and dependents of individuals with opioid use disorder. In this chapter we will look at the specific areas in which the opioid epidemic has had a very real, and very negative, effect on the world economy.

According to a 2021 study published in the journal *Drug and Alcohol Dependence*,[1] the costs related to opioid use disorder in the United States alone were estimated to be US$1.02 trillion, based on data from just one year, 2017. The majority of this economic burden was thought to be due to reduced quality of life and the value of life lost due to fatal opioid overdose. In October of 2019, the Trump White House announced the results of a report based on the same methodology used by Florence et al. but based on data from 2018.[2] According to the Council of Economic

[1] Florence et al. (2021).   [2] CEA (2019).

Advisers (CEA)[3] estimates, the economic burden of the opioid epidemic had increased to 3.4% of gross domestic product (GDP) and totaled more than US$2.5 trillion for the four-year period from 2015 to 2018. As the costs associated with this epidemic continue to increase, the consequences will continue to be felt throughout the economies of the world, sometimes in unexpected ways.

The Increased Financial Burden on the Criminal Justice System

The opioid epidemic has fueled a significant increase in drug-related crimes. With the increased demand for opioids, driven by increasing numbers of addicted individuals, comes increased supply from illicit sources. This trade, by definition, is illegal, and those involved on either side of the transaction risk involvement with the criminal justice system. On top of these transnational crimes, violent crimes, such as assault and attempted or actual murder related to turf wars conducted by suppliers vying for a greater share of the market, account for a significant portion of the increased burden. Customers in need of funds with which to procure the opioids they have become addicted to may commit robbery, burglary, or other property-related crimes. Additionally, the behavior associated with using opioids increases so-called "quality of life" or "drug nuisance" crimes, such as street prostitution, the establishment of drug houses or "shooting galleries," and the occupation and pollution of public spaces. All of these factors significantly increase the economic burden on the criminal justice system above that which existed prior to the opioid epidemic.

According to the 2017 report from the CEA, roughly US$14.8 billion of the increased economic burden attributable to the opioid epidemic was related to criminal justice spending that year.[4] These costs represent an increased burden that must be shared within the various parts of the justice system in a zero-sum distribution from year to year, so an increase in policing costs related to the enforcement of drug-related crime, for example, necessitates a decrease in the resources available to police non–drug-related crime. As an example, in a report published in 2019, J. D. Ropero-Miller and P. J. Speaker investigated the increased economic impact of the opioid epidemic on forensic laboratories.[5] The 2017 CEA report on these facilities estimated that the opioid epidemic accounted for an increase of US$270 million in expenses related to the need to

---

[3] The CEA is an agency within the Executive Office of the President of the United States, charged with offering the President objective economic advice on the formulation of both domestic and international economic policy.
[4] CEA(2017).   [5] Ropero-Miller and Speaker (2019).

process opioid-related laboratory samples. Ropero-Miller and Speaker point out that because "laboratory budgets did not grow at a rate capable of meeting this increased demand for forensic science services" the increased need to process these samples was paid for out of the limited budget intended to cover the cost of providing all forensic laboratory services, not just those related to drug chemistry and toxicology. This opportunity cost negatively impacted the laboratories' ability to provide these other services and dramatically increased the turnaround time for these other areas of investigation.

Another area of increased expenses is the cost of the law enforcement overdose response program, which provides police officers with the skills and equipment necessary to quickly treat and revive an opioid overdose victim on the scene. As, most often, police are the initial first responders to encounter someone who has overdosed, providing them with naloxone has significantly decreased the number of overdose deaths as well as reduced the number of overdose victims who would have otherwise required transport via ambulance and emergency hospital treatment. According to the National Institute on Drug Abuse (NIDA), "After a naloxone training session, the majority of police officers reported that it would not be difficult to use naloxone at the scene of an overdose (89.7 percent) and that it was important that other officers be trained to use naloxone (82.9 percent)."[6] This program, however, increases the financial burden on the criminal justice system, related to the costs of the naloxone kits, the costs of training, and related personnel costs. The cost of a single naloxone rescue kit ranges from approximately US$22 to US$60 for intranasal or auto-injector kits. While the cost related to law enforcement training for overdose reversal programs is generally not directly paid for out of departmental budgets, the government or private agency that provides the training must bear the costs with funds obtained from tax receipts or private donations.[7]

Direct Costs Related to Treatment for Opioid Use Disorder

The increased financial burden on the healthcare system directly attributable to the opioid epidemic can be broken down into two distinct categories of expense: the costs associated with emergent treatment related to opioid overdose, and the costs associated with chronic, preventative treatment for opioid use disorder. The costs associated with an opioid overdose vary widely, from the individual who is treated with naloxone by a friend or first responder and does not require or consent to transport for further treatment, to the individual

---

[6] NIDA (2021a).
[7] Bureau of Justice Assistance, United States Department of Justice (n.d.).

who is transported by ambulance to the hospital emergency room, admitted to the intensive care unit (ICU), and subsequently dies of multiple organ failure after a prolonged period of time. For individuals in treatment for opioid use disorder, the costs of detoxification, acute inpatient rehabilitation, and out-patient community treatment, often with medication-assisted treatment, can quickly add up. Residential treatment is expensive and the costs of this treatment, with either methadone or buprenorphine, are not insignificant.

An analysis of the costs related specifically to opioid overdoses during the period of October 2017 to October 2018 was conducted by Premier (Charlotte, NC), a healthcare consultancy affiliated with roughly 4,000 hospitals and health systems in the United States.[8] In this analysis, the experience of 647 facilities affiliated with the company was evaluated to determine the financial burden on the United States healthcare infrastructure. Extrapolation of the cost trends suggests that the total increased costs related to opioid overdose treatment alone are over US$11 billion annually, roughly 1% of all hospital expenditures, with US$7.4 billion of the expense borne by the federal Medicare and Medicaid programs. Just like there are regional variations in the numbers of patients requiring treatment for opioid overdose there are also variations in the costs for treatment depending on the acuity of the patient. In this analysis, an overdose patient who was treated and released might only cost the system around US$500, but the cost for a patient who required hospital admission quickly rose to over US$11,000, and to over US$20,000 if ICU care was indicated.

Opioid overdose patients that present to the emergency room, that is, those who require more than just treatment in the field, are by the nature of the acuity of their injury at a significantly high risk for multiple organ failure. According to the Premier analysis, while roughly 47% of patients were treated and released from the emergency room the majority (53%) required hospitalization. Of the patients who required hospitalization, almost 40% experienced organ failure and required ICU-level care. The costs associated with the delivery of critical care services associated with opioid overdose appear to be increasing. A study published in the *Annals of the American Thoracic Society* conducted by Dr. Jennifer P. Stevens of Beth Israel Deaconess Medical Center in Boston examined the costs of providing ICU-level care for patients admitted for opioid misuse between 2009 and 2015, and it found that the average cost per admission increased from US$58,500 to US$92,400 over the study period.[9] Sadly, the chances that a patient admitted to the ICU for opioid-related injury

---

[8] Premier (2019).   [9] Stevens et al. (2017).

will survive this admission have decreased over the same period: annual deaths in ICUs nearly doubled during the study period.

According to the US Commission on Combating Synthetic Opioid Trafficking, established under Section 7221 of the National Defense Authorization Act for Fiscal Year 2020, more than 100,000 people died of drug overdoses in the 12-month period from July of 2020 to June 2021, an increase of 30% from the pre-COVID period from July 2019 to June 2020.[10] The vast majority, almost two-thirds, of these overdose deaths were caused by synthetic opioids such as fentanyl and carfentanil. The commission estimated that opioid overdoses now cost the United States approximately US$1 trillion annually.

The costs associated with the non-acute treatment of opioid use disorder, a chronic relapsing disease, are significant as well and include the costs of medication and administration as well as inpatient treatment and ongoing therapy and counseling.[11] Cost estimates from the U.S. Department of Defense for treatment in a certified opioid treatment program (OTP) in 2016 were as follows:

- methadone treatment (daily visits): US$126.00 per week or US$6,552.00 per year;
- buprenorphine treatment (twice-weekly visits): US$115.00 per week or US$5,980.00 per year;
- naltrexone: US$1,176.50 per month or US$14,112.00 per year.

The costs for medication-assisted treatment include integrated psychosocial and medical support services, as well as the costs of administration provided in a certified OTP, which include drug administration and related services. By comparing these costs to the costs of treatment for other medical conditions it becomes clear that the opioid epidemic is rapidly becoming one of the most expensive healthcare concerns in the world. According to the 2014 Medical Expenditure Panel Survey, the annual cost for an individual with a chronic medical condition was only US $3,560 for those with diabetes mellitus and US $5,624 for those with kidney disease.[12]

According to the Kaiser Family Foundation, OTPs and the treatments offered through rehabilitation centers are expensive and the cost to consumers can vary widely depending on multiple factors. The average cost of a complete drug rehabilitation program in 2019 ranged from a low of US$5,000 to over US$80,000 depending on the length of treatment and the level of care required.

---

[10] Rand Corporation (2022).   [11] NIDA (2021b).
[12] Agency for Healthcare Research and Quality (2014).

In 2021, the estimated costs for different levels and length of treatment were estimated to be:[13]

- 30-day initial detoxification treatment costs US$250–900 per day.
- 3 months of outpatient treatment costs US$1,450–11,000 per quarter.
- 30 days of intensive outpatient treatment costs US$3,100–10,000 per month.
- Residential treatment (varies depending on length of stay): US$5,300–80,000.

As with most treatment for mental health-related conditions, the treatment for opioid use disorder is often not covered by health insurance or covered only at a 50% rate, with maximum usage well below the actual costs of treatment, leaving most patients with incomplete treatment due to inadequate access to care. Those who are able to obtain and complete treatment often find themselves burdened with debt comparable to the student loan debt carried by a new college graduate, but usually without the benefit of having learned the skills required to obtain the employment necessary to service it.

Indirect Costs for Treatment of Health Complications Related to Opioid Misuse

Individuals who have survived an opioid overdose that required ICU level care often require chronic medical care related to these injuries and remain at high risk for readmission to the hospital, even if unrelated to subsequent opioid misuse. Even those who have avoided an overdose often suffer from chronic medical conditions related to opioid misuse. People with opioid use disorder are significantly less likely to receive regular preventative medical care, more likely to suffer the medical consequences of poorly or uncontrolled chronic conditions such as diabetes, more likely to contract and transmit infectious diseases, and more likely to experience traumatic injuries. The cost for care and treatment of these conditions is significant, US$31.3 billion by one estimate,[14] and since most people with addiction-related illness do not have private medical insurance or the financial resources to pay for treatment, the burden of this increased cost is often shouldered by the government. In 2015, the average costs for a patient diagnosed with opioid use disorder were more than 550% higher (almost US$16,000 more per patient) than a patient without opioid use disorder.[15]

Opioid misuse (including opioid medications and illicit opioids such as heroin) has been linked to the transmission of several viral infections, such

---

[13] National Drug Helpline (2023).   [14] Florence et al. (2021).
[15] American Medical Association (2015).

as HIV and hepatitis C, as well as bacterial infections such as endocarditis and blood infections, often with antibiotic resistant organisms such as methicillin-resistant *Staphylococcus aureus* ("MRSA"). These infections are most commonly transmitted through the sharing of infected needles when the opioids are injected, but can also be transmitted through the mucous membranes of the nose through the sharing of straws or other devices used to insufflate the drug. Once established, these types of infections are hard and expensive to treat, often leading to subsequent medical issues that are also difficult and costly. According to the 2018 publication, *Facing Addiction in America: The Surgeon General's Spotlight on Opioids*, "approximately one in 10 new HIV diagnoses occur among people who inject drugs."[16] While the Center for Disease Control (CDC) has reported a steady decline in HIV diagnoses attributable to injection drug use since the 1990s, this decline appears to have leveled off and may be related to increased injection drug use, primarily heroin, over the last few years.[17] Unfortunately, cases of hepatitis C are increasing and have been linked to the opioid epidemic.[18] Because hepatitis C is difficult to cure, it often leads to a chronic infection and, in some cases, eventually leads to cirrhosis, liver failure, and the need for an organ transplant.

Neonatal abstinence syndrome (NAS), sometimes called neonatal opioid withdrawal syndrome (NOWS), occurs in newborns following exposure to drugs while in the mother's womb. Since opioids are able to cross the placenta, the developing fetus is exposed when her mother uses opioids for any reason, and, just like mom, will develop tolerance and dependence with repeated exposure. Once the baby has been born and is no longer physically attached to her mother, the same withdrawal syndrome that happens to anyone dependent on opioids begins. This is an expected and treatable condition but it may have long-term health consequences for the infant.[19] Just like adult opioid withdrawal, NAS signs include neurological excitability, gastrointestinal dysfunction, and autonomic dysfunction. Affected newborns may also have low birthweight and respiratory complications, and may experience developmental challenges.[20] Unfortunately, the incidence of NAS continues to increase as the opioid epidemic expands, affecting more and more children born to mothers with active opioid use disorder. According to the Boston Federal Reserve report, "the average cost to care for an infant with NAS in the first year of life alone is nearly US$70,000 more than the cost to care for an infant born without NAS."

[16] US Department of Health and Human Services (2018). [17] CDC (2022a).
[18] CDC (2022b). [19] Substance Abuse and Mental Health Services Administration (2018).
[20] Federal Reserve Bank of Boston New England Public Policy Center (2018).

Loss of Productivity Related to Opioid Use Disorder

The opioid epidemic has had a significant negative impact on local, regional, and national economies in the United States and around the world. In the United States, lost productivity for individuals with opioid use disorder was most recently estimated to be roughly US$23.5 billion (2017).[21] As the focus and motivations of affected individuals shift away from activities and behaviors that are generally seen as productive and contributing to the benefit of the economy as a whole and towards activities and behaviors solely directed towards the procurement and use of opioids, productivity necessarily suffers. People who misuse opioids have a significantly increased risk of coming into contact with the judicial system, as these drugs, and the funds required to purchase them, are often obtained illegally. People incarcerated for drug crimes do not participate in the economy to any appreciable extent during the course of their sentence, and often participation once released, especially if on parole or if their conviction was for the commission of a felony, is less than those who have not served time. Even if someone who misuses opioids does not end up in contact with the judicial system or is able to avoid incarceration through participation in a drug court or another alternative discipline program, their economic productivity while in residential or outpatient treatment programs is decreased.

According to a working-group report of the Federal Reserve Bank of Cleveland,[22] published in early 2019, the opioid epidemic has had widespread impacts on labor-force participation within the group most affected by the crisis: less-educated men. The working group defined less-educated as having achieved less than a Bachelor of Arts (BA) degree, which would include individuals who did not graduate from high school, hold only a high school diploma, attended or completed trade school, obtained an Associates (two-year) degree, or attended but did not graduate from college with a four-year degree. Using opioid prescription rates as a marker for increased opioid misuse in a given area, the group was able to correlate the extent to which increased availability of opioids in a given county in the United States affected labor-force participation by less-educated men, the subgroup most likely to be negatively impacted by increased availability of opioids. The group differentiated between White and non-White men and found that while abuse and mortality rates are generally higher in the group "White men with less than a BA," resulting in a greater negative impact on labor-force participation in this group, "the labor market outcomes of minority men with less than a BA are

---

[21] Florence et al. (2021).   [22] Federal Reserve Bank of Cleveland Working (2019).

even more impacted when exposed to high prescription rates." Sadly, the main reason for nonparticipation in the labor force is overdose fatality. According to a *New York Times* article by Josh Katz,[23] the average age at which someone was likely to experience an overdose fatality in 2017 was 41 years old. This is the prime working age in the United States, and someone who dies this early would likely have spent another 25 years in the labor force.

Insys Therapeutics, Subsys, and the Anti-Kickback Statute

Drug overdose has become the leading cause of death for Americans under 50, but even highly educated individuals without opioid use disorder can be prematurely removed from the labor force as a result of opioid misuse. In 2019, Geoffrey S. Berman, the United States Attorney for the Southern District of New York, announced an indictment[24] against five physicians, charging them with conspiracy to violate the Anti-Kickback Statute.[23] According to Berman, these physicians "engaged in a scheme in which they accepted bribes and kick-backs for prescribing a potent and highly-addictive fentanyl-based spray." Subsys, the fentanyl sublingual spray involved in the indictment, was developed by Insys Therapeutics, Inc. (Chandler, AZ) as a way to provide the powerful opioid pain reliever fentanyl to treat breakthrough pain in terminal and hospice patients with severe cancer pain while avoiding the need for repeated injections. At face value, the idea was based on a noble goal but, unfortunately, as we have seen with other opioid manufacturers, at some point greed got in the way. The target demographic accepted by the United States Food and Drug Administration (FDA) when it approved Subsys for clinical use was not large enough for Insys, and they soon worked to broaden the indications for the drug, pushing doctors to prescribe Subsys for chronic noncancer pain and other indications not approved by the FDA. Due to the resulting fraud perpetrated by Insys in their attempt to increase sales of this opioid, many people died, lost their jobs, and, in some cases, were sentenced to lengthy prison terms. The account that follows is only one example of the fallout that occurred nationwide when this scheme was uncovered by the United States Department of Justice.

According to the indictment, in 2012 Insys "established a 'speakers bureau' consisting of doctors selected and compensated by [Insys Therapeutics] purportedly to provide educational presentations regarding [Subsys]," so-called "speaker programs." While industry-sponsored educational events such as these speaker programs are a perfectly legal, if not morally questionable, marketing practice that is commonly employed by pharmaceutical companies

---

[23] Katz (2017).   [24] US District Court (2019).   [25] US Social Security Administration (n.d.).

in the United States, participants in these types of programs must adhere to strict guidelines regarding structure and execution. The structure of these types of programs is more or less the same across the industry: A company that produces a device or medication hires an independent healthcare professional, who does not work for the company but is familiar with the product, to speak to an audience about the device or medication. The healthcare professional is paid an "honorarium" for their time and effort (usually around US$1,000) and attendees receive a meal (not to exceed US$125 in value) for their participation. These programs are purportedly conducted "in order to help educate and inform other healthcare professionals about the benefits, risks, and appropriate uses of company medicines."[26] In reality, however, there is often less of an emphasis on education and more of an emphasis on entertainment, designed to associate the company's product in the minds of attendees with positive memories of a pleasant evening and implying a sometimes not so subtle quid pro quo.[27]

The United States Anti-Kickback Statute makes it a criminal offense to bribe (knowingly receive, offer, or pay any type of remuneration to induce or reward) physicians to prescribe a medication; but what, exactly, constitutes a bribe? Though there are some who have argued that taking a group of physicians out to a local restaurant and buying them an expensive dinner, complete with unlimited alcohol, while they watch a power-point presentation constitutes remuneration consistent with violation of this statute, prosecution has thus far been reserved for more flagrant violations. According to Berman, Insys Therapeutics' behavior went above and beyond the accepted industry standard for marketing pharmaceuticals. Insys allegedly "selected and compensated speakers not based on their qualifications, but rather to induce them to prescribe large volumes of [Subsys]," conducted these programs at "high-end restaurants where [often there was] no educational presentation whatsoever" and "lacked an appropriate audience of peer-level doctors with a professional reason to be educated about [Subsys]." The indictment alleges that there were several violations of the Anti-Kickback Statute perpetuated by Insys and the physician members of the speakers bureau. The bureau members were determined not to be the independent physicians required by the industry code of ethics, but in actuality, were physicians who were given one of these very lucrative speaking positions as a reward for their high volume of Subsys prescriptions. Appointment to the Insys speakers bureau and an opportunity to participate in these programs was an incentive for physicians to increase

---

[26] The Pharmaceutical Research and Manufacturers of America (2021).
[27] Department of Health and Human Services Office of Inspector General (2020).

their monthly prescribing of Subsys. These physicians were paid tens of thousands of dollars annually in speaker's fees, significantly more than the usual and customary amount, and, in some cases, the total compensation paid by Insys was well over US$100,000. Though these events were billed as educational programs, they were, in actuality, just a way for the company to kick back some of the profits generated by Subsys sales to their top prescribers. There were often no educational presentations unless an independent monitor was present in the audience, and the "audience" was made up not of qualified healthcare professionals with the ability to prescribe Subsys, who could benefit from their attendance, but instead was made up of Insys drug reps, the physicians involved in the scheme, and often their nonphysician employees, friends, and family members. Sadly, these events, which were held at expensive restaurants and, in some cases, adult entertainment venues, involved socializing with "attractive" members of the Subsys sales team, some of whom were previously employed as adult entertainers, the excessive consumption of alcohol, and the use of illegal drugs such as marijuana and cocaine but not, ironically, opioids.

While the specific details of what actually went on may seem sensational and, at times, salacious, it is important to understand the degree to which this epidemic continues to impact all of us, even those without opioid use disorder, in a significantly negative way. The far-reaching cost of the focus of these companies on increasing their profits at the expense of the patients who were supposed to benefit from their product is staggering. As a result of their participation in this scheme, five physicians specializing in pain management, emergency medicine, physical medicine and rehabilitation, hematology, and oncology will never practice medicine again. Dr. Dialecti Voudouris admitted to participating in the conspiracy by accepting US$119,400 in speaker fees and was sentenced to time served. Dr. Todd Schlifstein pleaded guilty to conspiring to violate the Anti-Kickback Statute by accepting US$127,100 from Insys and was subsequently sentenced to 24 months in prison. Dr. Jeffery Goldstein admitted to accepting US$196,000 and was sentenced to 57 months. Dr. Alexandru Burducea admitted to accepting US$68,400 in speaker program fees and was sentenced to 57 months as well. Dr. Gordon Freedman, the highest-paid Insys speaker in the United States, having received roughly US$308,600 in fees, did not take a plea deal, and was convicted following a jury trial. Dr. Freedman was subsequently sentenced to over 17 years in prison, three years of supervised release, ordered to forfeit the US$308,600 in fees he had received and pay a fine of US$75,000. He is currently awaiting trial on charges of overprescribing opioids related to the overdose death of one of his patients to whom he prescribed fentanyl. Each of these physicians was ordered to turn in their medical license as a result of these convictions. The cost to society in terms of the time, energy, and expense associated with the years of education and training in these five cases alone is considerable, as is the indirect cost of the years of lost future service, but this is only one example of the impact this conspiracy has had on the practice of medicine. Physicians who accepted bribes to prescribe Subsys to noncancer patients practiced all over the United States and similar stories are being told in Alabama, Michigan, Florida, Texas, Illinois, New Hampshire, Connecticut, and Arkansas. In one case, a doctor in Alabama was sentenced to 20 years in prison for accepting bribes from Insys and in Michigan another doctor was sentenced to 32 months.

The consequences for those who conceived and executed the conspiracy to bribe physicians to prescribe Subsys, and in some cases to switch patients from a different manufacturer's fentanyl-based product to Subsys, were equally severe. While Geoffrey S. Berman was aggressively pursuing the physicians who accepted bribes to prescribe, in his role as the United States Attorney for the Southern District of New York, a parallel investigation was taking place in the Southwest United States led by assistant US attorneys Nathaniel Yeager and Andrew Lelling.[28] As the alleged mastermind, Insys founder John Kapoor was convicted in federal court of racketeering conspiracy and subsequently sentenced to 66 months in prison, three years of supervised release, and ordered to pay forfeiture and restitution. Six other top Insys executives were also charged in federal court and accepted plea deals for reduced time in prison. According to the US district judge, Allison Burroughs, all seven defendants were considered culpable in the conspiracy, but Kapoor received the most severe sentence because of both his position as the leader and because he would not admit guilt to avoid a trial. Michael Gurry, former Insys vice president, was sentenced to 33 months in federal prison for his role and former Insys chief executive officer Michael Babich received 30 months. Those involved in sales also received lengthy prison terms, though considerably less than someone convicted of selling the same drug on the street would be expected to receive. Richard Simon, former Insys national director of sales, received 33 months in prison for his involvement in the scheme. Joseph Rowan, the company's regional sales director, received 27 months. Alec Burlakoff, former Insys vice president of sales, received 26 months and Sunrise Lee, former Insys regional sales director, was sentenced to one year and a day in prison. Insys Therapeutics ultimately settled with the Justice Department for US$225 million to end criminal and civil investigations, forfeiting US$28 million, and paying US$2 million in criminal fines and US$195 million to end the government's probe into False Claims Act

---

[28] United States District Attorney's Office for the District of Massachussetts (2020).

violations. The company subsequently filed for bankruptcy and is no longer operational.

Deaths directly attributable to Subsys aside (over 8,000 people died of overdoses after taking the drug), the financial costs involved with this one single conspiracy are astounding. It is important to remember that this is just an example, just one instance of this type of behavior which, no doubt, continues across the industry to this day. Over a 10-year period from 2012 to 2022, several law enforcement agencies, including the Drug Enforcement Agency, Federal Bureau of Investigation, as well as regional and local law enforcement agencies spent thousands of hours, and hundreds of thousands of dollars investigating Insys Therapeutics. United States attorneys and their staff in multiple districts were tasked with the same burden, and for those defendants who did not accept a plea, we must consider the cost of a trial on top of the investigation. For those who were convicted and sentenced to prison, there is the cost of incarceration. It all adds up.

The Economic Effect on Children of Parents with Opioid Use Disorder

As the opioid epidemic continues to devastate adults in the prime of their lives, the economic consequences of opioid addiction are felt by both the older and younger generations. According to Meredith Covington, community affairs manager at the St. Louis Federal Reserve, "there is a disproportionate number of people now that should be retiring who are going back and looking for second or third jobs. They're having to take care of their grandchildren because their children are struggling with opioid addiction. This issue not only affects those dealing with opioid addiction, but also their families. There are ramifications for the productivity of their parents, children, and siblings."[29] One aspect of the economic impact the opioid epidemic has had on families that deserves a closer look is the long-lasting impact on children and parents of people suffering from opioid use disorder.

The 2019 United Hospital Fund report entitled "The ripple effect: National and State estimates of the U.S. opioid epidemic"[30] breaks down the economic impact on children, focusing on the cumulative, lifetime cost of increased spending for healthcare, special education, child welfare, and the criminal justice system that result from the impact of parental opioid use disorder on a child's physical, mental, and social emotional health. Since this report did not consider lost productivity or missed opportunities, the actual cost is

[29] Federal Reserve Bank of St. Louis (2019).   [30] United Hospital Fund (2019).

considerably higher. Based on data from 2017, the authors estimate that there were 2.2 million children and adolescents who had a parent with opioid use disorder or who were themselves diagnosed. If current trends continue, they estimate, 4.3 million children will be in the same situation by the year 2030, at which point the cost of this "ripple effect" will be US$400 billion.

In summary, we have seen that the actual costs associated with the opioid epidemic are far greater than the substantial financial costs incurred by individuals, institutions, and governments. The fallout from the epidemic is considerable and continues to significantly impact all members of society, even those who do not suffer from opioid use disorder themselves, at an accelerating rate. While the impact on the poorest individuals and families is felt the greatest, the costs to all of us comes in the form of lost productivity, higher costs for healthcare, and increased burden of disease. Sadly, these costs are not a one-time charge as future generations will continue to make payments on this debt for decades to come. As the cautionary tale of Insys Therapeutics demonstrates, even the most educated among us have not been spared from the costs of the epidemic. Hundreds of physicians, biopharmaceutical executives, and support staff have been caught up in this web of deceit, driven by a desire to increase individual financial gain, at a considerable cost to those involved, but also to the rest of us. The costs associated with the loss of years of training and experience are substantial and difficult to calculate, as many of these healthcare professionals will likely never practice medicine again, and we are still suffering from a worldwide shortage of highly skilled workers. If we are to recover from the opioid epidemic it is essential that we rethink the attitudes which allow for the continued prioritization of profits over people and put in place policies that reflect a changing approach to healthcare.

References and Further Reading

Agency for Healthcare Research and Quality (2014). Medical expenditure panel survey: Methodology report. https://meps.ahrq.gov/data_files/publications/m r30/mr30.shtml

Aliprantis D, Fee K, Schweitzer ME (2019). Opioids and the labor market. Federal Reserve Bank of Cleveland, Working Paper no. 18-07 R. www.clevelandfed.org /publications/working-paper/wp-1807r-opioids-and-labor-market

Bureau of Justice Assistance, United States Department of Justice (n.d.). Law enforcement naloxone toolkit. https://bjatta.bja.ojp.gov/naloxone/what-are-typical-costs-law-enforcement-overdose-response-program Link to publication (accessed December 5, 2022)

CDC (2022a). HIV in the United States and dependent areas. www.cdc.gov/hiv/st atistics/overview/ataglance.html (accessed December 5, 2022)

CDC (2022b). New vital signs report: Hepatitis C is deadly, but curable. www .cdc.gov/media/releases/2022/t0809-vs-hepatitis-c.html

CEA (2017). The underestimated cost of the opioid crisis. https://trumpwhitehouse .archives.gov/sites/whitehouse.gov/files/images/The%20Underestimated%20C ost%20of%20the%20Opioid%20Crisis.pdf

CEA (2019). The full cost of the opioid crisis: $2.5 trillion over four years. Press release, October 28, 2019. https://trumpwhitehouse.archives.gov/articles/full-cost-opioid-crisis-2-5-trillion-four-years/

Department of Health and Human Services Office of Inspector General (2020). Office of Inspector General special fraud alert (SFA) on speaker programs, November 16. https://oig.hhs.gov/documents/special-fraud-alerts/865/SpecialF raudAlertSpeakerPrograms.pdf

Fair Health, Inc. (2016). The impact of the opioid crisis on the healthcare system: A study of privately billed services. FAIR Health White Paper. https://collections .nlm.nih.gov/catalog/nlm:nlmuid-101751547-pdf

Federal Reserve Bank of Boston New England Public Policy Center (2018). Report on the fiscal impact of the opioid epidemic in the New England states. www .bostonfed.org/publications/new-england-public-policy-center-policy-report/20 18/the-fiscal-impact-of-the-opioid-epidemic-in-the-new-england-states.aspx

Federal Reserve Bank of Cleveland (2019). Working paper on opioids and the labor market. WP 18-07R. www.clevelandfed.org/publications/working-paper/wp-18 07r-opioids-and-labor-market (accessed December 5, 2022)

American Medical Association (2005). The opioid crisis: Impact on healthcare services and costs. https://s3.amazonaws.com/media2.fairhealth.org/info graphic/asset/FH%20Infographic%20-%20The%20Opioid%20Crisis-59724533 a5ac5.pdf

Federal Reserve Bank of St. Louis (2019). The economic costs of the opioid epidemic. www.stlouisfed.org/open-vault/2019/september/economic-costs-opioid-epidemic

Florence C, Luo F, Rice K (2021). The economic burden of opioid use disorder and fatal opioid overdose in the United States, 2017. *Drug and Alcohol Dependence* 218: 108350.

Katz J (2017). Short answers to hard questions about the opioid crisis. *New York Times*, August 3.

Larochelle MR, Wakeman SE, Ameli O, et al. Relative cost differences of initial treatment strategies for newly diagnosed opioid use disorder. *Medical Care* 58(10): 919–926.

National Drug Helpline (2023). Report on the cost of drug and alcohol rehab in 2023. https://drughelpline.org/rehab-cost/ (accessed March 2023)

NIDA (2021a). Medications to treat opioid use disorder research report: Is naloxone accessible? https://nida.nih.gov/publications/research-reports/medications-to-treat-opioid-addiction/naloxone-accessible

NIDA (2021b). Medications to treat opioid use disorder research report. How much does opioid treatment cost? https://nida.nih.gov/publications/research-reports/medications-to-treat-opioid-addiction/how-much-does-opioid-treatment-cost

Pharmaceutical Research and Manufacturers of America (2021). Code on interactions with healthcare professionals, August 6. https://phrma.org/stem/code-on-interactions-with-health-care-professionals

Premier (2019). Opioid overdoses costing U.S. hospitals an estimated $11 billion annually. January 3, 2019. Report on the cost of opioid overdoses to United States Hospitals. www.premierinc.com/newsroom/press-releases/opioid-overdoses-costing-u-s-hospitals-an-estimated-11-billion-annually

Rand Corporation (2022). Commission on Combating Synthetic Opioid Trafficking: Annual report. February 8, 2022. www.rand.org/pubs/external_pu blications/EP68838.html

Ray B, O'Donnell D, Kahre K (2015). Police officer attitudes towards intranasal naloxone training. *Drug and Alcohol Dependence* 146: 107–110.

Ropero-Miller JD, Speaker PJ (2019). The hidden costs of the opioid crisis and the implications for financial management in the public sector. *Forensic Science International: Synergy* 1: 227–238.

Stevens JP, Wall MJ, Novack L, et al. (2017). The critical care crisis of opioid overdoses in the United States. *Annals of the American Thoracic Society* 14(12): 1803–1809.

Substance Abuse and Mental Health Services Administration(2018). Clinical guidance for treating pregnant and parenting women with opioid use disorder and their infants. HHS Publication No. (SMA) 18–5054. https://store.samhsa.gov/product/Clinical-Guidance-for-Treating-Pregnant-and-Parenting-Women-With-Opioid-Use-Disorder-and-Their-Infants/SMA18-5054

Sullivan R (2018). The fiscal impact of the opioid epidemic in the New England States. New England Public Policy Center, Policy Report 18–1. www.bostonfed.org/publications/new-england-public-policy-center-policy-report/2018/the-fiscal-impact-of-the-opioid-epidemic-in-the-new-england-states.aspx

United Hospital Fund (2019). The ripple effect: National and state estimates of the US opioid epidemic's impact on children. https://uhfnyc.org/media/filer_public/6e/80/6e80760f-d579-46a3-998d-1aa816ab06f6/uhf_ripple_effect_nationa l_and_state_estimates_chartbook.pdf

United States District Attorney's Office for the District of Massachussetts (2020). Massachusets announcing the sentencing of Founder and former chairman of the board of Insys Therapeutics sentenced to 66 months in prison. Press release, January 23, 2020. www.justice.gov/usao-ma/pr/founder-and-former-chairman-board-insys-thera peutics-sentenced-66-months-prison

U.S. Department of Defense, Office of the Secretary (2016). TRICARE; Mental Health and Substance Use Disorder Treatment. Federal Register. September 2, 2016. www.federalregister.gov/documents/2016/09/16/2016-22363/tricare-mental-health-and-substance-use-disorder-treatment

U.S. Department of Health and Human Services (2018). *Facing Addiction in America: The Surgeon General's Spotlight on Opioids*. Washington, DC: U.S. Department of Health and Human Services.

US District Court (2019). Indictment by the United States Attorney for the Southern District of New York of the five physicians accused of violating the Anti-Kickback Statutes. www.justice.gov/usao-sdny/press-release/file/1044111/download

US Social Security Administration (n.d.) Section 1128B(b)(1)–(2) of the Social Security Act; 42 U.S.C. § 1320a-7b(b)(1)–(2). www.ssa.gov/OP_Home/ssact/titl e11/1128B.htm

8 THE IMPACT OF THE OPIOID EPIDEMIC ON HEALTHCARE INFRASTRUCTURE

All countries are facing a dearth of medical resources. Developed countries struggle with access to specialized care, whereas their counterparts in developing nations are faced with a lack of healthcare workers, equipment, medication, and medical facilities. The coronavirus (COVID-19) pandemic has brought this issue to the forefront, spurring heated discussions about the ethical allocation of scarce resources such as ventilators and intensive care beds. Perhaps not publicized to the extent as the COVID-19 pandemic, the opioid epidemic has also placed significant strain on healthcare infrastructure. It is more difficult to quantify the burden that the opioid epidemic has had on healthcare services, but in this chapter we discuss the ways, both abstract and concrete, that increasing opioid misuse has led to fewer resources for other medical problems. We also examine some mitigation strategies that have and have not worked in an attempt to find the most effective path to follow forward.

Opportunity Costs

Whether you are living in a developing country or one with considerable resources and a robust healthcare infrastructure in place to provide services to most, if not all, of the populous, healthcare really is a zero-sum game. There is only so much money available to spend, resources are not unlimited, and when the incidence of opioid-related health issues increases, the funds and personnel necessary to address them must come from somewhere. Resources diverted in this manner negatively impact other healthcare services, reducing access to preventative treatments, increasing wait times for access to care, and increasing the already high burden on healthcare professionals.

Emergency rooms across the United States have been inundated with opioid-related injuries, including accidental overdoses, in the wake of the current opioid epidemic. Per the 2021 National Healthcare Quality and Disparity

Report, from 2005 to 2018, the rate of emergency room visits in the United States rose from 89.1 to 238.0 visits per 100,000 people; and, for those in the lowest income quartile, visits increased more dramatically to 348.1 visits per 100,000 people.[1] Another report found that between 2016 and 2017, emergency rooms in the United States, on average, experienced a 29.5% increase in opioid overdose visits, whereas in the Midwestern states specifically, the overdose rate increased by 69.7%.[2] This trend is not confined to the United States, however. Emergency room utilization in Finland and the Netherlands has tripled over a 10-year period, and Canada has seen a 150% increase in emergency room visits between 2010–2011 and 2016–2017. This influx of patients has only worsened issues of overcrowding. We know that overcrowding of emergency rooms results in higher mortality rates and worse outcomes, largely due to its downstream effects, such as extended wait times, delays in receiving care, and increased rates of medical errors, emergency room violence, and the likelihood of patients leaving prior to receiving all necessary medical care (also referred to as leaving "against medical advice"). These downstream effects impact all visitors to the emergency room, not just those with an opioid-related complaint, ultimately hindering care for anyone needing emergent care.

Because individuals in the emergency room often require inpatient treatment for medical or surgical issues, the hospital wards have also been taxed with a dramatic influx of opioid-related admissions. A similar story has been becoming increasingly common in hospitals across many countries: patients enter the hospital through the emergency room, are diagnosed with a problem that requires surgery, and taken to the operating room. Sometimes the need for surgery is directly related to opioid use, such as the acutely intoxicated individual who suffers traumatic injury, but oftentimes it is not. Even in a very busy urban hospital there are operating rooms available for urgent or emergent surgery, so there is often not a delay of care at this point, but once the surgery is finished the patient has to go somewhere to recover. The vast majority of patients in this situation will go to an intensive care unit (ICU) called the postanesthesia care unit (PACU), also commonly called the "recovery room," where they are monitored until they have recovered from the effects of anesthesia and can be transferred to a hospital ward for further treatment. But what if there are no hospital beds? With the increase in hospitalization rates related to fallout from the opioid epidemic it is increasingly common for many hospitals to operate above capacity; and, if there are no beds on the

---

[1] Agency for Healthcare Research and Quality (2021).
[2] Healthcare Cost and Utilization Project (2021).

wards, the post-surgical patients must wait in the PACU or, if the PACU is full, in the operating room until a bed becomes available. Aside from increasing the workload for a workforce that is increasingly becoming overburdened and burned out, the inability to efficiently downgrade a patient from a higher level of care, such as in the operating room where one patient is monitored by three healthcare professionals (a surgeon, an anesthesiologist, and a registered nurse), to a lower level of care significantly increases the costs associated with care and takes human resources away from other patients. In the PACU, for example, one physician anesthesiologist typically covers the entire unit with either a resident or physician assistant and each PACU nurse can care for two patients. On the regular floor, the nurse-to-patient ratio is even higher and, depending on the acuity of the patients involved, may be as high as one nurse to four or more patients. From 2005 to 2018, the rate of hospital inpatient stays in the United States solely related to opioid misuse doubled, growing from 136.8 to 286.1 admissions per 100,000 people. Canada has experienced a similar rise in hospitalizations that have resulted specifically from opioid-related behavioral health and mental disorders.[3]

However, not all patients are appropriate for a lower level of care. Even before the COVID-19 pandemic began, availability of ICU beds has been limited, especially for those living in rural areas or less-developed countries. Many individuals requiring hospitalization for their opioid use need medical care that is only offered in the ICU, such as mechanical respiratory support. One might argue that with more patients occupying ICU beds for opioid-related issues, even fewer beds are available for those with other concerns, for example those suffering from myocardial infarction, stroke, or traumatic injuries. And admission to the ICU is not inexpensive. In fact, it has been estimated that ICU stays for opioid-related causes, on average, cost around US$92,408, per a 2015 study.[4]

Secondary Effects

The opioid epidemic has resulted in an epidemic of poor health maintenance as well. Untreated opioid addiction invariably increases the part of the limited healthcare budget that must be allocated for treating otherwise preventable diseases or traumatic injuries. To illustrate this, consider Robert, a middle-aged man with diabetes and opioid use disorder. As a direct result of his chronic opioid misuse, Robert was unable to properly manage his blood sugar levels, frequently did not show up for scheduled appointments with his endocrinologist, and

---

[3] Canadian Institute for Health Information (2018).   [4] Stevens et al. (2017).

received medical care primarily during hospitalizations after being brought into his local emergency room. His poorly controlled diabetes greatly increased his risk for chronic infections, as did his intravenous heroin use, and he frequently developed skin infections in the area where he injected opioids. Had Robert been able to manage his diabetes better and receive treatment for his opioid use disorder in the primary care setting instead of the hospital, the cost to the system as a whole in terms of both the financial burden and the human resources required to manage his significant medical problems would have been considerably less.

Opioid misuse increases the demand for infectious disease treatment. Those who consume opioids are more likely to engage in certain behaviors, such as needle-sharing and unprotected sexual intercourse, that increase the likelihood of contracting certain diseases. For example, outbreaks of HIV, hepatitis B, and hepatitis C are frequently associated with the sharing of drug paraphernalia. Only recently, an outbreak of HIV and hepatitis C in the state of Indiana was facilitated by injection of an opioid known as oxymorphone, leading to US$100 million in medical costs. As a result, the number of diagnoses for hepatitis C has doubled between 2000 and 2014 in the United States, with three-quarters of new cases associated with a history of intravenous drug use.

Other types of infections, such as bacterial abscesses, endocarditis (infection of the heart and valves), osteomyelitis (infection of bone), and sepsis (widespread blood infection), are also on the rise. Not infrequently, individuals with these infections require medical services only found in the hospital setting, such as intravenous antibiotics, critical care support, and surgery. Between 2016 and 2018, for instance, hospitalizations in the United States for endocarditis, osteomyelitis, and sepsis rose by 33%, 35%, and 24%, respectively, ultimately resulting in more than 23,000 hospitalizations, 1,200 deaths and costs of nearly US$1.3 billion. In addition, because individuals who use intravenous drugs are more likely to leave the hospital against medical advice before completing treatment, they are more likely to require hospital readmission, further increasing the number of days that hospitalization is required.

The opioid epidemic has also driven increased rates of healthcare utilization among the pediatric population. The rate of neonatal abstinence syndrome, a consequence of opioid use during pregnancy, has increased significantly during the epidemic, rising from 1.2 cases per 1,000 hospital births in 2000, to 5.8 cases per 1,000 hospital births in 2012. Multiple states require all cases of neonatal abstinence syndrome to be reported to child protective services, sometimes requiring separation of child and mother. Increasing rates of home removal and foster care placement is attributed to increasing rates of child abuse and neglect associated with parental substance use.

Even when the child is not removed from the home, the opioid-addicted parent may still be absent, perhaps because of chronic intoxication or mental illness, incarceration, hospitalization, or death. As a result, other family members frequently accept the responsibility of childcare, affecting their lives in multiple ways. This obligation can require that work scheduled be adjusted or a change in living arrangements, and frequently negatively impacts the family finances. Additionally, this increased burden can impact the caregivers' physical health, causing anxiety, depression, sleep disturbances, and possibly premature death.

Diversion of Resources from Preventative Care

If we are reactive instead of proactive in our approach to disease management, medical care becomes much more expensive. As a direct result of the opioid epidemic, fewer resources are available for preventative care. This impacts people in less developed countries to a much greater degree, as most areas such as this have limited resources available to begin with and are unable to adapt to the significant requirement for reallocation of funds related to opioid misuse.

Addicted Healthcare Workers

In addition to the diversion of critical human resources away from preventative care and towards meeting the increasing demands on healthcare systems related to the opioid epidemic is the effect of the increasing number of healthcare professionals lost to opioid use disorder themselves. The epidemic has directly impacted all healthcare workers as we have discussed, but for some, the stress associated with working in this increasingly difficult environment, coupled with greater access to pharmaceuticals, has increased the risk for the development of opioid misuse by healthcare professionals. Physicians, nurses, and other members of the healthcare team work in demanding, high-stress environments with ready access to large quantities of highly addictive drugs and, for those at risk, the temptation may prove too great to avoid. While we generally hold these people to a higher standard, in reality, the chances that a healthcare professional will develop opioid use disorder is roughly the same as in the general population from where they come. Just like everyone else, while some people are able to use recreational drugs casually, others become addicted quickly, suggesting that genetic susceptibility plays a role in the development of addiction and substance abuse. In addition, individuals with novelty-seeking behavior traits may be both more likely to choose a particular medical specialty and more prone to the development of addiction. There is also an association between chemical dependence and other mental illnesses, such as depression or anxiety, that may contribute to the development of addiction in susceptible individuals. The observation that healthcare professionals are people too, and that they share the same genetic and experiential predisposition to developing opioid use disorder as everyone else, has historically been ignored, perhaps increasing the stress on these individuals who are routinely held to a higher standard than those in other industries. The main difference, however, is that when a healthcare professional misuses opioids the negative impact involves, just as with airline pilots, school bus drivers, big box store forklift operators, and others in so-called "safety sensitive" positions, the potential for a much greater number of casualties. While certainly a growing problem over the past two decades of the opioid epidemic, the stress of working in an environment with limited resources during the COVID-19 pandemic has no doubt accelerated this problem.

What Is Being Done About It?

In the United States, one of the most significantly impacted countries in the world, individual state governments have developed plans to combat the opioid epidemic, at both the state and local level, in an attempt to reduce the effects on an already overburdened healthcare system. Though only three years old at the time, North Carolina's 2019 Opioid and Substance Use Action Plan (OSUAP) was updated in May of 2021 to OSUAP 3.0.[5] Specific changes to the original plan reflect a reassessment of what was and what was not working and the need to broaden their approach in order to reach the most vulnerable among the population. For example, the recognition that fentanyl analogs are now responsible for many stimulant overdose deaths as well as opioid overdose deaths, the action plan broadened the scope to include polysubstance abuse, focusing not only on opioids but cocaine, methamphetamines, and other stimulants as well. Acknowledging that the systems in place have "disproportionately harmed historically marginalized people," a decision was made to "reorient those systems and increase access to comprehensive, culturally competent, and linguistically appropriate drug user health services."[6] Similar to other plans to combat the epidemic and reduce the strain on healthcare infrastructure, OSUAP 3.0 focuses on prevention, harm reduction, and increasing access to care for historically marginalized people. Learning from the successes and failures of others requires communication, and in New York State the Department of Health has established a coordinated approach to fight the opioid epidemic, which includes the sharing of relevant data between agencies and affected communities,

[5] OSUPA (2021).   [6] OSUPA (2021).

making their prescription-drug monitoring program easier for providers to access and use, and coordinating statewide and community programs to improve the effectiveness of opioid prevention efforts.[7]

The Commonwealth of Massachusetts' Health Policy Commission specifically recommended, in 2016, that "[T]he Commonwealth should systematically track the impact of the opioid epidemic on the health care system."[8] In order to do this, the Commission specifically analyzed the rate and volume of opioid-related hospital utilization and discovered that between 2007 and 2014 opioid-related hospital visits had increased by 84% and those visits related to heroin ingestion had increased by 201%. Faced with a rapidly escalating number of persons requiring hospital-level care for opioid-misuse-related medical issues the Commission, realizing that the rate of increase would not be sustainable under the existing system and circumstances, began to look for solutions. The recommendations for reducing the impact on the state's healthcare system included the mandate to continue tracking the impact of interventions to evaluate their efficacy and proposed increasing the access to and the effectiveness of "evidence-based opioid use disorder treatment by integrating pharmacologic interventions into systems of care." The proposal specifically stated that the organizations that set service rates, collect payments, process claims, and pay provider claims (health plan providers, Medicare, and Medicaid) have a duty to support this integration of opioid use disorder treatment into primary care by contracting with an adequate number of community-based behavioral health providers to meet the growing need. While this may sound like common sense, the fact that it took a state government health policy commission's report to urge that this type of action be taken is most likely reflective of the low reimbursement rates for mental health services in general and specifically for substance misuse treatment.[9] Most encouraging, however, was the commission's recommendation that the state should "test, evaluate, and scale innovative care models for preventing" opioid use disorder.

By the summer of 2020, only four years after the Massachusetts Health Policy Commission report, significant progress had been made, though opioid overdose deaths and hospital admissions continued to increase at an alarming rate. As recommended by the Health Policy Commission, many states had enacted policies that effectively increased access to treatment for opioid use disorder by increasing insurance coverage and payments for services. In the United States, healthcare insurance provided by the federal government is

---

[7] New York State Department of Health (n.d.).
[8] Commonwealth of Massachusetts' Health Policy Commission (2016).
[9] Pacula and Stein (2020).

limited to persons aged 65 or older and, in some cases, people under 65 with certain disabilities or conditions (Medicare). For the majority of the population aged 64 and younger, health insurance comes from private insurance plans, which are either purchased by the individual or provided as part of an employee benefit package. For some people with limited income and resources, Medicaid, a joint federal and state program, serves as a safety net that provides health insurance coverage to those with no other options. Traditionally, these state-run programs work with limited resources to cover a large population, and access to care, especially for substance misuse treatment, has been limited. By expanding Medicaid benefit coverage to include methadone, buprenorphine, and other nonpharmacological treatments, increasing reimbursement for screening, brief interventions, and referrals to treatment, and expanding eligibility criteria for Medicaid enrolment, states have been able to increase access to treatment and early intervention.[10]

Expanding access to treatment programs by increasing funding, however, is only part of the solution. The capacity of existing treatment facilities is the rate-limiting step in the drive to increase access to care, and for many people with opioid use disorder, the only effective method involves residential treatment. Individual states have been able to expand access to these facilities by increasing the capacity of existing facilities and creating new ones, through both federal block grant funding[11] and Medicaid Section 1115 IMD (institutions for mental disease) exclusion waivers.[12] Not all patients with opioid use disorder, however, require or qualify for inpatient treatment. By incentivizing providers to obtain DEA (drug enforcement administration) waivers to prescribe buprenorphine[13] to outpatients with opioid use disorder, and by increasing reimbursements rates for these services, outpatient treatment capacity has significantly expanded.

In addition to expanding capacity to existing services, and this is what will have the most significant impact on the opioid epidemic moving forward, we have begun to rethink the way treatment for opioid use disorder and other substance misuse is delivered. By integrating treatment for substance misuse with existing models of primary care for other chronic disease management, the

---

[10] Pacula and Stein (2020).

[11] Block grants are federal funds earmarked for specific state or local programs, supported by federal funds but administered by state or local governments for programs often meant to improve social welfare programs.

[12] Exclusion waivers enable Medicaid patients in states with these waivers to receive care in residential facilities specializing in mental health disorders, which would otherwise be excluded by federal statute.

[13] The Drug Addiction Treatment Act (DATA 2000) "waiver" legislation authorized the outpatient use of buprenorphine for the treatment of opioid use disorder.

separation between people with substance use disorder and those who don't carry the diagnosis begins to fade. By normalizing mental health disorders in general, those who were previously seen only in the context of their diagnosis, and received treatment for substance misuse issues in one facility separate from their primary medical care, are now able to access comprehensive care that treats both the substance misuse and their medical problems, related or unrelated to substance misuse. The hope is that this will be achieved by linking specialty substance use disorder treatment services with primary care and case management, by supporting information technology development and alternative payment models for care. According to Rosalie Liccardo Pacula and Bradley D. Stein of the Brookings Institution, "Payment reforms and delivery integration have the potential to fundamentally modify the type of care patients receive, not just for OUD [opioid use disorder], but for substance use disorders more generally. While the transition has been slow, incremental, and largely hidden from the public in ways that other opioid policies have not, the net effect of these changes will likely be quite substantial and enduring in the long run."[14]

According to the United States Congressional Budget Office, more than 500,000 opioid-involved deaths have occurred since 2000, and the United States has the world's highest number of opioid-involved deaths per capita, with deaths from opioid-involved overdoses among the leading causes of death in 2020.[15] The impact on this healthcare system has been immense, reducing access to care and more significantly impacting members of the population with limited resources and those in traditionally marginalized groups. While, as of 2022, opioid overdose deaths and the need for access to treatment continues to increase, the responses outlined above hold promise. By normalizing mental health and substance misuse and integrating these issues into a primary care model, we will be able to begin to become more proactive instead of reactive, focusing on prevention instead of treatment as the number of people with active substance misuse eventually declines.

References and Further Reading

Agency for Healthcare and Research Quality (2021). 2021 National Healthcare Quality and Disparity Report. www.ahrq.gov/research/findings/nhqrdr/nhqd r21/index.html

Bote S (2019). US opioid epidemic: Impact on public health and review of prescription drug monitoring programs (PDMPs). *Online Journal of Public Health Information* 11(2): e18.

---

[14] Pacula and Stein (2020)   [15] Congressional Budget Office (2022).

Blanco C, Wiley TRA, Lloyd JJ, Lopez MF, Volkow ND (2010). America's opioid crisis: The need for an integrated public health approach. *Translational Psychiatry* 10: 167. www.nature.com/articles/s41398-020-0847-1

California Health Care Foundation (2016). Changing course: The role of health plans in curbing the opioid epidemic. June 2016. www.chcf.org/wp-content/upl oads/2017/12/PDF-ChangingHealthPlansOpioid.pdf

Canadian Institute for Health Information (2018). *Types of Opioid Harms in Canadian Hospitals: Comparing Canada and Australia.* Ottawa, ON: Canadian Institute for Health Information.

Commonwealth of Massachusetts Health Policy Commission (2016). Opioid use disorder in Massachusetts, an analysis of its impact on the health care system, availability of pharmacologic treatment, and recommendations for payment and care delivery reform. www.mass.gov/doc/opioid-use-disorder-report /download

Congressional Budget Office (2022). The opioid crisis and recent federal policy responses. www.cbo.gov/system/files/2022-09/58221-opioid-crisis.pdf

Coyle JR, Freeland M, Eckel ST, Hart AL (2020). Infectious sequelae of the opioid epidemic. *Journal of Infectious Diseases* 222 (Suppl 5): S451–S457.

Crowley DM, Connell CM, Jones D, Donovan MW (2019). Considering the child welfare system burden from opioid misuse: Research priorities for estimating public costs. *American Journal of Managed Care* 25(13): S256–S263.

Grover S, McClelland A. Furnham A (2020). Preferences for scarce medical resource allocation: Differences between experts and the general public and implications for the COVID-19 pandemic. *British Journal of Health Psychology* 25: 889–901.

Hauser W, Buchser E, Finn DP, et al. (2021). Is Europe also facing an opioid crisis? A survey of European Pain Federation chapters. *European Journal of Pain* 25(8): 1760–1769.

Healthcare Cost and Utilization Project (2021). HCUP Fast Stats. September 2021. Agency for Healthcare Research and Quality, Rockville, MD.

Hedberg K, Bui L, Livingston C, Shields L, Van Otterloo J (2019). Integrating public health and health care strategies to address the opioid epidemic: The Oregon Health Authority's opioid initiative. *Journal of Public Health Management and Practice* 25(3): 214–220.

Meisner JA, Anesi J, Chen X, Grande D (2020). Changes in infective endocarditis admissions in Pennsylvania during the opioid epidemic. *Clinical Infectious Diseases* 71(7): 1664–1670.

National Academies of Sciences, Engineering, and Medicine (2017). Pain management and the opioid epidemic: Balancing societal and individual benefits and risks of prescription opioid use. In Phillips JK, Ford MA, Bonnie RJ (eds.) *Evidence on Strategies for Addressing the Opioid Epidemic*. Washington, DC: National Academies Press. www.ncbi.nlm.nih.gov/books/NBK458653

New York State Department of Health (n.d.). Addressing the opioid epidemic in New York State. www.health.ny.gov/community/opioid_epidemic/ (accessed December 10, 2022)

OSUPA (2021). North Carolina's opioid and substance use action plan: Updates and Opportunities. Version 3.0. www.ncdhhs.gov/nc-osuapopioid-and-substance-use-action-plan-3010192021/download?attachment

Patel S, Sheikh A, Nazir N, Monro S, Anwar A (2020). The opioid crisis: How to lessen the burden on emergency departments by at-risk populations. *Cureus* 12 (11): e11498.

Pacula RL, Stein BD (2020). State approaches to tackling the opioid crisis through the health care system: State approaches to tackling the opioid crisis through the health care system. brookings.edu/wp-content/uploads/2020/06/4_Pacula-Stein_final.pdf

Stevens JP, Wall MJ, Novack L (2017). The critical care crisis of opioid overdoses in the United States. *Annals of the American Thoracic Society* 14(12): 1803–1809.

Tyo MB, McCurry MK (2020). An integrative review of measuring caregiver burden in substance use disorder. *Nursing Research* 69(5): 391–398.

US Centers for Disease Control and Prevention (2016). HIV and injection drug use: CDC vital signs. www.cdc.gov/vitalsigns/pdf/2016-12-vitalsigns.pdf

Vine M, Staatz C, Blyler C, Berk J (2020). The role of the workforce system in addressing the opioid crisis: A review of the literature. www.dol.gov/sites/dol gov/files/OASP/evaluation/pdf/WorkforceOpioids_LitReview_508.pdf

Weier MA, Slater J, Jandoc R, et al. (2019). The risk of infective endocarditis among people who inject drugs: A retrospective, population-based time series analysis. *Canadian Medical Association Journal* 191: E93–E99.

Zibell JE, Asher AK, Patel RC, et al. (2018). Increases in acute hepatitis C virus infection related to a growing opioid epidemic and associated injection drug use, United States, 2004 to 2014. *American Journal of Public Health* 108(2): 175–181.

PART III
The Treatment Plan

9 DETOXIFICATION: HOW DO WE GET OURSELVES OFF OPIOIDS?

When an individual has been using opioids for some time, a natural phenomenon known as *physical dependence* develops within the body. When the body is repeatedly exposed to certain medications or substances, including opioids, the body adapts by changing physically and biochemically. With physical dependence, when this drug or medication is suddenly stopped, or when there is a significant decrease in dosage, the body is not able to immediately accommodate for the change, and so the person experiences a constellation of symptoms known as withdrawal. It is important to note that dependence and withdrawal are not specific to opioids or other abusable substances. In fact, the phenomenon of dependency can be seen when abruptly stopping certain blood pressure medications, antidepressants, and more. To confuse things further, the terms dependence and addiction are often used interchangeably; however, addiction (or substance use disorder, which is the currently preferred nomenclature as defined the DSM-V[1]), is characterized by the compulsive use of substances despite causing significant harm to self and others.

Opioid Dependence and Withdrawal

The symptoms of withdrawal can vary depending on the substance or medication being taken. For opioids, symptoms can appear as soon as four hours after the last dose and typically peak within two or three days, although this also depends on the type of opioid being used. Milder withdrawal symptoms include anxiety, loss of appetite, yawning, watery eyes, and insomnia. Symptoms can progress to shaking, nausea and vomiting, diarrhea, profuse sweating, elevated blood pressure and heart rate, aching muscles, and fever.[2] Clinical providers will typically use some sort of standardized assessment tool to quantify the severity of an individual's opioid withdrawal. One of the most frequently used assessment tools is the Clinical Opiate Withdrawal Scale (COWS), which is modified from

---

[1] American Psychiatric Association (2013).   [2] O'Malley and O'Malley (2020).

a similar scale used for alcohol withdrawal.[3] The COWS assesses the severity of 11 withdrawal symptoms and can classify the withdrawal as being mild, moderate, or severe based on a total points scale. This classification system not only identifies individuals who are experiencing the most severe withdrawal symptoms but also helps monitor an individual's progress and guides treatment decisions during withdrawal symptom management (Box 9.1).[4]

Although withdrawal from opioids may not be viewed to be as dangerous as alcohol withdrawal, it can still be extremely distressing. For those with underlying medical illnesses, such as heart failure, ischemic heart disease, and diabetes, or for the elderly population, opioid withdrawal can result in significant comorbidity or death. In addition, even for the healthy individual, opioid withdrawal symptoms can be so distressing that many resume opioid use to treat their discomfort.

History of Detoxification

Historically, the treatment of intoxication has been directed by law enforcement and the government and was largely unregulated. Drunk tanks, which are jail cells or facilities whose purpose is to hold intoxicated individuals until they become sober, are a quintessential example of this type of treatment. Although the idea behind these facilities is to protect the public and individual from behaviors that might occur while intoxicated, it can quickly become dangerous or life-threatening should the intoxicated person endure severe withdrawal. As a result, many countries around the world have either closed these facilities, or simply renamed them using less stigmatizing language such as a "sobering-up chamber" (in Switzerland), "welfare centre" (in the United Kingdom), or "protective care" (in Canada). Russia has recently reopened a series of drunk tanks to protect the large number of intoxicated individuals who freeze to death during its harsh winter season (see Figure 9.1).[5]

The concept of compulsory treatment is another punitive detoxification and treatment strategy that started to gain popularity in the mid-twentieth century and can still be found in the Soviet Union, the United States, and multiple countries in Asia. Treatment is considered compulsory if the individual does not have the right to refuse treatment, the process of ordering treatment is done without due process, or if the treatment violates human rights including social services and evidence-based treatment, and modern-day compulsory treatment centers frequently involve all three criteria. Today there are over 886

---

[3] Wesson and Ling (2003).   [4] Wesson and Ling (2003).   [5] Turner (2015).

Box 9.1 Parameters used in the COWS to assess opioid withdrawal severity

Resting pulse rate:	People in opioid withdrawal have higher pulse rates.
Gastrointestinal upset:	Opioid withdrawal is associated with stomach cramping, nausea, vomiting, and diarrhea.
Sweating:	Not explained by room temperature or patient activity. Chills, flushing, observable moistness and sweat are all associated with opioid withdrawal.
Tremor:	Tremor, either felt or observed, worsens with the severity of opioid withdrawal.
Restlessness:	This can range from difficulty sitting still to extraneous movements of legs/arms and the inability to sit still for more than a few seconds.
Yawning:	Observed frequency of yawning during assessment. People in opioid withdrawal tend to yawn frequently.
Pupil size:	The degree of pupil dilation is associated with the severity of withdrawal from opioids.
Anxiety or irritability:	The degree of irritability or anxiousness increases as the individual goes through opioid withdrawal.
Bone or joint aches:	Assuming someone did not have this type of pain before, bone pain, like the "growing pains" children experience, is common and specific to opioid withdrawal and may range from mild diffuse discomfort to severe debilitating pain.
Gooseflesh skin:	Piloerection (also known as goosebumps or gooseflesh) is a classic sign of opioid withdrawal.
Runny nose or tearing:	Nasal stuffiness or tearing in the eyes are associated with opioid withdrawal.

---

such treatment centers in East and Southeast Asia,[6] and they usually function as a method of punishment for a politically motivated "war on drugs." These centers are typically run by the military, police, or custodial staff, and they use

---

[6] In Cambodia, China, Laos, Malaysia, Philippines, Thailand, and Vietnam.

Figure 9.1 In this early drunk tank from 1914 in St. Petersburg, Russia, the newly delivered clients are piled up on the floor, while sobering men are sitting or standing up against the walls (from Wikimedia Commons).[7]

physical activity, unmedicated withdrawal, religious teachings, forced labor, or torture tactics as therapy. They can be overcrowded at over 400% capacity, and notably lacking are pharmaceutical treatments and social services. Some countries may spend up to 77% of their annual budget earmarked for drug dependence treatment on these compulsory facilities, despite promising to phase them out.[8] Some compulsory treatment centers, such as those that are found in the United States, are simply jails and prisons that have been renamed as "treatment facilities." These facilities force addicted individuals into abstinence, typically without any sort of medical supervision or treatment.[9] It is important to note that many countries have made efforts, albeit to varying degrees, to develop humane, community-centered treatment for substance use disorders.

As societal perceptions shifted and changes in policy were made, primarily in the early- to mid-twentieth century, the medical field began offering more humane treatment for those struggling with substance use. The concept of detoxification was created, and with that came two approaches. The medical model of detoxification is defined by the presence of medical personnel, including physicians and nurses, who monitor the symptoms of withdrawal, which are then treated with medication. On the other hand, the social model of detoxification opposes the use of medication, and rather focuses on social support in a nonmedical environment as the individual withdraws from a substance or substances. Since addiction is currently considered to be a biopsychosocial issue, meaning it results from the combination of biology,

---

[7] https://en.wikipedia.org/wiki/Drunk_tank.
[8] United Nations Office on Drugs and Crime (2022).
[9] Beletsky and Tomasini-Joshi (2019).

psychology, and social factors such as socioeconomic status and life experiences, you will rarely find detoxification services that are purely medical or social. Instead, you often find that current-day detoxification treatment combines the use of medication with the offering of psychological care and social services.

Nowadays, detoxification (also known as withdrawal management) can be defined as "a medical intervention that manages an individual safely through the process of acute withdrawal."[10] In other words, the detoxification process manages the unpleasant side effects of withdrawal when the individual initially discontinues their opioid use, often with the use of medication. The American Society of Addiction Medicine (ASAM) names three goals for detoxification. First, detoxification must "provide a safe withdrawal from the drug(s) of dependence and enable the patient to become drug free." Second, detoxification should "provide a withdrawal that is humane and thus protects the patient's dignity." Finally, detoxification needs to "prepare the patient for ongoing treatment of his or her dependence on alcohol or other drugs."[11]

It is very important to note that withdrawal management by itself is not treatment for the underlying substance use disorder, as the process is not designed to address the long-standing psychosocial dysfunction that co-occurs with drug and alcohol abuse. The likelihood of remaining abstinent from substances after detoxification alone is exceptionally low. For instance, one study found that only 6% of individuals who did not participate in post-detoxification treatment remained abstinent nine months later.[12] That being said, withdrawal management is frequently an important first step for an individual to cease opioid use and engage in the treatment and rehabilitation that is necessary to maintain sobriety.

An Overview of the Detoxification Process

Within the detoxification process are three essential and sequential steps that must take place: evaluation, stabilization, and fostering the individual's entry into substance use treatment. The first step, evaluation, assesses the individual's medical, psychiatric, and social histories, and obtains a detailed review of substance use. This step often also includes testing for underlying psychological issues and analyzing a urine or saliva sample for the presence of substances. The second step, stabilization, assists the individual through the withdrawal process, often with the use of medications but also support from peers and trained staff. Education is an important part of the stabilization

---

[10] McCorry et al. (2000).   [11] Wright et al. (2014).   [12] Ivers et al. (2018).

process, as this is when the individual and his or her support system learn about the disease of addiction and what course of action is most effective. Fostering entry into substance use treatment, the third essential step of detoxification, closely relates to the educational component of the second step. As the individual learns about treatment for their substance use, information about local resources can be given so that he or she continues working towards sobriety. Staff and family play an important part by repeating this information and encouraging engagement in post-detoxification treatment. Emphasis is on compassion and understanding so that the individual develops a sense of confidence with their medical team.[13]

There are multiple medications that can be used to alleviate the symptoms of opioid withdrawal during the detoxification process. A slow taper of opioids such as methadone, slow-release morphine, and buprenorphine are frequently used, especially in the inpatient setting. An opioid blocker known as naltrexone can be used to limit withdrawal symptoms and reduce the likelihood of opioid overdose, assuming the patient remains on the medication after detoxification has finished. Medications that suppress activation of the nervous system involved in one's "fight-or-flight" response, known as the autonomic nervous system, reduce symptoms such as muscle and joint pain, runny nose, watery eyes, and gastrointestinal distress. Finally, the use of anti-inflammatory drugs and muscle relaxants, anti-diarrheal medications, and sleep-promoting agents are effective for muscle aches and pains, diarrhea, and insomnia, respectively.

Historically, for those looking for a "painless" detoxification experience, individuals could undergo detoxification while under heavy sedation or general anesthesia, also known by various monikers such as rapid opioid detoxification under anesthesia (RODA), ultrarapid opioid detoxification (UROD), or simply "rapid detox." Although outcomes for this type of detoxification do not appear as superior to standard withdrawal management, and the risks of anesthesia may make this treatment modality unsafe for some, interest in rapid detoxification is increasing internationally in countries such as Iran and Germany.[14] For example, UROD in Iran gained exponential popularity in the early 2000s; however, shortly thereafter the government limited its use for educational and research purposes only, likely as a response to the unscrupulous advertising efforts promoting UROD as extremely safe and effective. As a result, much of the information we have currently stems from research performed in Iran. For instance, we now know that withdrawal symptoms do not instantly disappear at the completion of rapid detoxification methods, and

---

[13] Mee-Lee et al. (2013).   [14] Collins et al. (2005).

a syndrome of prolonged withdrawal symptoms such as drug craving, nausea and vomiting, diarrhea, and insomnia may occur for several months after. In addition, in a 2014 study by Forozeshfard, Hosseinzadeh Zoroufchi and others, the relapse rate after UROD appears to be extraordinarily high unless the individual is actively engaged in continued treatment after acute detoxification.[15,16]

Withdrawal Management as the First Step Towards Sobriety

As mentioned previously, withdrawal management is an important part of achieving abstinence from opioids, but by itself it is not effective in achieving long-term sobriety. Those who successfully complete withdrawal management and then continue to engage in substance use treatment, such as outpatient counseling, 12-step group participation, and psychiatric care, are more likely to remain abstinent than those who do not. Current evidence suggests that the use of medications for opioid use disorder, such as with methadone, buprenorphine, and naltrexone, gives individuals the best odds of maintaining prolonged abstinence from other opioids, and this concept is discussed further in Chapter 12 of this book, which discusses outpatient treatment options in detail.

Inpatient Treatment

Inpatient services often include detoxification but also encompass several other offerings. The inpatient treatment setting is defined as a location that offers 24-hour medical care in the short term, with the length of stay ranging from several days to three or four weeks. This care can occur in the general hospital, on a psychiatric ward, or in specialized hospitals that specialize in substance misuse. Opioid intoxication, withdrawal, medical comorbidities, and opioid-related disorders (such as psychosis and infectious disease) are treated by trained medical professionals who have access to any necessary diagnostic and treatment equipment and personnel. This environment also offers respite from the individual's social stressors and allows for a therapeutic alliance to develop between patient and provider.

---

[15] 100% of participants in the study relapsed within one month following UROD; Forozeshfard et al. (2014).
[16] Yassini Ardekani and Yassini Ardekani (2013).

Short-term, inpatient treatment can be most helpful for those who are at risk for severe withdrawal, which is typically determined by the type or amount of drug used, or if more than one substance is being misused. If withdrawal may be dangerous at home, for instance if the person has significant medical issues such as heart failure, ischemic heart disease, chronic obstructive pulmonary disease, psychotic disorders, or is of advanced age, then withdrawal management should be monitored and treated by medical professionals. Inpatient treatment is likely beneficial for those who are homeless or have unstable living environments, for example those who live with roommates who are drug users, or frequently need to move due to eviction or unsafe conditions. Those who have tried but failed to complete outpatient treatment previously likely require a higher level of care.

The World Health Organization has published international standards for the treatment of substance use disorders and list several necessary components of inpatient drug treatment. Some of these components include: a comprehensive assessment of an individual's drug use, medical history, and psychosocial background; development of individualized treatment plans; availability of medication-assisted withdrawal management and initiation of opioid agonist maintenance treatment; interventions to foster a desire to change behavior; treatment of underlying psychiatric or medical illnesses; and discharge planning to continue an individual's treatment and avoid relapse. This often includes referral to residential treatment, a type of inpatient treatment that typically does not include medical services, and peer support groups, such as any of the 12-step groups.[17]

The History of Residential Treatment

The historical development of residential treatment is closely linked to the societal trends occurring over time. In Europe, as well as most of the developed world, three waves of treatment have been noted. The first wave occurred between the early-nineteenth to mid-twentieth centuries in which a network of mental hospitals (or asylums) was erected across the continent. Many of those afflicted with mental illness could not care for themselves and required institutionalized housing and treatment. However, this mode of treatment was considered an improvement back then, as one must remember the terrible conditions that the mentally ill have been subjected to in the past, such as being locked up in cages or chained to stalls. During this time, we also saw the

---

[17] World Health Organization and United Nations Office on Drugs and Crime (2020).

early development of rudimentary community care, which included boarding homes for the mentally ill, psychiatric clinics for short-term inpatient stays, and finally some aspect of post-discharge care, which were often funded by private charities and organizations rather than the asylums themselves. For the mid to upper classes, spas and sanitoriums were created for cases of "nervous illness," "weakness and fatigue," and "hysteria," all terms being euphemisms for mental illness. The Battle Creek Sanitarium, founded in 1866 in Colorado Springs, Colorado, USA, was once such center, offering all sorts of dubious treatments including hydrotherapy, thermotherapy, and dietetics.

Starting at the end of World War II, Europe saw a gradual inclusion of mental health services in social insurance plans. Until this point, addiction was treated by the general health system and typically provided in the inpatient wards of psychiatric hospitals. However, the number of hospital wards for the treatment of addiction grew during the second wave of treatment reform. The Veterans Administration, the healthcare system that the United States offers its veterans, began establishing alcoholism treatment units in 1957. Dedicated treatment centers for those with addiction were extraordinarily rare, but include the "therapeutic farm" established in 1932 in Alsace, France, and federal "narcotics farms" in the United States starting in 1935.

The Narcotic Farm in Lexington, Kentucky was one of the first centers in the United States dedicated to the study and treatment of those addicted to drugs. The Narcotic Farm, also called "the Farm" or "Narco," served as both a prison and hospital, so that inmates could receive addiction treatment while serving out their sentences, all in hopes that the inmates would eventually be reintegrated into society as productive, law-abiding citizens. Although the majority of those receiving treatment at the Farm were convicted criminals with years-long sentences, up to one-third were volunteers, who could receive free treatment for a much shorter term. The prisoners and volunteers would participate in farming and animal husbandry, while the staff and their families lived in supplied housing, all located on the Farm's 1,050-acre estate. Although the prisoners worked hard on the Farm, they also had opportunities to participate in recreational activities, such as bowling, baseball, and art. Well-known jazz musicians such as Chet Baker, Sonny Rollins, Lee Morgan, and William Burroughs were incarcerated at the Farm, and it is rumored that some aspiring musicians checked themselves into the Farm for the opportunity to play with the masters. The Farm's Addiction Research Center (ARC) was the only laboratory in the world dedicated to studying drug addiction, although many of its methods are considered unethical by today's standards. Inmates willing to participate in the research would consume drugs such as heroin and lysergic

Figure 9.2 Narcotic Farm (from the University of Lexington Library).

acid diethylamide (LSD) and then be observed for the drugs' acute effects and subsequent withdrawal. The ARC also used the Farm's inmates to test for the addictive and withdrawal potential of medications already on the market, such as antidepressants, barbiturates, and painkillers. Unfortunately, participants in these experiments were compensated for their time with drugs, furthering their addiction. It is estimated that 90% of inmates relapsed after discharge from the Narcotic Farm. With its failure in treating addiction successfully, the program was discontinued in 1975.[18]

In the 1970s, a large push began towards deinstitutionalization of the mentally ill. Psychiatric hospitals either offered their own post-discharge care or were linked with outpatient clinics to continue treatment once the individual was discharged. More emphasis was placed on family and social environment during this time, which continued through the third wave of treatment reform.

This third wave is defined by emphasis on community care. In the 1970s and 1980s, heroin use reached epidemic proportions for many countries. In addition, adolescent drug users represented a new demographic of individuals needing substance use care but were without options for treatment. It was during this time that major changes in substance use treatment occurred. For instance, in 1968 Germany recognized addiction as a disease, and therefore its treatment must be covered under public insurance. Self-help groups, such as

[18] Olsen and Walden (2008).

Release in the UK, developed treatment programs in multiple countries. Religious-based treatment programs, such as Synanon as inspired by Alcoholics Anonymous, and the Phoenix House popped up in the United States, and were then subsequently adopted in Europe. The HIV/AIDS crisis further fueled the need for residential treatment centers, especially as viral transmission of HIV was linked to the intravenous use of heroin and other drugs.[19]

What Is Residential Treatment?

Modern-day residential treatment is a 24-hour level of care whose goal is to provide support and relapse prevention for those with substance use disorders and frequently co-occurring mental illness, but not in a hospital setting. The therapeutic interventions offered in the residential treatment setting are varied, although they all offer stable housing for the individual (hence the name "residential"). As a result, residential treatment programs can be quite beneficial for the homeless and for those with unstable living arrangements, such as for those who live with other drug users.

Other features aside from housing typically define a residential treatment program, making it an attractive option even for those without housing instability. Addiction and mental health personnel staff and organize programming for the residents and define policies and treatment protocols, as put forth by these personnel, which guide the operations of the facility and the treatment of the residents. Residential programs also host a variety of group meetings such as 12-step meetings and mutual support groups. Although some residential programs have medical staff on-site, most do not. Should significant medical or psychiatric issues arise, the staff must be able to recognize the issue and transfer the individual to a hospital or facility that offers medical care.

There are three primary therapeutic approaches that residential treatment centers in the United States, Europe, Canada, and Australia follow. These include the 12-step and Minnesota model, the cognitive–behavioral (or other) therapy-based intervention, and lastly the therapeutic community.

The 12-step model of treatment revolves around the 12 steps that were developed by the founders of Alcoholics Anonymous. A core component of the 12 steps is that the individual must surrender themselves to a "higher power," and that sharing experiences and support leads to strength and sobriety. Many 12-step rehabilitation programs are peer-run and organized, meaning those who formerly battled an addictive disorder are now in the position to help those who

---

[19] European Monitoring Centre for Drugs and Drug Addiction (2014).

continue to struggle. The Minnesota-style treatment model, which was initially developed at a state hospital in Minnesota, is also based on the 12 steps. The difference is that care under the Minnesota model is delivered by professionals and tends to be less reliant on self-help methods. However, both methods provide a highly structured, intense program of lectures and group meetings over a three- to six-week period and focus on factors that have contributed to the individual's development of an addictive disorder. Over 90% of rehabilitation programs in the United States are based on the 12-step method, whereas in Europe only 4% of programs are based on 12-step principles.[20]

The therapeutic community shares similarities with the 12-step model in that both methods focus on abstinence from mind-altering substances and see recovery from addiction as "requiring a restructuring of thinking, personality and lifestyle in addition to giving up drug-taking behavior."[21] The planned stay in a therapeutic community is much longer than other residential programs, typically between 6 and 12 months. In its essence, the therapeutic community uses the community itself (coined "community as a method") to address the underlying psychosocial contributors to addiction. Two features of the therapeutic community are that the community members (including residents and staff) participate in meetings and shared activities, and that community members are role models and a source of peer support. Daily life is extremely structured, and initially community members are not allowed interaction with the outside world, by prohibiting phone calls, internet access, or visitors. Those who exhibit traits such as honesty and reliability are promoted through the hierarchy, gaining more responsibility in the process, and ultimately becoming a role model for newcomers. This is the most common method employed in the residential programs found in much of Europe, whereas most residential facilities in Belgium, Bulgaria, Austria, and Norway employ the cognitive–behavioral therapy (CBT) model.[22] Saudi Arabia does offer a therapeutic community program; however, this is only for male patients.[23]

The CBT model uses a common therapeutic approach whose primary focus is to evaluate an individual's thinking errors that can lead to unwanted beliefs and behaviors. Thinking errors, also known as cognitive distortions, are irrational thoughts that we unknowingly reinforce over time, to the point we are unaware of them, and they cause more harm than good. By recognizing the erroneous thought patterns, the hope is to interrupt the unconscious thought process that leads to feelings of failure, depression, and use of substances.

[20] Substance Abuse and Mental Health Services Administration (2021).
[21] European Monitoring Centre for Drugs and Drug Addiction (2014).
[22] European Monitoring Centre for Drugs and Drug Addiction (2014).
[23] Alharbi et al. (2021).

Although a handful of studies have been conducted comparing the various approaches, it is not clear if one approach is more effective than another. Further research is needed to determine which components of residential treatment are most effective, and which type of treatment holds the highest likelihood of success, based on an individual's characteristics.

Access to Inpatient Treatment

It is well known that most individuals with a substance use disorder do not engage in treatment, and stigma plays a significant role. Not only might the individual with an opioid use disorder avoid treatment due to feelings of shame, but the perceived stigma originating from community members and healthcare providers, as well as the presence of sociolegal discrimination, create a substantial barrier to treatment. In addition, depending on the region, observance of strict religious principles may also be a barrier, such as in Muslim-predominant countries found in the Middle East and North Africa (also referred to as MENA), where the use of drugs and alcohol is not only prohibited but also frequently results in severe criminal punishments.[24]

As a result of these societal beliefs, law-enforcement efforts have been the customary approach to drug use in those countries in the MENA region. Policies that criminalize the consumption of opioids have led to a disproportionately high percentage of individuals being incarcerated. Certain countries in the MENA region, such as Iran, Libya, and Saudi Arabia, use corporal punishment (such as beating, caning, or whipping) in response to drug use. The death penalty has also been employed for drug offenses in several of these countries – it is estimated that over 10,000 individuals were executed for drug offenses between 1979 and 2011.[25]

Choosing the Right Type of Inpatient Treatment

To illustrate who best might benefit from inpatient treatment, let us consider the stories of two individuals, Mary and John:

Mary, a 23-year-old woman, started using opioids after a dental procedure as a teenager. When that prescription ran out, she began stealing medication from her grandmother. Over time, she progressed from using prescription pills to buying them "off the street." Once her parents learned of this, she was forced to leave

---

[24] Connery et al. (2020).   [25] Harm Reduction International (2018).

home and has been homeless since. Mary has been prostituting herself in exchange for heroin, which she now uses intravenously, multiple times a day. She only has access to shared needles. She has required two emergency room visits in the past to be treated with naloxone for overdose. She states that she no longer "gets high" from heroin but uses it to avoid severe withdrawal. She has also stopped treatment for her severe bipolar disorder.

John, a 35-year-old man, started using opioids after an orthopedic surgery. He found that he enjoyed the energy that the pills gave him and began using them to cope with long hours at work. His primary care physician became concerned, especially when he began calling the clinic for refills because he is running out of medication early. He also reported several lost prescriptions. Recognizing that he lacked the control to stop taking these opioids, he disclosed this information to his wife and boss, with whom he has a good relationship. His primary reason to discontinue his opioid use is so that he can start a family and continue working at a job he loves.

Both individuals meet the criteria for a diagnosis of an opioid use disorder, and both of their disorders began using prescription opioids. However, there are some significant differences. Mary's use of opioids appears to be much riskier than for John. She has experienced several overdoses, and she is engaging in dangerous behaviors such as prostitution and sharing needles. She also lacks a network of people who can support her through the early stages of sobriety. John, on the other hand, has a supportive spouse and boss. In addition, his desire to start a family and continue working are factors that can enhance John's motivation to change.

The ASAM has created a guide for clinicians to identify the most appropriate location for someone's addiction treatment, the patient placement criteria (PPC-2 R).[26] These criteria consider six "assessment dimensions" to match individuals to treatment, which include:

- acute intoxication and withdrawal potential;
- biomedical conditions and complications;
- emotional, behavioral, or cognitive conditions and complications;
- readiness to change;
- relapse, continued use, or continued problem potential;
- recovery/living environment.

By looking at these criteria and considering Mary and John's stories, one can begin to systematically identify who might require more intensive treatment such as inpatient or residential.

---

[26] Substance Abuse and Mental Health Services Administration (2021).

The PPC-2 R also guides the clinician to choose the most appropriate treatment location and, from an international perspective, the World Health Organization has similar recommendations.[27] For those at risk for severe withdrawal, who have severe underlying biomedical and/or psychological illnesses, who continue to use opioids in very dangerous ways, and for those in poor living environments, an inpatient setting is likely most appropriate. Mary is once such person who would qualify for inpatient treatment. For those without as many risk factors, such as John, outpatient treatment can be both efficacious and economical. The next chapter discusses outpatient treatment in more detail.

References and Further Reading

American Psychiatric Association (2013). *Diagnostic and Statistical Manual of Mental Disorders*, 5th Edition (DSM-5). Washington, DC: American Psychiatric Association.

Alharbi FF, Alsubaie EG, Al-Surimi K (2021). Substance abuse in Arab world: Does it matter and where are we? In Laher I. (ed.) *Handbook of Healthcare in the Arab World*. Cham: Springer, pp. 2371–2398.

Beletsky L, Tomansini-Joshi D (2019). 'Treatment facilities' aren't what you think they are. *New York Times*, September 3.

Center for Substance Abuse Treatment (2006). *Detoxification and Substance Abuse Treatment.Treatment Improvement Protocol (TIP) Series*. No. 45. HHS Publication No. (SMA) 15–4131. Rockville, MD: Center for Substance Abuse Treatment.

Collins ED, Kleber HD, Whittington RA, Heitler NE (2005). Anesthesia-assisted vs buprenorphine- or clonidine-assisted heroin detoxification and naltrexone induction: A randomized trial.*JAMA* 294(8): 903–913.

Connery HS, McHugh RK, Reilly M, Shin S, Greenfield SF (2020). Substance use disorders in global mental health delivery: Epidemiology, treatment gap, and implementation of evidence-based treatments. *Harvard Review of Psychiatry* 28(5): 316–327.

European Monitoring Centre for Drugs and Drug Addiction (2014). *Residential treatment for drug use in Europe, EMCDDA Papers*. Luxembourg: Publications Office of the European Union.

Forozeshfard M, Hosseinzadeh Zoroufchi B, Saberi Zafarghandi MB, Bandari R, Foroutan B (2014). Six-month follow-up study of ultrarapid opiate detoxification with naltrexone. *International Journal of High Risk Behaviors & Addiction* 3(4):e20944.

Harm Reduction International (2018). Regional overview of the Middle East and North Africa. www.hri.global/files/2018/12/10/MiddleEastNorthAfrica-harm-reduction.pdf

---

[27] World Health Organization and United Nations Office on Drugs and Crime (2020).

Ivers JH, Zgaga L, Sweeney B, et al. (2018). A naturalistic longitudinal analysis of post-detoxification outcomes in opioid-dependent patients. *Drug and Alcohol Dependence* 37(Suppl. 1): S339–S347.

McCorry F, Garnick GW, Bartlett J, Cotter F, Chalk M (2000). Developing performance measures for alcohol and other drug services in managed care plans. Washington Circle Group. *Joint Commission Journal on Quality Improvement* 26 (11): 633–643.

Mee-Lee D, Shulman GD, Fishman MJ, Gastfriend DR, Miller MM (2013). *The ASAM Criteria: Treatment Criteria for Addictive, Substance-Related, and Co-Occurring Conditions*, 3rd ed. Carson City, NV: The Change Companies.

O'Malley GF and O'Malley R (2020). Opioid toxicity and withdrawal. Merck manual, professional version. www.msdmanuals.com/professional/special-subjects/illicit-drugs-and-intoxicants/opioid-toxicity-and-withdrawal/?autoredirectid=20985

Olsen JP, Walden L (2008). *The Narcotic Farm* [Video]. King Love Films and the Independent Television Service. https://vimeo.com/91392115

Reif S, George P, Braude L (2014). Residential treatment for individuals with substance use disorder: Assessing the evidence. *Psychological Services* 65(3): 301–312.

Substance Abuse and Mental Health Services Administration (2021). *National Survey of Substance Abuse Treatment Services (N-SSATS): 2020. Data on Substance Abuse Treatment Facilities*. Rockville, MD: Substance Abuse and Mental Health Services Administration.

Turner A (2015). Alternatives to criminalizing public intoxication: Case study of a sobering centre in Calgary, AB. *SPP Research Papers* 1–8(27).

United Nations Office on Drugs and Crime (2022). *Compulsory Drug Treatment and Rehabilitation in East and Southeast Asia: Executive Summary*. Bangkok, Thailand: UNODC Regional Office for Southeast Asia and the Pacific.

Wesson DR, Ling W (2003). The clinical opiate withdrawal scale. *Journal of Psychoactive Drugs* 35(2): 253–259.

World Health Organization and United Nations Office on Drugs and Crime (2020). *International Standards for the Treatment of Drug Use Disorders: Revised Edition Incorporating Results of Field-Testing*. Geneva, Switzerland: WHO and UNODC.

Wright TM, Cluver JS, Myrick H (2014). Management of intoxication and withdrawal: General principles. In Ries, RK, Fiellin DA, Miller SC, Saitz R (eds.) *The ASAM Principles of Addiction Medicine*, 5th ed. Philadelphia, PA: Wolters Kluwer, pp. 625–634.

Yassini Ardekani SM, Yassini Ardekani S (2013). Ultrarapid opioid detoxification: Current status in Iran and controversies. *International Journal of High Risk Behaviors & Addiction* 2(3): 96–99. https://doi.org/10.5812/ijhrba.13140

10 OUTPATIENT TREATMENT MODALITIES

Inpatient and residential treatment for individuals with an opioid use disorder has certain advantages, as it provides a safe space for recovery, increases access to comprehensive medical and psychiatric treatment services, and prepares the individual for the sometimes-difficult transition to outpatient treatment. However, when an individual completes inpatient or residential treatment, the journey towards sobriety does not end. Outpatient care is almost always recommended as the next step in treatment for someone with an opioid use disorder. Additionally, some people may not require inpatient or residential treatment at all. Instead, management of the substance use disorder can be performed safely and effectively in the outpatient setting. Those at low risk for severe withdrawal, people who are otherwise relatively healthy, and those who have a high level of motivation, good insight, and a strong positive support system in place can often be treated in the outpatient setting. Outpatient treatment for those with an opioid use disorder holds multiple benefits as well. It is cost-effective, allows patients to maintain social obligations and (in many cases) employment during treatment, and also has the advantage of providing the opportunity to experience recovery in a real-world setting.[1] Just as the types of inpatient and residential treatment are varied, so too are the types of treatment and the locations in which they occur. Partial hospitalization programs, intensive outpatient program/treatment programs, psychosocial interventions and peer support groups are discussed here. Medication for the treatment of opioid use disorders is also frequently part of an outpatient treatment plan and will be discussed in detail in the upcoming chapters.

Partial Hospitalization and Intensive Outpatient Programs

Partial hospitalization programs (PHPs), which are sometimes referred to as "day treatment" programs, are less time intensive when compared to inpatient programs. The programming in a typical PHP involves a minimum of 20 hours

---

[1] Alam and Martorana (2011).

of skilled treatment per week, such as individual, group, and family counseling, medication management, vocational and educational services, and recreational therapy. Basically, people in these types of programs participate in the same curriculum as people in residential treatment programs but at the end of the day they go home. Participants have access to a variety of medical services, including treatment by physicians and psychiatrists, laboratory testing, and toxicology services such as urine drug testing, but don't benefit from the complete separation from the environment in which they used to misuse. Complete separation is considered essential for some cases such as persons who have relapsed multiple times and have been unable to refrain from using after prior treatments, and in some industries this is considered mandatory for persons with employment in high-intensity "safety sensitive" jobs such as physicians, nurses, pharmacists, and other healthcare professionals, or police officers, firefighters, paramedics, and other first responders. The mandatory assignment to inpatient programs for these individuals is, in the United States anyway, not consistent across the board and has a lot to do with the individual case and the desire to return to work in the same profession. As an example, an anesthesiologist who is in treatment for fentanyl misuse would be more likely to be assigned to an inpatient program, given the extremely addictive nature of the drug and the (somewhat) unrestricted access to it should they return to work in the operating room. The firefighter with an alcohol problem, however, might not be remanded to inpatient treatment, even if their intent is to return to work in the firehouse, as the option of intensive outpatient treatment may be perceived as having less risk for both the patient and society. In both cases, the risk of injury to the individual and the risk to society must be considered, as well as the cost associated with the level of treatment.

For those determined to be an acceptable risk for outpatient treatment, emergency services must still be available, though typically they are only accessible via phone call after hours as the patients are not on-site at that time. Since the risk for relapse, especially with people who are in treatment for opioid misuse, is greatest within the first few months of treatment, outpatient programs typically have an affiliation with such programs that provide naloxone training to both patients in treatment as well as individuals in their support network. Additionally, these programs should be able to provide transfer to a more intensive level of care when this is deemed appropriate by the treating staff. Despite the considerable risk for relapse, the goal of all treatment programs is to eventually reintroduce patients into society. For many people in treatment, the transition from inpatient to partial hospitalization to intensive outpatient treatment represents a step towards independence and an opportunity to begin to live an opioid-free life, often in the same community where they once regularly misused opioids. The determination of when this should happen (either at the initiation of treatment or after a period of inpatient treatment) is difficult and often made after consultation with multiple healthcare providers as well as members of the individual's external support network. Unfortunately, as we have seen, the process is expensive and, many times, the treatment plan is interrupted by the seemingly arbitrary decision made by an anonymous employee at an insurance company, who has decided that since the company has already paid enough for treatment the patient does not require further care. In the United States and countries without universal healthcare, as well as in the countries where little or no healthcare is available, this is how it is done. Partial hospitalization programs tend to work best for those who require more intensive treatment but do not qualify, are unable to afford, or lack the desire to participate in a higher level of care.

Intensive outpatient treatment programs (IOPs) are similar to PHPs; however, they will usually be less time intensive and therefore are generally reserved for those with a more stable, less severe opioid use disorder. Traditionally, IOPs consisted of nine hours of scheduled treatment per week, often divided into three 3-hour days. Currently, these programs can range anywhere from 6 to 30 hours per week, depending on available resources and funding. Many services are offered at these programs including comprehensive biopsychosocial assessment, individual, group, and family counseling, drug testing, 24-hour crisis coverage, medical treatment, vocational and educational services, and medication management. The goals of these IOPs include maintaining abstinence from opioids, helping patients with identifying individual relapse triggers and teaching them how to manage opioid cravings, addressing the underlying psychological issues that might be driving opioid use, increasing resilience to personal stressors, and helping patients to develop a sobriety maintenance plan to be used after discharge.[2] IOPs are supposed to act as a bridge from the protected environment of early treatment back into the "real world," so it is essential that they not only provide services designed to help individuals cope with issues related to prior opioid misuse and avoid relapse, but also provide real-world skills such as job training and conflict resolution, increasing the chances for success once discharged.

Based on the evidence available thus far, it appears that partial hospitalization and IOPs are just as effective as residential treatment, at least for those with less severe opioid dependence, though it is possible that the length of treatment, rather than the type, is what influences an individual's success in treatment.[3] Every person is unique, as are the circumstances that surround

---

[2] Center for Substance Abuse Treatment (2006).   [3] McCarty et al. (2014).

their history of opioid misuse. Determining the course of treatment for someone in this situation requires the careful assessment of all of these factors and
a "one size fits all" approach rarely works for the majority of patients. The ideal
program involves a careful and systematic evaluation of each case with consideration of the goals of treatment.

Group and Individualized Therapy

There are a variety of outpatient treatment modalities available, which serve
as alternatives to the more intensive programs discussed above, or, in many
cases, allow graduates of these programs to maintain contact with
a therapeutic community on the "outside" in a less intensive manner.
Many of these programs have demonstrated a degree of success, especially
in motivated patients regardless of prior intensive treatment, and they are
the most ubiquitous options given their lower cost and widespread availability. Group therapy, for instance, is not only cost-effective but also provides
opportunity for peer support and development of interpersonal relationships.
Depending on the group format, the focus may be on education, relapse
prevention, stress management, or may simply provide a forum for persons
in recovery from opioid misuse to speak candidly about their personal experiences in a supportive and nonjudgmental forum.[4] Other outpatient treatment services include medical and psychiatric care, individual and family
therapy, and involvement with mutual support groups. Comprehensive
treatment of opioid use disorders requires a combination of resources, as
depicted in Figure 10.1.

Certain types of psychosocial interventions that are often provided during
individualized therapy have proven to be helpful for patients in recovery
from opioid misuse. Cognitive behavioral therapy (CBT) is based on the
idea that dysfunctional behaviors are driven by negative thought patterns.
The idea is that by learning to identify these potentially negative thought
patterns, the individual can recognize and then interrupt them and, as
a result, decrease the likelihood of the individual engaging in undesired
behavior such as relapse and opioid misuse. Contingency management
refers to a type of therapy in which an individual is rewarded for positive
behaviors, for example if the individual maintains perfect attendance for
group therapy, he or she receives a gift card to a restaurant or coffee shop.
Drug testing is typically used to track an individual's progress and encourage
honesty. Motivational enhancement therapy employs a communication

---

[4] Lo Coco et al. (2019).

Components of Comprehensive Drug Abuse Treatment

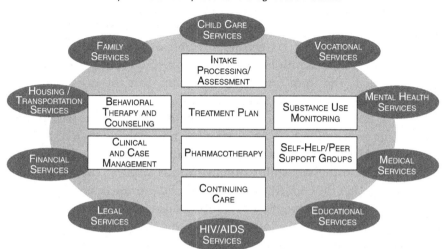

Figure 10.1 Components of a comprehensive substance misuse treatment program. The best treatment programs provide a combination of therapies and other services to meet the needs of the individual patient.[5]

technique known as motivational interviewing, which is aimed at increasing motivation for change and resolving any ambivalence one might have about changing their behaviors.

Mutual Support Groups and the 12 Steps

Mutual support groups, such as those based in the "12 steps," are frequently recommended as part of an outpatient treatment plan. These programs are available worldwide but are more popular in the United States and, because of their basis in Christian spirituality, are less popular in areas where Christianity is not the dominant religion. The origins of Alcoholics Anonymous and its 12 steps can be traced back to the United States in the 1930s. Bill Wilson, a broker's representative traveling from New York to Akron, Ohio, found himself struggling with cravings for alcohol when he reached out to a surgeon with similar struggles, Dr. Robert Smith. Bill W. and Dr. Bob, as they are colloquially known, met to discuss and share their experiences with alcohol on May 12, 1935. During this meeting, the two men made three discoveries that subsequently built the foundation of

---

[5] From the National Institutes of Health (NIH) Free Library (United States).

all 12-step groups. The first discovery was spirituality's role in sobriety: for instance, the two men met through a minister associated with the Oxford Group,[6] and Bill W. had a "spiritual conversion" while hospitalized for his alcohol use a year earlier. The second principle was to "carry the message": both Bill W. and Bob Smith believed that, to remain sober, one must help others in need. The third and final realization was the need to identify oneself through the process of telling and listening to stories. Together, Bill W. and Dr. Bob created a fellowship of individuals struggling with alcohol use to share experiences and derive strength from one another. Bill W. also created the 12 steps after gathering the positive experiences that both he and others had witnessed while working towards sobriety. The two founders went on to author the book, *Alcoholics Anonymous*, whose intent was to carry the message to others struggling with alcohol use.[7,8]

The same year that Alcoholics Anonymous was founded, so too was a prison and hospital for those addicted to narcotics in Lexington, Kentucky, known as Narcotic Farm (see previous chapter). Residents of Narcotic Farm learned of Alcoholics Anonymous and wondered if these principles could be applied to them. Twelve years later, in 1947, these residents formed a group based on Alcoholics Anonymous called Addicts Anonymous. Members of Addicts Anonymous were in regular contact with those of Alcoholics Anonymous, and multiple articles regarding the use of narcotics were published in the Alcoholics Anonymous newsletter, "The Grapevine." When one of its members, known as Danny C., was discharged from Narcotic Farm in 1953, he moved back to New York City and brought Addicts Anonymous with him, changing the name to Narcotics Anonymous in the process.[9] The members of Narcotics Anonymous authored their own version of Alcoholics Anonymous' text, frequently referred to as the *Basic Text*. Multiple informational pamphlets and guides have also been published, all free of charge on the organization's website.[10,11] The 12 steps of Narcotics Anonymous are listed in Box 10.1. Note that the original version of the "Twelve Steps," as published in the book *Alcoholics Anonymous*, uses the terms alcohol (instead of our addiction) and alcoholics (instead of addicts).

---

[6] The Oxford Group was a Christian fellowship whose tenets became the foundation on which Alcoholics Anonymous was built.

[7] Also known as the "Big Book," whose nickname was derived from the printer's use of thick paper, making the book appear to be of higher value.

[8] Kurtz and White (2003).

[9] Danny C. changed the name to Narcotics Anonymous (NA), so that there was no confusion between Addicts Anonymous and Alcoholics Anonymous, both of which used the abbreviation AA.

[10] www.na.org.   [11] White et al. (2011).

The 12 steps of Narcotics Anonymous

1. We admitted we were powerless over our *addiction* – that our lives became unmanageable.
2. We came to believe that a Power greater than ourselves could restore us to sanity.
3. We made a decision to turn our will and our lives over to the care of God as we understood Him.
4. We made a searching and fearless moral inventory of ourselves.
5. We admitted to God, to ourselves, and to another human being the exact nature of our wrongs.
6. We were entirely ready to have God remove all these defects of character.
7. We humbly asked Him to remove our shortcomings.
8. We made a list of all persons we had harmed, and became willing to make amends to them all.
9. We made direct amends to such people wherever possible, except when to do so would injure them or others.
10. We continued to take personal inventory and when were wrong promptly admitted it.
11. We sought through prayer and meditation to improve our conscious contact with God as we understood Him, praying only for knowledge of His will and the power to carry that out.
12. Having had a spiritual awakening as a result of these steps, we tried to carry this message to *addicts*, and to practice these principles in all our affairs.

An Overview of Narcotics Anonymous

The beliefs, teachings, and meeting structure of Narcotics Anonymous are all based on its predecessor, Alcoholics Anonymous, and can now be found in 144 countries, with over 70,000 meetings per week. Membership is open to any individual struggling with a drug addiction. Despite the common misconception that 12-step meetings are based in religion, the true emphasis is on spiritual principles; in fact, some 12-step meetings are designed specifically for those who identify as atheist or agnostic. Narcotics Anonymous does not affiliate itself with other organizations, is completely funded by member donations (which are optional), does not offer medical or legal services, and operates on the condition of anonymity. In addition, Narcotics Anonymous has "no opinion on outside issues, including prescribed medications," which is in contrast to another common misconception that group members cannot take medication for substance use.

The primary service that Narcotics Anonymous offers is group meetings. Most groups rent meeting space from churches or schools, although some own their own property. Group members share stories and offer support, and work together to manage finances, participate in community service, distribute literature, and visit schools and prisons. The meeting itself typically runs 60–90 minutes. The format of the meetings can be varied, although they typically begin with the Serenity Prayer, followed by member introductions and presentation of key tags, which are used to celebrate those who have achieved sobriety in specific time intervals. The format for the remainder of the meeting can be varied, although it frequently involves a discussion of the 12 steps or a sharing of experiences. In addition, members who are further along their journey in sobriety, the sponsors, are encouraged to support newcomers, the sponsees, a concept referred to as sponsorship. The goal is for both the sponsor and sponsee to benefit from the relationship by maintaining contact with a single person who can be relied on to answer questions, offer support during trying times, and guide the individual through the teachings of the organization. Although a sponsor may have more than one sponsee, the opposite is not necessarily the case. There are no limitations as to who can be a sponsor, though it is traditionally recommended that the sponsor and sponsee are of the same sex. This is primarily intended to reduce the chances that an individual in early recovery, since this is typically a time of increased vulnerability, develops a sexual relationship with their sponsor, one with a necessarily unequal power dynamic. Current recommendations are that individuals in early recovery seek out and obtain a sponsor who identifies with a different gender and sexuality than they themselves do. For instance, it is now common to have a straight woman sponsor a gay man, or a nonbinary individual sponsor another nonbinary individual with opposite sexual attractions. The point is to remove the potential for a "conflict of interest" to develop and maintain the focus of the relationship on the recovery of the sponsee.

Alternative Support Groups

Although Alcoholics Anonymous has tried to include those from all religious or spiritual backgrounds by using the term "Higher Power" rather than "God," many would-be participants still struggle with the perceived religious undertones. As a result, there are many international alternative support groups that have become available to those who might benefit from the mutual support within their communities. By far the most popular, completely secular peer support group is Self-Management and Recovery Training, also referred to as SMART Recovery. The basis of SMART Recovery's approach is what has been coined the "4-Point Program": building and maintaining the motivation to change; coping with urges to use; managing thoughts, feelings, and behaviors in an effective way without addictive behaviors; and living a balanced, positive, and healthy life.[12] The organization is run by volunteers and funded by donations. Trained facilitators direct meetings and are free of charge, and its methods are based on psychotherapeutic techniques such as CBT. Like the 12-step groups, SMART Recovery does not associate itself with other organizations, and is accepting of medical treatment for substance use disorders. As of today, there are over 3,000 SMART Recovery meetings in 23 countries. There are several publications available online, including the primary resource, *The Smart Recovery Handbook*.

A number of other secular support groups have gained popularity in the past half century and are therefore worth mentioning. Women for Sobriety, founded by sociologist Jean Kirkpatrick in 1976, focuses on common experiences that women share, such as issues with self-esteem, shame and guilt, and trauma. Secular Organizations for Sobriety, founded in 1985, is based on the concept of "sober priority," that being the concept that anyone can maintain sobriety if it is made the primary concern in one's life. LifeRing Secular Recovery is another peer support group who uses the concepts of "Sober Self" and "Addict Self" to empower change. There are also mutual support groups based on specific spiritual or religious ideologies, based on the understanding that shared cultural or religious beliefs can be a very strong motivation for some people to maintain sobriety and that these people may find support in these places. Refuge Recovery and the Buddhist Recovery Network offer peer support meetings that are based on Buddhism, Celebrate Recovery focuses on Christian beliefs, and Millati Islam is based on Islamic principles.

Biofeedback and Acupuncture

Although the individual undergoing treatment for an opioid use disorder may be abstinent from opioids, the cravings to use drugs can often linger for months and, as we have seen, for years in some cases. Not only are cravings unpleasant, but they are also frequently a precursor for relapse, as it is often these visceral desires that drive continued opioid misuse during active use and spur relapse when they return, seemingly without reason in many instances. In an effort to reduce the frequency or intensity of these cravings in people in

---

[12] www.smartrecovery.org/our-approach.

recovery from opioid misuse there has been increasing interest in the use of biofeedback to manage emotional lability, distress intolerance, and these cravings for opioids. Biofeedback is a technique that increases an individual's control over his or her autonomic nervous system, which is responsible for the "fight-or-flight response." By learning to control certain bodily functions that are overactive at times of distress, for example breathing, heart rate, and muscle tension, an individual can reduce the amount of stress felt when in situations that would otherwise trigger cravings.

Acupuncture, a treatment originating from China several thousand years ago, has been studied as a possible treatment for opioid use disorder in the United States since the 1970s. At that time, it was discovered that acupuncture can trigger a release of natural (endogenous) opioids, which are always present in the brain. Although acupuncture needles were used in the original studies, the more common practice nowadays is to place small electrodes on the skin. The effect is the same. The technique of transcutaneous electrical acupoint stimulation involves the administration of small amounts of electrical stimulation, which are delivered to specific points on an individual's ear. The desired result is to lessen withdrawal symptoms and reduce the intensity of the cravings associated with opioid withdrawal.[13,14] An agency founded in the United States, known as the National Acupuncture Detoxification Association, has created a standardized protocol for ear acupuncture, which carries the name AcuDetox. This method is being employed in certain addiction treatment centers in the United States, Europe, Canada, and China.

Treatment in the Digital Age

As technology continues to advance, the practice of medicine continues to evolve, more rapidly in recent years, spurred on by increasingly busy lifestyles, more access to computers and other technology, and, most recently, safety concerns associated with the coronavirus pandemic. The inevitable push towards telemedicine has brought the future of substance use disorder treatment into the present.[15] The past five years alone has seen a significant increase in the percentage of substance use disorder treatment provided using telehealth in the United States. Even prior to the pandemic, treatment services provided online increased significantly: from 13.5% in 2016 to 17.4% in 2019. Telemedicine services, including those for substance use disorder,

---

[13] Eddie et al. (2015).   [14] Han et al. (2011).

[15] Also sometimes referred to as "telehealth," telemedicine is defined by Merriam-Webster as "medical care provided remotely to a patient in a separate location using two-way voice and visual communication (as by computer or cell phone)."

have necessarily increased from 2020 numbers, though access to mutual support groups for those without access to broadband internet have significantly decreased in areas where meeting in person was not possible due to the pandemic. Because addiction treatment can be difficult to access in normal times and often carries a perceived stigma, treatment offered in the privacy of the home or office can be quite appealing. It is likely that telemedicine treatments for opioid use disorder will only increase as we return to a post-pandemic degree of normalcy as this process not only benefits the individual seeking treatment but can also be of benefit for the medical provider by increasing efficiency of care coordination, alleviating the burden of workforce shortages, and reducing burnout and fatigue. Costs for telemedicine are lower and most insurance companies are now willing to cover these costs. Additionally, telemedicine now offers access to care in areas that have been traditionally without on-site access to physicians and, provided that reliable internet access can be established, offers the promise of hope for treatment and recovery in some of the largest in-need populations. Despite these benefits, there remain large populations of individuals who are unable to participate in telemedicine, primarily those who lack access to smartphones, a computer, or the internet, or for those with low technological literacy.[16]

Evidence to date strongly suggests that a telehealth approach to treatment for substance use disorders is equally effective as an in-person approach. There appears to be no differences in retention and attendance rates, client satisfaction, or client and provider ratings of therapeutic alliance using a telehealth and in-person hybrid approach when providing medication treatment for substance use disorders. In addition, the use of telehealth in the treatment of post-traumatic stress disorder, which is not an uncommon diagnosis among those struggling with substance use, appears to be at least as effective in reducing symptoms and, at the same time, reduces utilization costs while increasing client satisfaction.[17] Telehealth also encompasses non-patient-facing technology, such as mobile applications that can be downloaded on a smartphone or tablet. Several examples of such applications for the treatment of opioid use disorders include A-CHESS (via the Connections application), DynamiCare, and reSET-O. These applications typically use a combination of CBT and contingency management, and may also facilitate communication between client and physician, send alerts based on GPS location, or request the completion of drug tests. Some insurance policies cover the use of these applications, although many still do not. One major reason for this

---

[16] Substance Abuse and Mental Health Services Administration (2021). pp. 1–7.
[17] Substance Abuse and Mental Health Services Administration (2021), pp. 13–26.

is the current lack of evidence to suggest that these applications are either cost-effective or help improve patient outcomes.[18]

Virtual reality has recently emerged as a potential treatment for substance use disorders, specifically management of cravings. Virtual reality cue exposure therapy (VR-CET) uses virtual images (or cues) known to trigger cravings in the participant. As the participant is repeatedly exposed to such cues, a reduction in cravings is experienced, which hopefully reduces the risk for future relapse.[19] Just as with mobile applications, VR-CET does not have an abundance of evidence supporting (or refuting) its use. As society focuses on increasing the accessibility of substance use disorder treatment while balancing its financial impact, our experience with electronic resources will continue to grow.

References and Further Reading

Alam DA, Martorana A (2011). Addiction treatment: Level of care determination. *Primary Care: Clinics in Office Practice* 38: 125–136.

Center for Substance Abuse Treatment (2006). *Detoxification and Substance Abuse Treatment. Treatment Improvement Protocol (TIP) Series.* No. 45. HHS Publication No. (SMA) 15-4131. Rockville, MD: Center for Substance Abuse Treatment.

Eddie D, Vaschillo E, Vaschillo B, Lehrer P (2015). Heart rate variability biofeed-back: Theoretical basis, delivery, and its potential for the treatment of substance use disorders. *Addiction Research and Theory* 23(4): 266–272.

Han J, Cui C, Wu L (2011). Acupuncture-related techniques for the treatment of opiate addiction: A case of translational medicine. *Frontiers of Medicine* 5(2): 141–150.

Kurtz E, White W (2003). Alcoholics Anonymous. In Blocker J, Tyrell I (eds.) *Alcohol and Temperance in Modern History.* Santa Barbara, CA: ABC-CLIO, pp. 27–31.

Lo Coco G, Melchiori F, Oien V, et al. (2019). Group treatment for substance use disorders in adults: A systematic review and meta-analysis of randomized-controlled trials. *Journal of Substance Abuse Treatment* 99: 104–116.

McCarty D, Braude L, Lyman DR, et al. (2014). Substance abuse intensive outpatient programs: Assessing the evidence. *Psychiatric Services* 65(6): 718–726.

Substance Abuse and Mental Health Services Administration (2021). *Telehealth for the Treatment of Serious Mental Illness and Substance Use Disorders.* SAMHSA Publication No. PEP21-06-02-001. Rockville, MD: Substance Abuse and Mental Health Services Administration.

---

[18] Tice et al. (2020).   [19] Tsamitros et al. (2021).

Tice JA, Whittington MD, Fluetsch N, et al. (2020). Health technologies as an adjunct to medication assisted therapy for opioid use disorder: Evidence report. Institute for Clinical and Economic Review. https://icer.org/wp-content/uploads/2020/08/ICER_Digital_Therapeutics_for_OUD_Evidence_Report.pdf

Tsamitros N, Sebold M, Gutwinski S, et al. (2021). Virtual reality-based treatment approaches in the field of substance use disorders. *Current Addiction Reports* 8: 399–407.

White W, Budnick C, Pickard B (2011). Narcotics Anonymous: Its history and culture. *Counselor*, 12(2), 10–15, 22–27, 36–39, 46–50. https://counselormaga zine.com/en/columns/2013/columns/narcotics-anonymous/

11 THE TRUE COST OF OPIOID ADDICTION TREATMENT

Access to Treatment

As we learned in Chapter 7, the opioid epidemic has resulted in significant socioeconomic costs worldwide. Much of this may stem from the fact that although we currently have effective treatments for opioid use disorder, the majority of those with an opioid use disorder do not engage in treatment. In the United States alone, it is estimated that only about 10% of Americans who have been diagnosed with opioid use disorder are actively engaged with any kind of a treatment program. The numbers in countries with socialized medicine (and presumably better access to care) are better, though not by much, and only 30% of Canadians with an opioid use disorder are engaged with a treatment program. For low-income regions of the world with more limited resources and access to care, the number is even less. Of those individuals who are currently engaged in treatment, only about 8% are receiving one of the most effective interventions available – medications for opioid use disorder (MOUD).[1,2] The reasons for this disparity are numerous, but the barriers keeping people from finding help can be categorized at either the personal or systemic level. Personal-level barriers are related to either an individual's vulnerabilities, such as a mental illness preventing someone from participating in treatment, or an individual's beliefs, for example the perceived stigma surrounding addiction or its treatment. On the other hand, according to Hall et al., structural barriers "are factors and practices rooted in social, political, legal, and service systems," which prevent specific groups of people from accessing medical care.[3] Some examples of structural barriers include the inability to access treatment due to geographical location or homelessness, or the failure to identify the presence of an opioid use disorder by healthcare professionals, which can be the result of poor access to healthcare or the healthcare provider's lack of training. There may also be issues with the way the treatment is provided; for example, long wait times can be discouraging. If the treatment offered cannot be tailored to the

---

[1] Methadone, buprenorphine, and naltrexone.   [2] Hall et al. (2021).   [3] Hall et al. (2021)

individual, many will find the treatment ineffective, or will be unable to engage at all (as for those who require childcare services). Racial, ethnic, and religious disparities are another significant barrier for many, as studies have noted differences in diagnosis and referral rates, as well as access to treatment, between different races or ethnicities, and these issues specific to systemic racism were discussed in greater detail in Chapter 3.[4] Finally, the financial burden of addiction treatment itself hinders access to treatment, whether that comes from limited insurance coverage or lack of public funding.

Financial Costs of Treatment

The financial costs of addiction are enormous, with one report published by the Recovery Centers of America estimating that, as of 2019, substance use disorders have cost the United States close to 3.7 trillion US dollars (US$) thus far. This estimate includes both the direct healthcare costs associated with treatment and the indirect costs of addiction such as lost productivity, costs related to legal issues and incarceration, and the funding of income assistance and other social safety-net programs for patients who cannot work because of their opioid misuse. In contrast, this same report estimated that the total cost of treating every individual with a substance use disorder in the United States would be approximately US$2.5 trillion, resulting in over US$1.2 trillion of savings.[5]

Costs for an individual seeking treatment depend heavily on the type of treatment being provided and the country in which it is obtained, although in general residential and inpatient treatment will be much more expensive than what is offered as an outpatient. The United States' Surgeon General's Report on Alcohol, Drugs, and Health from 2016 estimated that the average cost of treatment required to assist one person in achieving abstinence is $28,256 for inpatient treatment versus only US$11,411 for outpatient therapy with medications. The implication is that although the average cost per person across all treatment types is $US22,460, it may be cost-effective to treat individuals in the outpatient setting, assuming it can be done in a safe manner.[6] Another more recent study published in 2021 found that the average cost of participation in a residential treatment program in the United States was $618 per person per day, and that, not surprisingly, the cost for participation in a for-profit program was significantly higher, at $718 per person per day, versus $357 per person per day for not-for-profit programs.[7] Treatment costs in Europe where socialized medicine has increased access to care for a greater percentage of the

---

[4] Priester et al. (2016).   [5] Recovery Centers of America (2020), p. 37.
[6] US Department of Health and Human Services (2016).   [7] Beetham et al. (2021).

population are considerably less than for the United States, and previous reports estimate a single day of inpatient detoxification treatment averages to be the equivalent of €199 per person per day in the United Kingdom and €247 per person per day in Germany. The estimated daily cost per patient for residential treatment ranges anywhere from 56 to 288 EUR in the United Kingdom (depending on the study cited), whereas Sweden's cost of daily treatment is €404 and for Norway is €234.[8]

The costs for outpatient treatment involving the use of MOUD vary greatly depending on the country in which they are being prescribed, and these costs are primarily related to the costs of labor, medication, and urine and blood testing. The costs for treatment with a single medication alone can vary considerably. In Afghanistan, the estimated total treatment cost per person treated with naltrexone is US$610, whereas in Australia the total treatment cost is US$5,750, and in the UK it is US$5,840. Treatment with buprenorphine is more expensive, with the total cost of treatment per person being US$1,090 USD in Afghanistan, US$6,620 in Australia, and US$7,200 in the UK.[9] At a more granular level, the total treatment cost per person in the United States has been estimated to be the following: $631 USD for behavioral intervention, $766 USD for medical management with naltrexone (which is one type of MOUD), and $1,183 USD for naltrexone plus behavioral intervention.[10]

Multiple cost–benefit analyses to date have demonstrated that treatment for substance use disorders is cost-effective, no matter what treatment modality is used. For instance, the Washington State Outcomes Project found the average cost of treatment per person to be US$4,912, whereas the total economic benefit was US$21,329.[11] Another study has estimated that the cost *savings* per person treated with cognitive behavioral therapy is US$136.41, US$33.71 USD for contingency management, US$41.10 for motivational interviewing, US$2.18 for methadone maintenance treatment and US$1.30 for buprenorphine treatment.[12] A study in Australia found that a person remaining abstinent from heroin for one year would cost close to 7,000 Australian dollars (A$) for treatment using pharmacotherapy and A$18,000 for residential treatment. When compared to the cost of incarceration for that same individual over the same period of time (approximately A$60,000) it becomes clear that either treatment type is still significantly more cost-effective than sending someone with an opioid use disorder to jail, and probably more likely to result in a productive member of society who is able to contribute as a result of their

---

[8] Lievens et al. (2014).   [9] Ruger et al. (2012).
[10] US Department of Health and Human Services (2018).   [11] French et al. (2002).
[12] US Department of Health and Human Services (2018).

treatment and not require as much social and financial support as someone with a criminal record.[13]

Although treatment of addiction results in spared lives and financial savings, depending on insurance status and country of residence the individual seeking treatment may find that they are personally responsible for most, if not all, of the cost associated with treatment. In fact, a recent survey conducted in the United States by the Substance Abuse and Mental Health Services Administration found that over 20% of respondents did not seek substance abuse treatment in the past year specifically because of the cost, often due to a lack of adequate insurance coverage.[14] Although less than 50% of health treatment in the United States is publicly financed, public funding is the primary source of payment for substance use disorder treatment.[15, 16] With the passage of the Affordable Care Act in 2010, the 21st Century Cures Act in 2016, and the Mental Health Parity and Addiction Equity Act in 2018, both public and private insurance companies are now required to cover treatment for substance use disorders, and there is no yearly or lifetime limit on the number of times someone can return to treatment. However, the amount of coverage offered varies on the insurance plan, and the copayment or deductible alone can be a barrier to treatment for some, especially individuals from lower socioeconomic groups or those who, often as a result of chronic opioid misuse, no longer have the financial resources to afford care. At the same time, this expansion of coverage in the United States has had unintended consequences, and certain individuals have figured out ways in which to exploit the system designed to help people in need for their own personal financial gain.

Addiction Treatment as a Business

As we learned earlier, the average daily charge for residential treatment in the United States is US$618 per person per day; however, for-profit programs typically charge significantly more than not-for-profit programs. Organizations with a financial incentive are also more likely to use aggressive recruitment techniques such as follow-up phone calls or offer transportation to the facility for new patients who will be admitted for residential treatment. Additionally, these programs typically require significantly larger upfront payments (over US$17,000 on average) when compared to nonprofit programs, and require regular weekly cash payments, leaving the patient with the task of trying to

---

[13] Moore et al. (2007).
[14] Substance Abuse and Mental Health Services Administration (2020).
[15] Lievens et al. (2014).   [16] Reif et al. (2017).

obtain reimbursement from their insurance company.[17] Considering that the average operating cost of residential treatment has been previously estimated to be US$162.53 daily per patient (adjusted to 2021 US dollars),[18] the potential for significant profits immediately becomes quite apparent. This profit margin is likely one reason why the percentage of treatment centers in the United States categorized as "private, nonprofit" has continued to decline (between 2010 and 2020 the number of private not-for-profit treatment centers dropped from 58% to 50% by the end of the decade), while the number of treatment centers categorized as "private, for-profit" rose during that same decade from 30% in 2010 to 41% as of 2020. Government agencies operate the small remainder of facilities and have remained steady over time, making up approximately 10% of available treatment centers in the United States.[19]

Unfortunately, it is not just the opportunity for access to the considerable revenue to be made by providing legitimate substance abuse treatment services that has driven the recent increase in industry activity. Certainly, an argument can be made that we do not have enough of these types of facilities and that the great need for addiction treatment generated by the opioid epidemic has to be filled, but this massive growth has unfortunately resulted in several instances of behavior that ranges from the questionably legal to the blatantly unethical. One such example is the practice of "patient brokering" or "body brokering," in which patients are either given cash directly, or the patient's financial responsibility (such as with a copayment or deductible) is waived in order to influence which treatment facility they chose to go to. Once admitted, some treatment centers will routinely overcharge insurance companies for necessary laboratory testing or will conduct this testing much more frequently than is typically required. Lohse et al. reported in 2018 that the owners of several sober-living homes and "half-way" houses have also participated in excessive drug testing and kickback schemes designed to generate increased profits at the expense of patients and health insurance companies.[20]

The quintessential example of fraud in the substance abuse industry occurred in the state of Florida, fueled by the previously mentioned Affordable Care Act (ACA). With its fee-for-service model and elimination of restrictions on the number of times someone can re-enter treatment, the ACA unintentionally created an opportunity for residential treatment centers to become revolving-door facilities generating a regular stream of revenue at the expense of patients with opioid use disorder. The first step in the

[17] Beetham et al. (2021).   [18] French et al. (2002).
[19] Substance Abuse and Mental Health Services Administration (2021).
[20] Lohse et al. (2018).

scheme is to fill as many inpatient beds as possible with patients who have "good" medical insurance. Staff at some of these facilities were incentivized to actively recruit such individuals desperately looking for addiction treatment, enticing them with benefits such as reduced up-front costs and transportation to the facilities, even providing, in some cases, a one-way plane ticket to get there. Once there the patient receives the standard treatment services, but billed at the higher for-profit rate. At some point, when the patient meets criteria for discharge from the residential portion of treatment, and this often coincides with a decision by the insurance company to refuse to pay for continued treatment, the patient is discharged to a sober living facility. The sober living facility pays a fee to the inpatient treatment center for the referral (an illegal payment referred to as a kickback as was discussed in Chapter 7) and the sober living facility receives payment from the patient, their insurance or government support until they move on. It should be noted that these sober living facilities do not offer any medical treatment services, and so are not required to be regulated by any governmental agency. As a result, some sober living homes more closely resemble flop houses and may be rife with frequent drug use and prostitution. Unbeknownst to the patient, part of the ongoing relationship between the sober home and the treatment facility involved patients being transported back to the treatment facility for ongoing outpatient therapy and (often excessive) laboratory testing, and the owner of the sober home receives financial kickbacks in return. In some cases, the rent required to live in these homes was reduced or waived entirely if the patient continued treatment with that specific treatment center, encouraging people not to leave, and once insurance benefits were exhausted for the round of treatment, the patient is discharged, only to start the cycle again once the person relapsed and the insurance benefits can be used again. In the most egregious cases, opioids were actually provided to patients in these so-called "sober" homes in order to get them back into treatment sooner.

Many people have become victims of this so-called "Florida Shuffle" (Figure 11.1), and the overdose death rate in certain parts of Florida has quadrupled as a result.[21] In response to the ongoing fraud within the state, the Florida legislature passed the Practices of Substance Abuse Service Providers Act in 2017, which updated the credentials required for a provider or facility to be accredited, expanded the criteria of what is considered fraudulent activity (including patient brokering), created a minimum fine of US$50,000 for patient brokering, and required licensing of all substance abuse marketing providers.[22]

---

[21] Seville et al. (2017).   [22] Lohse et al. (2018).

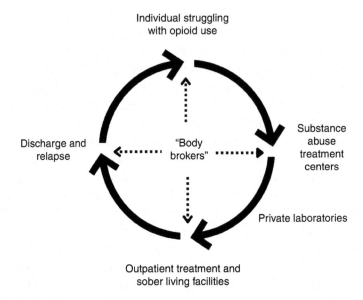

Figure 11.1 Body brokering and the "Florida Shuffle."

Subsequently, the Opioid Addiction Recovery Fraud Prevention Act of 2018 was passed, giving the Federal Trade Commission authority to seek civil penalties for any fraudulent or deceptive actions performed by addiction treatment centers.

References and Further Reading

Beetham T, Saloner B, Gaye M, et al. (2021). Admission practices and cost of care for opioid use disorder at residential addiction treatment programs in the US. *Health Affairs (Millwood)* 40(20): 317–325.

European Monitoring Centre for Drugs and Drug Addiction (2011). *Cost and Financing of Drug Treatment Services in Europe: An Exploratory Study.* Luxembourg: Publications Office of the European Union.

French MT, Salome HJ, Carney M (2002). Using the DATCAP and ASI to estimate the costs and benefits of residential addiction treatment in the State of Washington. *Social Science & Medicine* 55: 2267–2282.

Hall NY, Le L, Majmudar I, Mihalopoulos C (2021). Barriers to accessing opioid substitution treatment for opioid use disorder: A systematic review from the client perspective. *Drug and Alcohol Dependence* 221: 108651.

Lievens D, Vander Laenen F, Christiaens J (2014). Public spending for illegal drug and alcohol treatment in hospitals: An EU cross-country comparison. *Substance Abuse Treatment, Prevention, and Policy* 9: 26.

Lohse J, Ashpole L, Epperson KJ (2018). Behavioral health care: The new frontier of fraud and abuse? AHLA Connections. sharepoint.healthlawyers.org/News/Con nections/Documents/2018/Feature/January-February2018_Feature1.pdf.

Moore TJ, Ritter A. Caulkins JP (2007). The costs and consequences of three policy options for reducing heroin dependency. *Drug and Alcohol Review* 26: 369–378.

Priester MA, Browne T, Iachini A, et al. (2016). Treatment access barriers and dispar-ities among individuals with co-occurring mental health and substance use dis-orders: An integrative literature review. *Journal of Substance Abuse Treatment* 61: 47–59.

Recovery Centers of America (2020). Economic cost of substance abuse Disorder in the United States, 2019. http://recoverycentersofamerica.com/resource/eco nomic-cost-of-substance-abuse-disorder-in-united-states-2019/.

Reif S, George P, Braude L (2014). Residential treatment for individuals with substance use disorder: assessing the evidence. *Psychological Services* 65(3): 301–312.

Reif S, Creedon, TB, Horgan CM, Stewart MT, Garnick DW (2017). Commercial health plan coverage of selected treatments for opioid use disorders from 2003 to 2014. *Journal of Psychoactive Drugs* 49(2): 102–110.

Ruger JP, Chawarski M, Mazlan M, et al. (2012). Costs of addressing heroin addic-tion in Malaysia and 32 comparable countries worldwide. *Health Research Educational Trust* 47(2): 865–887.

Seville LR, Schecter A, Rappleye H (2017). Florida's billion-dollar drug treatment industry is plagued by overdoses, fraud. NBC News. www.nbcnews.com/feature/ megyn-kelly/florida-s-billion-dollar-drug-treatment-industry-plagued-overdoses-fraud-n773376.

Substance Abuse and Mental Health Services Administration (2020). *Key Substance Use and Mental Health Indicators in the United States: Results from the 2019 National Survey on Drug Use and Health.* HHS Publication No. PEP20-07–01-001, NSDUH Series H-55). Rockville, MD: Center for Behavioral Health Statistics and Quality, Substance Abuse and Mental Health Services Administration.

Substance Abuse and Mental Health Services Administration (2021). *National Survey of Substance Abuse Treatment Services (N-SSATS): 2020. Data on Substance Abuse Treatment Facilities.* Rockville, MD: Substance Abuse and Mental Health Services Administration.

US Department of Health and Human Services(2016). *Office of the Surgeon General, Facing Addiction in America: The Surgeon General's Report on Alcohol, Drugs, and Health.* Washington, DC: US Department of Health and Human Services.

US Department of Health and Human Services (2018). *Facing Addiction in America: The Surgeon General's Spotlight on Opioids.* Washington, DC: US Department of Health and Human Services.

12 HARM-REDUCTION, LEGAL ISSUES, DRUG COURT AND OTHER ALTERNATIVES TO DISCIPLINE

What Is Harm Reduction?

In the 1990s, having come to recognize the considerable harm drug misuse was having on an increasing percentage of the population, leaders in the majority of European countries began to shift their focus away from fighting the "war on drugs" by attacking the supply side and instead focused on policies designed to reduce demand. A "four pillars approach" was developed to reduce the harm caused by the illegal drug trade and the size of the market for these drugs, with the idea that if the customer base is decreased then increased supply would not be as much of an issue. This approach is focused on *prevention* (efforts to reduce harmful use of drugs or alcohol before addiction develops), *treatment* (developing effective treatment options and increasing their availability), *enforcement* (reduction of criminal activities associated with drug misuse, and response to related medical emergencies in the community, such as overdose), and *harm reduction*.[1] Subsequently, after considerable success in Europe, other countries, including Canada and the United States, began to adopt this strategy or develop similar policies, which moved away from their historical attempts at supply reduction.

Harm reduction can be defined as a set of strategies aiming to limit the negative consequences of drug use without requiring abstinence.[2] In an ideal world, individuals struggling with an opioid use disorder would be able to achieve and maintain abstinence from opioids with ease. In reality, there are some people who are either unable or unwilling to discontinue their opioid use and, when this is the case, the focus of treatment changes toward reducing the negative consequences of opioid use. Most harm-reduction efforts are aimed at achieving three goals: reducing the risk of overdose, limiting transmission of disease, and increasing access to treatment. Many types of harm reduction achieve more than one of these goals.

[1] MacPherson (2001).   [2] Gugala et al. (2022).

Harm-Reduction Strategies

Naloxone

When someone overdoses on opioids, they generally stop breathing, or their respiratory rate slows to the point where the lungs become ineffective at bringing much needed oxygen into the body. In technical terms this is called "opioid-induced respiratory depression" and occurs because there are opioid receptors at specific sites in the central nervous system (specifically the pre-Bötzinger complex in the pons, a part of the brainstem where our natural respiratory rhythm is generated). When opioids bind to these receptors in the brainstem they reduce the natural drive to breathe and, in the case of an opioid overdose, eliminate it all together. When this happens, the individual who has overdosed has only minutes before all of the oxygen left in their lungs and in their blood is used up. Without oxygen, the brain begins to die and the heart becomes starved for oxygen. Without intervention, the person will suffer a cardiac arrest and die.

Naloxone is an opioid *antagonist*, meaning it blocks (or antagonizes) the effects of opioids such as heroin, fentanyl, or oxycodone. It works because it has a much higher affinity for the opioid receptors than actual opioids, meaning it can push the opioids off their receptors and then, since it binds more tightly to them, this prevents the opioids from regaining access. When naloxone is given to someone who has recently overdosed on opioids, the opioids remain in the body but can no longer exert their effects on the brain stem, immediately restoring the drive to breathe. Naloxone also reverses the other effects of opioids, including euphoria and sedation, resulting in the symptoms of withdrawal. The end result is a person who is awake and breathing but also suffering from opioid withdrawal. As unpleasant as that may be, using naloxone saves lives. In the United States, for example, states that have implemented naloxone access laws have seen a 14% decrease in overdose deaths.[3] More potent opioids, such as fentanyl, often require multiple doses of naloxone, which is why it is important to contact emergency medical services when an overdose occurs.

Although we know how beneficial naloxone can be, many people are afraid to use it. Some people fear that, when naloxone is administered, the person receiving the naloxone may become violent and dangerous. However, this is extraordinarily rare, especially if the naloxone is administered by someone known to the victim.[4] Others are afraid to use naloxone because they have never given it before. However, with some simple training, anyone can

---

[3] NIDA (2017).   [4] Indiana State Department of Health (n.d.).

administer certain formulations of naloxone like the nasal spray. In addition, naloxone is a very safe medication: you cannot overdose on naloxone, if given to someone who has not used opioids it will not hurt them, and there are no serious adverse reactions associated with the drug. Furthermore, some might not know how to get naloxone. In some areas of the United States, a pharmacist can dispense naloxone without a prescription, otherwise it can be prescribed by a healthcare provider. Europe has "take home naloxone" programs, supplying naloxone to people in the community in case of emergency, and such programs can also be found in Ukraine, Kazakhstan, the United States, and Canada. In 2019, France began supplying injectable naloxone at pharmacies without a prescription.[5]

Good Samaritan Drug Overdose Laws

Many countries in Europe, as well as in the United States and Canada, have implemented laws protecting individuals from prosecution if they have witnessed an overdose and are seeking medical assistance. Those who have witnessed an overdose may be hesitant to contact emergency services over concerns that police involvement might lead to serious consequences for either themselves or the person who has overdosed. Sadly, this fear is not unfounded; there have been reports of police harassment, arrest, and loss of child custody or subsidized housing following a phone call for help.[6] By implementing Good Samaritan laws, the hope is more people will call for help without fear of repercussions.

Fentanyl Testing Strips

The rate of fentanyl-associated overdose deaths in the United States has increased exponentially since 2013. Between April 2020 and May 2021, almost two-thirds of drug overdose deaths in the United States involved synthetic opioids such as fentanyl, and three-quarters of overdose deaths from cocaine in 2021 were associated with fentanyl.[7, 8] Fentanyl (and its analogs carfentanyl and acetylfentanyl) are cheap, highly potent, synthetic opioids currently being used as adulterants in the illicit drug trade. As discussed in earlier chapters, because of fentanyl's high potency, a smaller amount is required to achieve the same effect as a larger amount of heroin, and these smaller amounts make drug trafficking easier for dealers. In addition, fentanyl is cheap, and so selling fentanyl mixed with a bulking agent (such as baking soda) leads to greater profits compared with selling the same amount of heroin. Unfortunately, fentanyl's high potency also means that even a tiny amount can easily result in an unintended overdose.

---

[5] EMCDDA (2020).   [6] Moaleff et al., p. 2.   [7] Kounang (2021).   [8] Miller (2022).

Fentanyl testing strips were first developed to detect the presence of the drug in urine but are now also being used to detect the presence of fentanyl in illicit substances. The idea is that if someone can test the substance before ingestion, they might adjust the amount of drug they consume, should fentanyl be present. These strips have been utilized for this purpose in Europe since the 1990s, and individuals in certain European countries and Canada can have their drugs checked at special consumption facilities.[9] More recently, fentanyl testing strips have gained popularity in the United States. Surprisingly, fentanyl testing strips are considered illegal in half of states in the United States, typically under decades-old drug paraphernalia laws, which have not been updated to reflect their current use. Despite this, these test strips can still be easily ordered from internet sites and delivered via mail.[10]

Studies demonstrating the efficacy of fentanyl testing strips in preventing overdose are limited. However, there is anecdotal evidence that people do change their drug use behaviors if the testing strip is positive for fentanyl.[11] Further research is required to fully understand how fentanyl testing strips influence safety and risk of overdose.

Syringe Services Programs

It is well known that sharing drug paraphernalia, such as needles and syringes, is associated with a high transmission rate of serious diseases, including infective endocarditis, hepatitis B, hepatitis C, and HIV. Syringe services programs (SSPs), also referred to as needle and syringe programs or needle exchange programs, are community-based services that aim to reduce disease transmission by providing access to clean syringes and needles (Figure 12.1). They may also provide other services such as syringe and needle disposal, naloxone kits, fentanyl testing strips, screening for hepatitis and HIV, and referrals for the treatment of infectious disease and substance use.

A common misconception is that SSPs increase the rate of drug use and crime. According to research funded by the National Institute on Drug Abuse, this does not appear to be true. In fact, those who utilize the services at SSPs are *more likely* to enter treatment.[12] In addition, studies thus far have not been able to demonstrate increased crime rates in communities with SSPs. Other proven benefits of SSPs include: decreased transmission of blood-borne diseases; significant cost savings when compared to the costs of hospitalization, treatment of disease, and incarceration; reduced paraphernalia litter; and increased enrollment in treatment for both infectious disease and opioid use disorders.[13]

---

[9] Goldman et al. (2019).   [10] Miller (2022).   [11] Goldman et al. (2019).
[12] Surratt et al. (2020).   [13] Centers for Disease Control and Prevention (2019).

Figure 12.1 Poster for a syringe exchange program found in the Bay View neighborhood of Milwaukee, Wisconsin, United States.

Despite the strong evidence demonstrating a relationship between SSPs and reduced transmission rates of HIV and hepatitis, significant stigma remains. For example, of the countries comprising the Middle East and North Africa, only 8 of 19 have at least one SSP. To make things more difficult, prejudice can hinder the success of these programs, as procurement of clean supplies is hindered by pharmacists who refuse to sell them.[14] Unfortunately, SSPs will likely not be widely accepted until the stigma associated with drug use and addiction is effectively addressed.

Supervised Injection and Consumption Facilities

Supervised injection facilities (SIFs) are facilities that allow people to use illicit substances intravenously under the supervision of trained professionals who can respond to an overdose. Supervised consumption facilities (SCFs) are

[14] Harm Reduction International (2018).

similar to SIFs, except they also allow the use of non-injectable drugs. These facilities do not supply drugs, but rather provide a safe environment to use them.

SCFs and SIFs were initially developed in Europe as a response to the rapid spread of HIV and AIDS in the 1980s. Most of the legally sanctioned SIFs are located in Europe, but are also found in Canada and Australia. The United States also has several SIFs, but unlike in other countries they are not legally sanctioned, so significant controversy has prevented further expansion.[15] Those who oppose SIFs and SCFs argue that these facilities create public safety risks, increase crime rates, destroy the surrounding community, and facilitate drug use and addiction, even for future generations.[16] Despite this opposition, there is growing evidence of the benefits of SIFs and SCFs, including lower overdose death rates, decreased rates of using shared needles, and an increased likelihood of enrolling in addiction treatment. Studies from Vancouver, Canada, and Sydney, Australia have found that rates of crime, public drug use, and injection-related litter decreased with a SIF or SCF in the vicinity.[17] Unfortunately, just as with syringe services programs, stigma is a primary hindrance to expansion of these facilities.

Medications for Opioid Use Disorder

Medications for opioid use disorder (MOUD), also frequently referred to as medication-assisted treatment or, in certain circumstances, opioid agonist therapy, is the use of pharmacotherapy to treat individuals struggling with an opioid addiction. Three medications are primarily used for this purpose: methadone, buprenorphine, and naltrexone. All three of these medications are supported by the World Health Organization for the treatment of opioid use disorders and can be found on their Essential Medicines List, which has been published biennially since 1978. In addition, several other medications have also been utilized for the treatment of opioid use disorder, which are discussed below.

METHADONE

Historically, the first medication used for the treatment of an opioid use disorder was methadone. Methadone is a synthetic opioid that was originally developed in Germany during World War II as a pain reliever for soldiers wounded in combat. Several decades later, Drs. Vincent Dole, Marie Nyswander, and Mary Jeanne Kreek began treating patients addicted to heroin with methadone. They noted that methadone relieved "narcotic hunger" and

---

[15] Levengood et al. (2021).   [16] Rosenstein (2018).   [17] Levengood et al. (2021).

blocked the euphoric effects of other opioids. Combining methadone treatment with psychosocial rehabilitation, their patients returned to school or work, and mended broken relationships with family members,[18] and so the "Dole–Nyswander treatment of heroin addiction" was born.

Like opioids such as heroin, fentanyl, and oxycodone, methadone is considered an "opioid agonist," meaning it binds to and activates opioid receptors found throughout the human body. As the dose of methadone increases, activation of the receptor and the medication's effects will also increase at a similar rate. It is a long-acting medication, although the length of its effects can be quite variable. Because of this variability, individuals taking methadone may not experience its full effects for several days. In addition, methadone has many drug interactions which need to be taken into consideration. It is exceptionally important that increased doses are performed at a slow rate, as increasing the dose too quickly can result in oversedation, cardiac arrhythmias, respiratory depression, or death. It is for this reason that methadone is considered one of the more dangerous opioids on the market, unless prescribed by an experienced provider. More common side effects of methadone include nausea, vomiting, constipation, and excessive sweating.

In the United States, methadone prescribed for the treatment of opioid use disorder must be supplied by a Substance Abuse and Mental Health Services Administration-certified opioid treatment program (OTP). The methadone used in OTPs is most frequently formulated as a liquid and is usually given once daily. In the beginning of treatment, methadone must be taken under direct observation to limit the likelihood of diversion. As treatment progresses, the OTP may provide the individual with "take home" doses of methadone, which can be a considerable motivator for people to remain compliant with treatment recommendations. There is no known optimal length of treatment with methadone, although those who stay in treatment longer have better outcomes, whereas the risk of overdose and death increases for those who leave treatment.[19]

BUPRENORPHINE

Buprenorphine, discovered in 1966, is a synthetic opioid initially marketed as an analgesic for acute and postoperative pain. Thirty years later, buprenorphine was adopted as treatment for opioid use disorder in France, subsequently approved in the United States in 2002, and is now used in more than 45 countries.[20] Buprenorphine is classified as a "partial agonist," meaning it

---

[18] Dole and Nyswander (1965).
[19] Substance Abuse and Mental Health Services Administration (2021).
[20] Shulman et al. (2019).

binds to opioid receptors, but it does not activate them to the same extent as opioid agonists like heroin and methadone, especially at higher doses. With less activation of receptors, the chance for someone experiencing the negative consequences expected with ingestion of large amounts of opioids, such as respiratory depression, is diminished. This phenomenon is referred to as a "ceiling effect," and is thought to increase buprenorphine's safety profile. Buprenorphine can also be classified as an "antagonist," as it blocks activation of the kappa opioid receptor, which is a specific opioid receptor subtype. When someone starts buprenorphine for the first time, they are often asked to abstain from all opioids for a specific period of time or until withdrawal symptoms begin. The danger of taking buprenorphine shortly after using other opioids is that it may cause severe withdrawal symptoms, which is called "precipitated withdrawal." Therefore, it is very important to follow the prescriber's instructions when beginning this medication.

Known colloquially as "bupe," buprenorphine for the treatment of opioid use disorder comes in a variety of formulations. The most frequently prescribed formulation of buprenorphine is a dissolvable medication film (or "strip"), which is placed under the tongue and allowed to dissolve. The medication naloxone is also added to these films as an abuse deterrent. As mentioned earlier, naloxone is an opioid antagonist that reverses the effects of opioids in the case of overdose. The purpose of naloxone in these strips is different, however. When buprenorphine films are taken as prescribed, very little of the naloxone is absorbed through the mucosa in the mouth and therefore has no effect on the body. But if the strips are adulterated and injected intravenously, the naloxone reverses the effects of opioids in the body and severe withdrawal symptoms will occur.[21] Buprenorphine, either with or without naloxone, can also be found as a tablet, and certain insurance plans offer better coverage for the tablets rather than the strips. Buprenorphine is not associated with cardiac arrhythmias and has a lower overdose risk when compared to methadone.[22] The more common side effects of sublingual buprenorphine films include nausea, constipation, dry mouth, sedation, and excessive sweating.

Buprenorphine subdermal implants are also available, although less popular than other formulations. Four small, plastic rods impregnated with

---

[21] Interestingly, although rates of buprenorphine injection are low in the United States, where heroin and other opioids are readily available, this has not been the case in other countries. Finland, for example, experienced a surge of buprenorphine-addicted patients when the supply of heroin from Afghanistan dropped in the late 1990s, whereas in Malaysia rapid expansion of opioid use disorder treatment resulted in poorly trained providers prescribing buprenorphine with financial incentives (Lofwall and Walsh 2014).

[22] Sofuoglu et al. (2019).

buprenorphine are inserted under the skin of the upper arm through a small incision performed in a doctor's office. These rods remain in the arm for six months, at which time they must be surgically removed and replaced. Because the implant requires a small surgical procedure that necessitates special training to perform, and with the real possibility of individuals removing the implants themselves, there are few doctors who continue to offer this option.[23]

Most recently, an injectable version of buprenorphine has been developed, exciting the addiction community. This formulation is injected by a healthcare provider into the fatty layer of the abdomen monthly. This form of administration eliminates the possibility of diversion or missed dose and supplies a constant amount of buprenorphine throughout the day, avoiding the highs and lows associated with the buprenorphine strips. Some patients say they feel "tied down" by taking a medication every day, and so enjoy the freedom the injectable version offers. Some common side effects of injectable buprenorphine include injection-site reactions, constipation, and fatigue.

Buprenorphine can be supplied at an OTP, but it can also be prescribed by a provider with a special prescribing license and either picked up at a pharmacy (for the tablets or films) or administered in the clinic (for implants and injections). Many people find this appealing, especially those with families or full-time jobs, as it doesn't require daily visits to obtain the day's worth of medication. Just as with methadone, there is no ideal length of time that someone should remain on buprenorphine. However, longer lengths of treatment are associated with better outcomes.

NALTREXONE

Naltrexone is a close cousin of naloxone, as it is classified as an "opioid antagonist" and therefore can reverse the effects of opioids. Unlike naloxone, however, naltrexone is not used as an emergency medication or combined with buprenorphine. Rather, it is given as a monthly intramuscular injection (in the case of extended-release naltrexone) or taken daily as an oral tablet. The benefits of naltrexone are twofold, as it blocks the effects of opioids, protecting the individual from an opioid overdose and reducing any cravings for opioids. To avoid the possibility of withdrawal, the patient is typically asked to wait up to seven days before naltrexone is initiated. Alternatively, under close supervision in a clinic or hospital, very small amounts of naltrexone are administered, sometimes within hours of opioid ingestion, until the total therapeutic dose has been reached, a practice referred to as "micro-dosing." The injectable form of naltrexone is generally better tolerated than the oral

---

[23] Author's observation.

version, but some of the common side effects are nausea, dizziness, and injection-site reactions. Because naltrexone is metabolized in the liver, those with severe liver disease need to be monitored with occasional blood tests.

COMPARISON OF METHADONE, BUPRENORPHINE, AND NALTREXONE

There have been several recent trials comparing buprenorphine and methadone for the treatment of opioid addiction. These results suggest there is better treatment retention, and therefore a lower dropout rate, with methadone compared to buprenorphine. Several theories have been postulated as to why this might be. For example, methadone clinics in the United States provide more support and structure when compared with office-based buprenorphine treatment, encouraging people on methadone to stay in treatment. In addition, methadone (an opioid agonist) is highly reinforcing and is associated with severe withdrawal when discontinued, motivating people to remain on methadone. In comparison, buprenorphine (a partial opioid agonist) might not be as reinforcing as methadone, but it is associated with milder withdrawal, making it easier to discontinue. That being said, both methadone and buprenorphine seem to be equally effective in reducing illicit opioid use, as long as the individual taking the medication remains in treatment.

Another multi-site study compared intramuscular, extended-release naltrexone to buprenorphine–naltrexone tablets. Significantly more people struggled at the beginning of treatment with naltrexone; however, once naltrexone therapy was established, the rates of relapse and retention in treatment were comparable.[24]

ALTERNATIVE MEDICATIONS FOR OPIOID USE DISORDER

Although methadone, buprenorphine, and naltrexone are the most frequently prescribed MOUD, other medications and supplements have been used with promising results. In countries where opium is commonly found and socially accepted (such as in Iran and Afghanistan), those with an opioid use disorder might be treated with an opium tincture.[25] In Persian medicine, an herbal compound known as *Hab-o Shefa* has been used for both withdrawal management and opioid use disorder treatment.[26] For people who continue to relapse while on methadone, "heroin-assisted treatment" is available in multiple European countries and Canada. Heroin in this case is used to supplement methadone treatment by enhancing treatment retention and hopefully limiting the use of illicit opioids. Other opioids, such as hydromorphone and delayed-release morphine, have also been used in a similar way.[27]

[24] Sofuoglu et al. (2019).   [25] Noroozi et al. (2021).   [26] Moosavyzadeh et al. (2020).
[27] Bond and Witton (2017).

Table 12.1 Summary of the most common medications for opioid use disorder[28]

	Methadone	Buprenorphine	Naltrexone
Pharmacology	Opioid receptor agonist	Opioid receptor partial agonist	Opioid receptor antagonist
Route of administration	Oral	Oral; subcutaneous extended-release injection; subdermal implant	Oral; intramuscular extended-release injection
Frequency of administration	Daily	Daily (oral); monthly (subcutaneous injection); every six months (subdermal implant)	Daily (oral); every four weeks (intramuscular injection)
Misuse/ diversion potential	Low with directly observed administration; moderate with take-home doses	Low in settings with directly observed administration; moderate when given at home	None
Risk of sedation or respiratory depression	Low, unless dose is increased too quickly or when combined with other sedating substances	Low, unless combined with other sedating substances	None
Withdrawal symptoms on discontinuation	Present, can be worse than for opioid receptor partial agonists	Present, can be less than for opioid receptor agonists	None
Common side effects	Gastrointestinal distress, sweating, sedation	Gastrointestinal distress, sweating, insomnia	Insomnia, gastrointestinal distress, muscle aches, elevated liver enzymes

[28] Modified from source: Substance Abuse and Mental Health Services Administration (2021).

Levo-alpha-acetylmethadol (LAAM) has been previously used in the United States and Europe for the treatment of opioid use disorder, although it is no longer available or approved for use in most markets (including Europe, Canada, and Australia). LAAM's chemical structure resembles methadone but it has an even longer half-life, so that it only needs to be administered two to three times weekly. Also, like methadone, LAAM is associated with cardiac arrhythmias, ultimately leading to its removal from the European market in 2001. The United States followed suit in 2003 when the only pharmaceutical company that manufactured LAAM discontinued its sale. Interestingly, LAAM continues to be approved by the Federal Drug Administration, should manufacturing of the drug resume.[29]

MOUD IN PREGNANCY

As rates of opioid abuse and addiction in the general population have increased over the past decade, so too has it increased among pregnant women. In the case of pregnancy, opioid use disorder impacts both the woman and child. Treatment of opioid use disorder in pregnancy is therefore of utmost importance and will typically fall into one of two categories.

Medication-assisted withdrawal is the first option. Medication-assisted withdrawal refers to the practice of giving medications to alleviate withdrawal symptoms while the person abstains from their opioid of choice. Only certain medications for the management of withdrawal have been approved for use in pregnancy, and methadone and buprenorphine have been used successfully for this purpose. This method is not preferred because most women who undergo medication-assisted withdrawal will relapse before delivery.[30]

Because of this serious risk, the preferred treatment method is to continue MOUD throughout the pregnancy. Methadone has been the medication of choice for decades, but now, with years of experience, we know that buprenorphine can be used safely and effectively as well. Pregnant women tend to require higher doses of methadone as the pregnancy advances because their biochemical makeup changes. Because there are not enough data to determine if naloxone or naltrexone is safe during pregnancy, the buprenorphine–naloxone films and naltrexone formulations are not usually recommended for use in pregnancy unless under close supervision.

Both methadone and buprenorphine appear also to be safe for the fetus, especially when compared to illicit opioids. Babies born to mothers using heroin or other illicit opioids can experience stunted growth while in the uterus and are born underweight, possibly resulting from repeated toxin exposure,

---

[29] Jaffe (2007).   [30] Klaman et al. (2019).

opioid-related inhibition of various growth hormones, and maternal malnutrition. Although these risks are also present for the mother taking methadone or buprenorphine, it is less likely to occur or will otherwise occur to a reduced degree.

When a pregnant woman uses opioids, a certain portion of the drug crosses the placenta into the fetus. Once the baby is born and is no longer receiving opioids from the mother, the baby will go through a withdrawal period. This is referred to as neonatal abstinence syndrome (NAS). NAS has been portrayed frequently in the media, often seemingly to dramatize the suffering of the neonate and "scare" women to not use opioids. Of course, the only way to absolutely avoid NAS is to never use opioids while pregnant, but for women with an active opioid use disorder, this can be difficult if not impossible. Neonatologists have vast experience treating neonates with NAS, and typically treat the withdrawal with small doses of morphine. Breast feeding is also encouraged, as it reduces the need for treatment, and if treatment is required, it reduces the length of time treatment is required. It does not appear that there are differences between methadone and buprenorphine as to likelihood of NAS, and the dose of methadone does not affect these odds either. The American Academy of Pediatrics recommends that the infant should be monitored for five to seven days after birth to ensure treatment is given, if necessary. When breastfeeding, both methadone and buprenorphine can be detected in the breast milk, albeit very low levels and therefore unlikely to harm the child. Currently, breastfeeding while on MOUD is encouraged and may help to reduce the symptoms of NAS.[31]

Harm-Reduction Approaches in the Criminal Justice System

Drug Decriminalization

Drug decriminalization, which will be discussed in further detail in Chapter 16, refers to "the removal of criminal sanctions for possession of small amounts of illegal substances."[32] The theory behind decriminalization is that by removing legal sanctions on drug use, and replacing these sanctions with safer options like safe injection facilities and treatment referrals, the harms typically associated with illicit drug use will decrease.

Prisons and Jails

Although some countries have decriminalized the use or possession of drugs, most of the world continues to address drug-related offenses in a punitive manner. Of the approximately 10 million individuals who are incarcerated around

[31] Klaman et al. (2019).   [32] Canadian Centre on Substance Use and Addiction (2021).

the world, at least one in five are imprisoned for drug-related offenses (and in some countries, such as in the Philippines and Thailand, this proportion reaches 50% and 72%, respectively).[33] Therefore, it comes as no surprise that individuals engaged in the criminal justice system have disproportionately high rates of substance use – up to four times greater than the general population. Opioids are a significant contributor to this estimate, as approximately 11% of males and 21% of females in United States prison have reported daily opioid use within the six months prior to incarceration. In addition, approximately 10% of prisoners reported a lifetime history of opioid use disorder, and 8% were currently struggling with an opioid use disorder.[34] Sadly, this translates to an exceptionally high rate of overdose, especially when first released from prison; one study found that within two weeks of release, male and female prisoners are 29 times and 69 times more likely to die from an overdose when compared to those who have not been incarcerated.[35]

The World Health Organization, the United Nations Office on Drugs and Crime, and the Joint United Nations Program on HIV/AIDS all recommend the use of harm-reduction measures in prisons. Unfortunately, only a small minority of individuals receive this kind of treatment, which is considered by many as evidence of unethical and inhumane treatment.[36] Needle and syringe programs are the least utilized form of harm reduction internationally. The use of MOUD is more common but still rare, especially in the United States where 68% of jails and prisons don't offer any type of MOUD, and only 7% offer all three types of MOUD (methadone, buprenorphine, and naltrexone).[37] To make things worse, many of the US prisons limit the use of MOUD for certain individuals, such as pregnant women or those already taking MOUD. Rhode Island in the United States is one exception: MOUD is offered to all prisoners, and as a result has seen a 61% decrease of post-incarceration overdose deaths.[38] Other countries, such as Canada, have implemented naloxone training in prisons, and give naloxone kits to individuals once released.[39]

Police Diversion Programs

Police diversion programs replace legal sanctions for drug possession or consumption with less punitive measures, such as informal warnings or fines, as well as referral to treatment. One example of a police diversion program is the Drugs Education Programme in the United Kingdom, where those found in possession of drugs are given the option of attending an educational class

---

[33] Sander et al. (2019), p. 106.   [34] Cropsey and Schiavon (2019).
[35] Sander et al. (2019), p. 111.   [36] Sander et al. (2019), p. 108.   [37] Scott et al. (2021).
[38] Sander et al. (2019), p. 110.   [39] Sander et al. (2019), p. 112.

rather than spending time in jail. In Australia, multiple diversion programs are in place to connect people with education and treatment services. The Law Enforcement Assisted Diversion program in the United States is similar in concept.[40] A study performed in the state of Washington determined that, over a 10-year period, its police diversion program reduced the incidence of HIV by 3.4%, hepatitis C by 3.3%, overdose deaths by 10%, and the incarcerated population by 6.3%, translating to a savings of US$25,000 per quality-adjusted life year.[41]

Drug Treatment Courts

Drug treatment courts (also called "recovery courts" or "drug courts") are based on the theory that individuals who commit crimes often have underlying pathologies, such as an opioid addiction, that predispose them to engage in criminal behavior. Therefore, to reduce the criminal activity associated with opioid use, the underlying addiction needs to be addressed. When an individual is arrested for criminal activity, he or she is screened for underlying substance use and other psychological issues. If a substance use disorder is present, then the individual may be referred to a drug treatment court in lieu of incarceration. The typical drug treatment court includes a combination of substance use treatment with oversight from case management, frequent drug and alcohol screening, and weekly hearings with judicial supervision.[42] If the treatment program is successfully completed, the underlying criminal offenses are usually expunged from the person's record.

By interlinking the criminal justice system with substance use disorder treatment, the hope is to decrease drug use and recidivism while increasing rates of treatment participation and sustained sobriety. Research from the National Institute of Justice found that, when compared to their peers, court participants were much less likely to resume drug use. In addition, drug treatment courts significantly reduced the rates of crime and incarceration.[43] Because of the positive outcomes associated with this intervention, the European Monitoring Centre for Drugs and Drug Addiction has given drug courts the rating of "likely to be beneficial" and is supported by the United Nations Office on Drugs and Crime.[44, 45] There are over 3,000 drug courts currently in operation in the United States, and they can also be found in many countries in Europe and South America, as well as in Canada and Australia.

---

[40] Jesseman and Payer (2018).   [41] Bernard et al. (2020).
[42] Cropsey and Schiavon (2019).   [43] Rossman et al. (2011).
[44] European Monitoring Centre for Drugs and Drug Addiction (n.d.).
[45] United Nations Office on Drugs and Crime (2006).

References and Further Reading

Bernard CL, Rao IJ, Robison KK, Brandeau ML, (2020). Health outcomes and cost-effectiveness of diversion programs for low-level drug offenders: a model-based analysis. *PLoS Medicine* 17(10): e1003239.

Bond AJ, Witton J (2017). Perspectives on the pharmacologic treatment of heroin addiction. *Clinical Medicine Insights: Psychiatry* 8: 1–10.

Canadian Centre on Substance Use and Addiction (2021). Evidence-based decriminalization (policy brief). www.ccsa.ca/evidence-based-decriminalization-policy-brief.

Centers for Disease Control and Prevention (2019). Summary of information on the safety and effectiveness of syringe services programs (SSPs). www.cdc.gov/ssp/syringe-services-programs-summary.html.

Cropsey KL, Schiavon SP (2019). Criminal justice system and addiction treatment. In Johnson B (ed.) *Addiction Medicine: Science and Practice*, 2nd ed. Elsevier, pp. 628–637.

Dole VP, Nyswander M (1965). A medical treatment for diacetylmorphine (heroin) addiction. *JAMA* 193(8): 80–84.

European Monitoring Centre for Drugs and Drug Addiction (2020) Take home naloxone, factsheet. www.emcdda.europa.eu/publications/topic-overviews/take-home-naloxone_en.

European Monitoring Centre for Drugs and Drug Addiction (n.d.). Drug court programmes to reduce recidivism. www.emcdda.europa.eu/best-practice/evidence-summaries/drug-court-programmes-reduce-recidivism_en.

Goldman JE, Waye KM, Periera KA, et al. (2019). Perspectives on rapid fentanyl testing strips as a harm reduction practice among young adults who use drugs: a qualitative study. *Harm Reduction Journal* 16: 3.

Gugala E, Briggs O, Moczygemba LR, Brown CM, Hill LG (2022). Opioid harm reduction: A scoping review of physician and system-level gaps in knowledge, education, and practice. *Substance Abuse* 43(1): 972–987.

Harm Reduction International (2018). Regional overview of the Middle East and North Africa. www.hri.global/files/2018/12/10/MiddleEastNorthAfrica-harm-reduction.pdf.

Indiana State Department of Health (n.d.). Naloxone myths debunked. www.in.gov/health/overdose-prevention/files/47_naloxone-myths-debunked.pdf.

Jaffe JH (2007). Can LAAM, like Lazarus, come back from the dead? *Addiction* 102: 1342–1343.

Jesseman R, Payer D (2018). Decriminalization: Options and evidence. Canadian Centre on Substance Use and Addiction Policy Brief. 6/2018. www.ccsa.ca/sites/

default/files/2019-04/CCSA-Decriminalization-Controlled-Substances-Policy-Brief-2018-en.pdf.

Klaman SL, Isaacs K, Leopold A, et al. (2019). Treatment women who are pregnant and parenting for opioid use disorder and the concurrent care of infants and children: Literature review to support national guidance. *Journal of Addiction Medicine* 11(3): 178–190.

Kounang N (2021). This strip of paper can help prevent a drug overdose. *CNN Health*, December 1. http://edition.cnn.com/2021/12/01/health/fentanyl-test-strip/index.html.

Levengood TW, Yoon GH, Davoust MJ, et al. (2021). Supervised injection facilities as harm reduction: A systematic review. *American Journal of Preventive Medicine* 61 (5): 738–749.

Lofwall MR, Walsh SL (2014). A review of buprenorphine diversion and misuse: The current evidence base and experiences from around the world. *Journal of Addiction Medicine* 8(5): 315–326.

Macpherson D (2001). Framework for action: A four-pillar approach to drug problems in Vancouver. www.researchgate.net/publication/242480594_A_Four-Pillar_Approach_to_Drug_Problems_in_Vancouver.

Mielau J, Vogel M, Gutwinski S, Mick I (2021). New approaches in drug dependence: Opioids. *Current Addiction Reports* 8(2): 298–305.

Miller A (2022). As overdoses soar, more states decriminalize fentanyl testing strips. https://khn.org/news/article/states-decriminalize-fentanyl-testing-strips/.

Moaleff S, Choi J, Milloy MJ, et al. (2021). A drug-related Good Samaritan law and calling emergency services for drug overdoses in a Canadian setting. *Harm Reduction Journal* 18: 91.

Moosavyzadeh A, Mokri A, Ghaffari F, et al. (2020). Hab-o Shefa, a Persian medicine compound for maintenance treatment of opioid dependence: Randomized placebo-controlled clinical trial. *Journal of Alternative and Complementary Medicine* 26(5): 376–383.

National Institute on Drug Abuse (2017). Naloxone for opioid overdose: Life-saving science. https://nida.nih.gov/publications/naloxone-opioid-overdose-life-saving-science.

Noroozi A, Kebriaeezadeh A, Mirrahimi B, et al. (2021). Opium tincture-assisted treatment for opioid use disorder: A systematic review. *Journal of Substance Abuse* 129: 108519.

Rosenstein RJ (2018). Fight drug abuse, don't subsidize it. *New York Times*, August 27. www.nytimes.com/2018/08/27/opinion/opioids-heroin-injection-sites.html.

Rossman SB, Rempel M, Zweig JM, Rempel M , Lindquist CH (2011). *The Multi-Site Adult Drug Court Evaluation: The Impact of Drug Courts*, volume 4. Washington, DC: National Institute of Justice.

Sander G, Shirley-Beavan S. Stone K (2019). The global state of harm reduction in prisons. *Journal of Correctional Health Care* 25(2): 105–120.

Scott CK, Dennis ML, Grella CE, Mischel AF, Carnevale J (2021). The impact of the opioid crisis on U.S. state prison systems. *Health and Justice* 9: 17.

Shulman M, Wai JM, Nunes EV (2019). Buprenorphine treatment for opioid use disorder: An overview. *CNS Drugs* 33(6): 567–580.

Sofuoglu M, DeVito EE, Carroll KM (2019). Pharmacologic and behavioral treatment of opioid use disorder. *Psychiatric Research and Clinical Practice* 1(1): 4–15.

Substance Abuse and Mental Health Services Administration (2021). *Medications for Opioid Use Disorder.* Treatment Improvement Protocol (TIP) Series 63 Publication No. PEP21-02–01–002. Rockville, MD: Substance Abuse and Mental Health Services Administration.

Surratt HL, Otachi JK, Williams T, et al. (2020). Motivation to change and treatment participation among syringe service program utilizers in rural Kentucky. *Journal of Rural Health* 36(2): 224–233. doi:10.1111/jrh.12388.

United Nations Office on Drugs and Crime (2006). Drug treatment courts work! www.unodc.org/pdf/drug_treatment_courts_flyer.pdf.

PART IV
Recovery

13 STOPPING THE CYCLE OF RELAPSE

What Is Relapse?

Relapse prevention is a significant part of addiction treatment, but what exactly is relapse? The definition primarily depends on what is considered a success or failure regarding an addictive behavior. According to the Alcohol and Drug Foundation, "A relapse happens when a person stops maintaining their goal of reducing or avoiding use of alcohol or other drugs and returns to their previous levels of use."[1] Many addiction specialists describe "relapse" on a continuum of behaviors, which begins when someone previously in recovery starts to rationalize their return to drug use, long before actually "picking up" their drug of choice, and ends when the individual returns to active substance use. For many, the terms "slips" or "lapses" refer to a short period of substance misuse, not associated with the potentially devastating consequences of a full-blown relapse, but indicative of a continuing problem that needs to be addressed. Some addictionologists describe relapse as the change in behaviors or thought patterns that allow for rationalization of future substance misuse but do not actually involve use. Although the term "relapse" is frequently associated with substance misuse in the common vernacular, it is actually a common medical term, which describes a phenomenon associated with many other medical conditions or treatments including cancer, diabetes, or even attempts to adhere to a healthy diet. Sadly, too often when people hear that an individual with substance use disorder has "relapsed" the initial thought is that the individual has failed, while when someone with cancer has "relapsed" the initial thought is that the treatment has failed. The treatment of the disease of addiction, like the treatment for many other chronic, relapsing diseases, involves successes and failures, but for diseases of the brain our understanding must be more nuanced. In our minds it is often easier to define diseases such as cancer, heart disease, hypertension or diabetes in terms of success or failure, based on outcomes and

[1] https://adf.org.au/reducing-risk/relapse.

empirical data; but why we have such a difficult time defining success with addiction treatment may be at the core of our societal biases toward behaviors which we see as based on choices and not in response to impulses beyond the individual's control. It is in this context that we examine the phenomenon of "relapse" as it relates to substance use disorder.

Why Do People Relapse?

Opioid use disorder is a chronic illness, and therefore life-long treatment is typically required even after someone discontinues their use of opioids. If the individual wishes to maintain sobriety, they must learn how to manage cravings,[2] avoid triggers[3] associated with their drug use, and address the psychological, environmental, and social factors that have contributed to their opioid addiction. This is certainly not an easy task, and relapse is "par for the course". In fact, one frequently cited study found that 91% of patients relapsed after completing an inpatient detoxification program, with 59% returning to opioid use within a week.[4] Another study found that among Americans who reported the resolution of a substance use problem, the average number of attempts required to achieve sobriety was 5.35, with a range of 1 to over 100 attempts, although most surveyed individuals required one or two attempts.[5]

We are only beginning to elucidate the factors that influence an individual's risk for relapse, as these multifactorial external and internal influences often include many more variables than are involved with the medical diseases mentioned earlier. Clinical trials have demonstrated that treatment with medications for opioid use disorder (MOUD) significantly reduces the risk of relapse, regardless of these variables, although some people relapse even while receiving MOUD, and yet others are able to successfully abstain from opioid use even without medication treatment. When researchers Dr. Robin Clark, Dr. Jeffrey Baxter, and others studied a group of Americans with opioid use disorder who were receiving the governmental insurance Medicaid, they published some interesting findings.[6] According to their study, those receiving MOUD were less than one-half as likely to relapse when compared to individuals receiving other treatments, suggesting that MOUD is an effective treatment for opioid use disorder, at least when effectiveness is defined as the

---

[2] An overwhelmingly strong desire or need to use a drug, a central component of opioid use disorder and other substance misuse disorders.
[3] Persons, places, or things including smells or tactile sensations that encourage the individual to return to substance misuse.
[4] Smyth et al. (2010).   [5] Kelly et al. (2019).   [6] Clark et al. (2015).

prevention of relapse. Regarding co-occurring non-opioid substance misuse, individuals with alcohol misuse or alcohol use disorder relapsed at four times the rate of those without a history of alcohol misuse, and addiction to other non-alcohol substances doubled the rate of relapse. This suggests that the risk for relapse for individuals with opioid use disorder, even if participating in an effective recovery program which includes MOUD, is increased when the individual has a history of polysubstance misuse. The misuse of other psychoactive substances increases the chances for relapse even when in treatment for opioid use disorder. On the other hand, each year of treatment received, even for patients in high-risk populations such as this, significantly decreased the rate of relapse by up to 30%. When individuals with previous treatment were examined separately, it appears that their prior treatment experience did not impact their relapse rate to a significant degree, but this suggests that those with multiple prior attempts at maintaining sobriety were more likely to have a longer history of disease.

Mental illness also plays a role in relapse. Carrying a psychiatric diagnosis of schizophrenia, bipolar disorder, or other psychoses was shown to increase the likelihood that an individual in treatment for opioid use disorder would relapse by almost 80%. It is unclear to what extent untreated, undiagnosed, or co-existing mental illness complicates the treatment of opioid use disorder; however, it is clear that many individuals with mental illness unrelated to substance misuse commonly use psychoactive substances, either as a form of self-treatment or convenience, and that this co-existing misuse contributes to the increased risk for relapse. Recognizing this, many institutions have established so-called "mentally ill and chemically addicted" (MICA) or "dual-diagnosis" units for the treatment of patients with both substance use disorders and psychiatric illnesses, addressing the treatment challenges unique to this population.

Even though relapse is common for those struggling with opioid misuse, it can still be quite discouraging for any number of reasons. For instance, it is a common misconception that relapse is equivalent to failure, and not infrequently the expectation of how one's recovery will unfold does not match with reality. The discouragement and shame that individuals might feel after relapse can also be amplified with a type of cognitive distortion known as "all-or-nothing" or "black-or-white" thinking. Engaging in this type of thought process leads individuals to evaluate things or situations in extreme terms without any middle ground. To illustrate, let's consider a common practice found in 12-step groups such as Narcotics Anonymous. At the beginning of each meeting, a token (such as a coin or key chain) is given to members who achieve a sobriety for a specific length of time, whether that be days, months, or years. However, when relapse occurs, the sobriety clock restarts at day 0, subtly suggesting that any prior treatments and introspective analyses have been for naught. This is not to suggest that 12-step groups are harmful, but for some who utilize "all-or-nothing" thinking, the discouragement they experience can be so severe that some may assume recovery is unachievable and stop trying.

In order to avoid such cognitive distortions, we would argue that normalization of relapse is an important part of opioid misuse treatment and should be included with relapse prevention and recovery education and planning. As DiClemente and others remark, "Relapse ... is not so much a failure as an opportunity to learn what went wrong and what was missing in the unsuccessful process of change."[7]

How Does Relapse Happen?

Prior to the twentieth century, addiction was viewed as a moral failing that could be overcome with sheer willpower and a strengthened sense of morality. However, with the acceptance of the disease model of addiction, the stigma associated with addiction began to be reduced and efforts were refocused on promoting more effective and compassionate treatments. As the term "addiction" slowly changed from its prior classification as a moral failing to one as a disease of the brain, efforts to understand and prevent relapse became more common. The concept of relapse prevention developed over the course of the twentieth century, and in 1985 the Relapse Prevention (RP) model by G. A. Marlatt and J. Gordon was developed.[8]

The tenet of the RP model is that relapse is not a sudden event but rather a gradual process occurring over weeks to months. Marlatt and Gordon noted that the predictable sequence of events leading to substance misuse was often triggered by a "high-risk situation," such as a divorce, sudden illness, loss of employment, or other traumatic event. In reality though, multiple factors impact the likelihood of relapse, and the RP model has been updated to include the consideration of factors such as genetics, familial influences, drug metabolism, and personality. The RP model postulates that, for an individual to maintain abstinence, they must develop a degree of self-efficacy, which is the ability to control one's behaviors. However, when the individual encounters a high-risk situation combined with other risk factors, this sense of self-control can be lost, ultimately endangering the person's sobriety.

[7] DiClemente et al. (2010), p. 554.   [8] Larimer et al. (1999).

Marlatt and Gordon also described a version of all-or-nothing thinking, to which they assigned the term: "abstinence violation effect." In this model, those who attribute a relapse to a personal failure or lack of willpower are more likely to continue misusing substances primarily to avoid feelings of guilt. In addition, those who subscribe to this all-or-nothing thinking may decide to give up on sobriety entirely, as their recovery trajectory no longer fits within the established paradigm. On the other hand, those who view their relapse as a learning opportunity may be more likely to subsequently develop better coping skills for dealing with stressful situations and unexpected challenges and be more likely to avoid relapse in the future.

Although the RP model was a significant step toward understanding relapse, its use of technical jargon can cause confusion for many of us. In response, psychiatrist Dr. Melemis describes relapse as an evolving process over three sequential stages: *emotional relapse*, followed by *mental relapse*, and finally *physical relapse*.[9] To understand this process in more detail, let's consider an example. Dawn, a 38-year-old female, has struggled with an opioid use disorder for many years. She began using opioids after she was prescribed prescription painkillers for whiplash after a motor vehicle accident. These painkillers not only relieved the pain from her injury, they also gave Dawn an unexpected burst of energy, eliminated her social anxieties, and reduced her feelings of depression. Even though her pain subsided, Dawn's physician continued to prescribe these pain medications without question for years. However, when she moved to another town, she couldn't find a provider who was willing to continue her prescriptions since she no longer had pain from that injury, which happened over 10 years ago. Soon after taking her last pill, the withdrawal began with symptoms of anxiety, nausea, tremor, insomnia, and intense cravings. She found these symptoms so intolerable that, unable to continue to get these medications legitimately, she sought out an alternative source. A local drug dealer couldn't supply her with the opioid pills she had become dependent on but could provide heroin, which she soon discovered was cheaper and much more effective. Her heroin use progressed rapidly, from snorting heroin two or three times daily to injecting it intravenously multiple times a day. After an accidental overdose she realized she needed to get help for her addiction and, with encouragement from her family, she made the difficult decision to enter treatment. Dawn successfully completed a residential treatment program and was discharged with a personalized relapse prevention plan, designed to help her remain sober. She established a relationship with an addiction psychiatrist and a therapist in

---

[9] Melemis (2015).

her town and became an active member of Narcotics Anonymous, always attending two or more meetings a week.

Dawn followed all of the plans that her treatment team had given her and was, by all accounts, doing well. That is, until her husband, Brian, filed for divorce. Dawn felt ashamed that she was unable to keep the marriage together, especially since her mother was always pestering her about having children. She also didn't feel comfortable speaking to her friends since many of them were friends with Brian before they met her. Rather than talk about the divorce, she started avoiding situations in which her husband might be mentioned. Soon, Dawn started skipping her Narcotics Anonymous meetings as well. Her sponsor was concerned about how Dawn was isolating herself, but Dawn began to make excuses, telling her that she was just too busy with work while promising that she was secure in her recovery.

Based on Dr. Melemis' relapse model, Dawn is exemplifying the *emotional relapse* stage. During this stage, people such as Dawn are not explicitly thinking about substance use and so it is very difficult for people in this situation to recognize warning signs themselves, though their move away from recovery-related activities may elicit concern from others, such as Dawn's sponsor. Since Dawn is unable to recognize her own personal behavioral red flags, it is only natural for her to deny that anything is wrong, and often during this stage concern expressed by others may be met with accusations of "hovering" and "judgment." The hallmark feature of the emotional relapse stage is a lack or absence of *self-care*. As Melemis states, "The common denominator of emotional relapse is poor self-care, [including] emotional, psychological, and physical care." In Dawn's case, an example of emotional self-care might be spending time with supportive friends and family and setting appropriate boundaries between herself and people who are not supportive of her choice to remain in recovery. Psychological self-care for Dawn might be meditation, therapy, or any activities that promote an internal sense of well-being, and physical self-care would include maintaining adequate sleep, a healthy diet, and exercise as appropriate to her physical condition.

Needless to say, Dawn was not taking good care of herself. Over the coming weeks, all the while ruminating about her failed marriage, Dawn began feeling more and more depressed. She found that completing even the simplest of tasks required more energy than she could muster. She failed to show up for the last appointment with her psychiatrist and was now without a prescription for her antidepressant. Dawn recognized she was not following the relapse prevention plan that she had created while in residential treatment, but even so, she felt ashamed about her noncompliance. As this shame festered inside of her, she started daydreaming about her past. She remembered how opioids had given her energy throughout the day and erased much of the sadness she felt after fighting with her husband. In fact, when she was taking opioids, she could easily sleep a full eight hours a night. Dawn began to idealize her past opioid use, remembering it in a positive light while minimizing the consequences of her past experience with opioid addiction. With the negative consequences a distant memory she devised a plan to use again. Dawn had rationalized opioid use within her mind to the point that she had convinced herself that she was "cured" of her addiction and would be able to control her opioid use "like a normal person." She thought to herself, "I'm not going back to heroin – that's for junkies. I'm going to get a legitimate prescription from a doctor. I'll have no problems following the instructions on the prescription bottle, and once the divorce has been finalized, I will just stop taking the pills. It is as simple as that. I just need these to get through the next several months." She began reading reviews on the internet of various local providers, hoping to find one who would give her a prescription for opioids without much effort on her part.

Dawn has entered the *mental relapse* stage. The lack of self-care typically leads to significant levels of mental exhaustion, which in turn lessens someone's ability to effectively cope with stressful situations and resist cravings for opioids. At the same time, any way to escape this mental exhaustion (like substance use) becomes more attractive. As mentioned above, Dawn is not only thinking about opioid use, but she is glamorizing any positive effects while downplaying potential consequences. She justifies her need for opioids and creates rules for using opioids so that she has a sense of control. In addition, she is actively looking for ways to relapse, which in this case is finding a physician who can provide the prescription she wants.

Dawn eventually succeeded in finding a provider who was willing to prescribe opioids to her. She stopped at the pharmacy on her way home and took her first pill before leaving the pharmacy parking lot.

This is the *physical relapse* stage, which is when someone resumes the use of substances like opioids. Dr. Melemis refers to the physical relapse stage as "relapses of opportunity," meaning individuals typically relapse when they don't think they will get caught. As an individual progresses toward physical relapse, it becomes increasingly more difficult to stop the process. It would have been near impossible for Dawn not to relapse once she received the prescription for opioids. However, if warning signs were recognized much earlier, she may not have progressed down this path. The most effective way of preventing someone from entering the stage of physical relapse is to intervene before that even becomes a possibility, but that requires maintaining a strong support network capable of detecting a change in behavior before those changes result in active use.

What Influences the Likelihood of Relapse?

Understanding the relapse process and its warning signs are important, but what makes someone more or less likely to relapse? In order to answer this question, we need to consider the circumstances surrounding those who have been able to successfully avoid relapse after treatment and also the circumstances that surround those who have not. The desire to discover the factors that push some people toward relapse behaviors and the factors that pull others away from relapse has spawned a significant amount of scientific inquiry. After years of research, the majority of investigators have divided these influential factors into two separate camps: intrapersonal factors (that occur within oneself) and interpersonal factors (that occur between others).

Intrapersonal Factors

Motivation to actualize change, an ability to cope with stressful situations, and having confidence in one's ability to achieve sobriety (referred to as self-efficacy) are key characteristics for successful abstinence. Most are familiar with the phrase "You can lead a horse to water, but you can't make him drink" and, in the context of sobriety, that translates into "While you can provide encouragement and resources to someone with an opioid use disorder, you can't force him or her to fully engage in treatment unless they have made the decision to change for themselves." The inability to recognize that there is a problem that requires solving precludes the ability to take steps toward sobriety, and without this insight, relapse prevention becomes exceedingly difficult. Dr. DiClemente uses a five-stage motivation model to describe how a change in behavior occurs and this model rings true for many in sobriety. Dr. DiClemente's model is based on the assumption that, for an individual to successfully become abstinent from substances for an extended period of time, they must be guided through these stages with help from treatment professionals, but the stages apply to anyone attempting to recover from opioid use disorder. Anyone personally attempting to recover from opioid use disorder or anyone with a friend, family member, or partner who is doing the same can potentially recognize these stages and encourage their significant other to self-motivate and enlist the help of trained professionals

For those with an opioid use disorder, opioids become a primary strategy for dealing with stressful experiences. If someone hasn't developed alternative coping strategies when a crisis occurs, they are more likely to resort to substance use instead. Examples of coping strategies include positive self-talk, avoidance of risky situations, contacting a trusted support person, or mindfulness-based exercises (which is discussed later in this chapter). In structured recovery programs, these types of coping strategies are frequently taught and persons in these programs are encouraged to employ them when cravings occur.

Those who effectively employ alternative coping strategies begin to develop heightened levels of self-efficacy, or feelings of competence and confidence in oneself to be successful in the future. As self-efficacy increases so too does the likelihood of avoiding relapse. On the other hand, those who relapse may doubt their abilities, leading to a weaker sense of self-efficacy. The presence of negative emotional states of negative emotional states also increases the likeihood increases the likelihood of relapse. Loneliness, boredom, and fatigue are well-documented triggers for relapse. These feelings are separate from clinical depression and any other diagnosable mental illnesses that frequently coexist with opioid use disorder (and also increase the risk for relapse), and they are specific to both acute and chronic withdrawal syndromes. To avoid relapse in recovery from opioid use disorder, it is essential to employ appropriate strategies to avoid triggers to relapse, mitigate the consequences when a trigger is experienced, and recognize when a change to the recovery plan needs to occur.

Interpersonal Factors

An essential component of maintaining recovery and avoiding relapse is the establishment of external support systems. For many people, prior to the cessation of active opioid use, the presence of people who supported their continued use of opioids, either directly, perhaps by shared use experiences, or indirectly, by enabling their continued use, allowed them to normalize this behavior. In recovery, the presence of persons who support not using opioids can help to normalize recovery and support attempts to avoid relapse. Humans are social creatures and it is natural to follow the direction of others in an attempt to fit in and feel comfortable. If the others that surround the individual attempting to avoid relapse are supportive of this goal, that makes relapse much less likely to occur. For many people in recovery, having friends without a substance use disorder significantly increases one's success for sobriety through shared experiences and common goals, which is one of many reasons why mutual support groups can be so beneficial.

While the choice to associate with individuals either supportive or unsupportive of recovery can help or hinder attempts to avoid relapse, making these choices can be difficult when it comes to family. The relationships that bind family members together, either through blood or partnership, often have the potential to more significantly impact an individual's recovery, for better or worse. Certain family dynamics can significantly increase someone's potential to relapse into opioid use, especially if a significant other is also using opioids and does not support this change in behavior. Even if a family member does not themselves use opioids and supports the persons recovery, they may not fully understand what someone goes through when they are withdrawing from opioids, the process of recovery, the risk for relapse, or even how to differentiate the behaviors that are normal and expected during this time from the behaviors that suggest an increased risk for relapse. This is one of the many reasons why mutual support groups for family and friends of those going through recovery should be considered for those who are part of the extended social support group for anyone in recovery, especially if they do not have any personal experience or knowledge surrounding the issue.[10, 11]

How Can We Prevent Relapse?

For a relapse prevention strategy to be effective, it needs to be focused on the intrapersonal and interpersonal characteristics that we discussed above, which have been associated with maintaining long-term sobriety. Multiple relapse prevention strategies are usually employed together, as each individual case is as unique as the circumstances that surround the person in recovery. A single strategy is unlikely to be effective for all individuals or in all situations. Drs. Douaihy, Daley, Marlatt, and Donovan have outlined 10 key strategies to help reduce the risk of lapse and relapse, which apply broadly to a number of circumstances and can be applied to the majority of individuals in recovery:[12]

Strategy 1: Understand the relapse process and learn to identify warning signs. The
   first strategy involves an in-depth review of the person's relapse history
   (Have they attempted recovery before? If so, what worked and what didn't?),
   education about the relapse process (such as the one penned by
   Dr. Melemis), and identifying the warning signs associated with an
   impending relapse, as these signs are often specific to the individual and can
   more effectively be used to identify relapse-specific behaviors sooner rather
   than later.

Strategy 2: Identify high-risk situations and develop effective coping strategies. The
   goal of this strategy is to identify situations in which the person feels vulnerable for substance use and find effective methods to cope with these
   situations.

*Strategy 3: Enhance communication skills and interpersonal relationships, and
   develop a recovery social network.* Positive family and social relationships
   promote long-term recovery, and so work must be done to identify who
   these people are (if they already exist) or where they might be found (if

---

[10] DiClemente et al. (2010).   [11] Menon and Kandasamy (2018).
[12] Douaihy et al. (2014).

social support is currently lacking). Peer support groups encourage the repair of strained relationships while also providing a source of social support.

Strategy 4: Identify, reduce, and manage negative emotional states. Negative emotional states, such as depression, anxiety, hunger, loneliness, and fatigue, all contribute to an increased chance for relapse. Approaches to manage feelings such as these depend on the individual but could include psychiatric care for depression or self-care strategies to combat fatigue.

Strategy 5: Identify and manage cravings. The goal of this strategy is to reduce the likelihood that a craving for a substance will lead to actual substance use. Cue exposure treatment involves the identification of someone's drug triggers and repeatedly shows these triggers so that the individual can develop ways to effectively limit the intensity and frequency of cravings. Mindfulness-based relapse prevention uses meditation practices as a response to cravings.

Strategy 6: Identify and manage cognitive distortions. This strategy usually involves identification of maladaptive thinking patterns (such as all-or-nothing thinking, catastrophizing, or overgeneralization), and then develop ways to counteract the thoughts when they occur.

Strategy 7: Work toward a balanced lifestyle. Encourage self-care and a healthy lifestyle through diet, exercise, and hobbies.

Strategy 8: Consider the addition of medications. MOUD are a highly effective treatment and reduce the risk of relapse. Further discussion about MOUD can be found in Chapter 12.

Strategy 9: Improve the transition between higher and lower levels of care. If someone fails to continue with treatment after completing inpatient or residential care, the risk for relapse increases. By enhancing someone's desire to continue treatment after discharge, they are more likely to adhere to recommendations and maintain their sobriety.

Strategy 10: Improve adherence to medications and treatment. People who remain in treatment are more successful than those who drop out. Various strategies have been employed effectively to keep people engaged in treatment.

Creating a Relapse Prevention Plan

Most relapse prevention plans address several core topics. First, the individual completing the plan is instructed to evaluate his or her history with drug use, previous recovery attempts, and the details surrounding any prior relapses. Second, the person will then create a list of relapse warning signs and triggers.

In addition, ideas for coping strategies, types of self-care, and plans for ongoing treatment will be written down. Lastly, an action plan is developed should the individual find themselves heading toward relapse.

To witness a relapse prevention plan in action, we can revisit Dawn's story. Several years after her relapse, Dawn returned to residential treatment for opioid use disorder. As her discharge date approached, Dawn began meeting with her counselor to develop a relapse prevention plan. To assist her in the process, her therapist gave her a workbook[13] to complete prior to their next meeting. The workbook guided Dawn through a series of questions with the intent to increase Dawn's awareness of her triggers and relapse warning signs. She was asked to make a "pros and cons" list for her drug use, including how her addiction impacted her family and friends. She identified people she could reach out to for support, coping strategies that could be used in stressful situations, and ways she could practice self-care. The workbook also discussed common cognitive distortions, such as all-or-nothing thinking, and ways to combat those thoughts. Reviewing her completed work, she began to feel more confident in her ability to remain sober. She also met with the facility psychiatrist and was started on buprenorphine for her opioid use disorder. Altogether, Dawn felt motivated to continue treatment after discharge and was referred to an outpatient treatment program. Now three years sober, Dawn's relapse recovery plan has helped her manage cravings and appropriately deal with stress, all without resorting to the use of opioids.

References and Further Reading

Clark RE, Baxter JD, Aweh G, et al. (2015). Risk factors for relapse and higher costs among Medicaid members with opioid dependence or abuse: Opioid agonists, comorbidities, and treatment history. *Journal of Substance Abuse Treatment* 57: 75–80.

DiClemente CC, Holmgren MA, Rounsaville D (2010). Relapse prevention and recycling in addiction. In Johnson B (ed.) *Addiction Medicine*. Springer, New York, NY.

Douaihy A, Daley D, Marlatt A, Donovan DM (2014). Relapse prevention: Clinical models and intervention strategies. In Ries, RK, Fiellin DA, Miller SC, Saitz R (eds.) *The ASAM Principles of Addiction Medicine*, 5th ed. Philadelphia, PA: Wolters Kluwer, pp. 553–565.

---

[13] The *MISSION Consumer Workbook* is an excellent example of a relapse prevention workbook; Smelson et al. (n.d).

Kakko J, Alho H, Baldacchino A, et al. (2019). Craving in opioid use disorder: From neurobiology to clinical practice. *Frontiers in Psychiatry* 30(10): 592.

Kelly JF, Greene MG, Bergman BG, White WL Hoeppner BB (2019). How many recovery attempts does it take to successfully resolve an alcohol or drug problem? Estimates and correlates from a national study of recovering U.S. adults. *Alcohol Clinical and Experimental Research* 43(7): 1533–1544.

Larimer ME, Palmer RS, Marlatt GA (1999). Relapse prevention: An overview of Marlatt's cognitive–behavioral model. *Alcohol Research and Health* 23(2): 151–160.

Melemis SM (2015). Relapse prevention and the five rules of recovery. *Yale Journal of Biology and Medicine* 88: 325–32.

Menon J, Kandasamy A (2018). Relapse prevention. *Indian Journal of Psychiatry* 60 (Suppl 4): S473–8.

Smelson DA, Kline A, Marzilli A, Tripp J (n.d.). The MISSION Consumer Workbook. www.umassmed.edu/contentassets/58c9d438c9ef4f7f8a4a44e9452d471a/mission-consumer-workbook.pdf.

Smyth BP, Barry J, Keenan E, Ducray K (2010). Lapse and relapse following inpatient treatment of opiate dependence. *Irish Medical Journal* 103(6): 176–179.

14 RETHINKING ANTI-DRUG POLICIES AND CHANGING DRUG EDUCATION

Picture this: It's 1986 and you're living in Northern California (United States) during the height of the "crack" cocaine epidemic. Cocaine has always been around and you're familiar with the problems that come with excessive use. In fact, maybe as a suburbanite you've even tried it yourself, but this new "crack" cocaine seems to be an "inner-city" problem, far removed from you, that is until now. During the commercial break from your weekly comedy, drama, or sitcom you're asked to stay tuned for an exclusive report after the show.[1] The 10 o'clock news is broadcasting a special on the crack epidemic and KPIX (San Francisco, California) plays the following teaser: *a closeup shot of a police officer's gloved hand holding what appears to be some rocky white substance obtained during a raid. A dramatic voice identifies the substance as "crack." The video transitions to a woman in a jungle farm, "the harvest" explains the voice, then to a speedboat, "the journey" we are told, then to cash being counted out on the table, "the sale," and finally to an image of a young boy in the suburbs smoking crack through a glass pipe, "the addiction."* As the teaser unfolds you see a series of dramatic and choppy video images of people involved with the production, sale, and use of the drug. All the while the dramatic voice narrates: "From their jungle to our streets. Men. Women. Children. Where is it from? How does it get here? What is being done to stop it? Crack: Pipeline to the Bay Area. Tonight, at eleven, only on KPIX 5."

The United States' "War on Drugs" and Its Effect on Anti-Drug Policy

In the late 1960s, recreational drug use in the United States began to creep into the suburbs. As the children of White, middle-class Americans began to adopt this practice, two things happened. First, the social stigmatization previously associated with recreational drug use began to fade as it became associated with protest and social rebellion in the era's atmosphere of political unrest.

---

[1] KPIX television evening news teaser (www.youtube.com/watch?v=ZIdEBfrQIw0).

No longer was heroin seen as relegated to the seedy underbelly of society and something that suburban families need not worry about. Second, these children's parents began to demand that their government do something about it. In 1968, President Johnson formed the Bureau of Narcotics and Dangerous Drugs, basically a consolidation of several anti-drug agencies that already existed, purportedly intended to improve communication, and increase efficiency, in response to this public demand. Recreational drug use was hardly a new issue in the United States, and opioid misuse and addiction had been endemic for decades prior to these actions, but once again these concerns reached the parents, relatives, and friends of citizens with access to legislators. In 1969, psychiatrist Dr. Robert DuPont's study of inmates entering a jail system in Washington, DC found that 44% of these people tested positive for heroin.[2] With the link between opioid misuse and crime "scientifically" established, the race to protect the public from the scourge was on.

Based on the success of Dr. DuPont's work providing methadone to incarcerated peoples addicted to heroin (one year after the program was started, burglaries in Washington, DC decreased by 41%), in 1970 President Nixon provided funding for the Narcotics Treatment Administration, which increased access to methadone treatment beyond the prison system. This same year the United States Congress passed the Comprehensive Drug Abuse Prevention and Control Act, which consolidated all of the previous anti-drug laws and strengthened law enforcement by allowing police to conduct "no-knock" searches. Included in this act is the Controlled Substances Act (CSA), which established the five categories, or "schedules," for regulating drugs based on their medicinal value and potential for addiction. The CSA was intended to separate substances that had "legitimate" medicinal use from those that did not. Substances that were deemed to have "potential for addiction" were classified as "controlled substances" and subsequently ranked according to the degree of misuse potential. At the time, the United States was deeply entrenched in the Vietnam War, in a region where opium production, as we have discussed, was and remains today a cash crop. Politicians in the United States at the time expressed considerable concern about the growing heroin epidemic among their servicemen returning from the war. According to one report, 10–15% of the servicemen either residing in or returning from Vietnam were addicted to heroin, and President Nixon declared drug abuse to be "public enemy number one." On June 17, 1971, during a press conference, President Nixon announced the United States' "war on drugs" had begun. The President announced the creation of the Special Action Office for

[2] PBS Frontline (2000).

Drug Abuse Prevention, which was to be headed by a doctor with significant experience in using methadone as a treatment for opioid addiction, and initially it seemed the "war" would focus on treatment instead of law enforcement. Unfortunately, however, it wasn't long before the focus, and funding allocations, changed directions.

In 1972, President Nixon established the Office of Drug Abuse Law Enforcement (ODALE), which allowed for cooperation between federal and local law enforcement agencies. Task forces were created to fight the drug trade at the street level, changing the strategy from treatment of the end user (reducing demand) to eliminating access to illicit drugs (reducing supply). In 1973, the Drug Enforcement Administration (DEA) was established, consolidating agents from the Bureau of Narcotics and Dangerous Drugs, United States Customs and Border Protection (CBP), the Central Intelligence Agency, and ODALE. For the 50 years that followed, this consolidation of the United States DEA would be at the forefront of America's war on drugs as policy remained staunchly focused on enforcement, battling the supply side at the expense of funding efforts to reduce demand. In the early years of the war, some efforts were made to address the demand side of the equation. In 1975, President Ford, who became president when Nixon resigned, released the White Paper on Drug Abuse composed by the Domestic Council Drug Abuse Task Force, which urged that efforts be focused on both supply and demand reduction and recommended specifically that marijuana be classified as a low-priority drug as opposed to heroin. Jimmy Carter, who became president in 1976, actually campaigned on the decriminalization of marijuana and was in favor of relinquishing federal criminal penalties for possession of up to one ounce of marijuana, but in the late summer of 1976 the anti-drug "parents' movement" began. Spurred on by the new organization called "Families in Action," Dr. Robert DuPont, the head of the National Institute on Drug Abuse (NIDA), abandoned his support for decriminalization of marijuana.

By the end of the decade, governmental efforts in the United States had shifted significantly and appeared entirely focused on reducing supply. Efforts to reduce demand by treating the end users of illicit opioids had been relegated to the states, and without funding, floundered. In 1978, the Comprehensive Drug Abuse Prevention and Control Act was amended to allow law enforcement to seize all money and other things of value "furnished or intended to be furnished by any person in exchange for a controlled substance [and] all proceeds traceable to such an exchange." As a result, anyone associated with a "drug crime" would legally have to forfeit property, automobiles, and other assets to law enforcement. Many of these high-profile seizures made the evening news and police departments around the country routinely paraded seized vehicles in public as an example of what using or dealing drugs will cost.

By the beginning of the 1980s, the war on drugs had been raging for only a decade but had already been overseen by four presidents from both sides of the aisle. Democrats and Republicans alike bowed to pressure from concerned citizens' groups demanding action and, in 1982, President Ronald Regan formed the South Florida Drug Task Force, designed to address the increasing violence related to the drug trade in Miami. The cabinet-level task force, headed by Vice President George Bush, combined agents from the DEA, CBP, Federal Bureau of Investigation, Bureau of Alcohol, Tobacco, Firearms and Explosives and the Internal Revenue Service, with the United Stated Army and Navy to combat the trafficking of illicit drugs into the country. President Reagan subsequently authorized the creation of several other regional task forces in different areas of the country with similar problems related to drug trafficking. In an effort to address the demand side of the equation, First Lady Nancy Reagan began an anti-drug campaign targeted primarily at school age children. The "Just Say No" campaign became a centerpiece of the Reagan administration's anti-drug campaign, but was funded by corporate and private donations, while the government continued to fund law enforcement efforts. In October of 1986, however, President Reagan signed The Anti-Drug Abuse Act of 1986, appropriating US$1.7 billion to fight the drug crisis. The bill is heavily weighted to fund the demand side (US$97 million is allocated to build new prisons, US$200 million for drug education and US$241 million for treatment) but the creation of mandatory minimum penalties for drug offenses disproportionately affected minority communities and increased racial disparities in the prison population.

Refocusing Anti-Drug Policy on the Demand Side

The past 50 years have proven that an exercise focused on eliminating the supply of illicit drugs is an exercise in futility. Where there is money to be made, people will find a way to make it. The only effective way to fight the opioid epidemic is to focus on the demand side of the equation. Addiction is a chronic, relapsing disease that is often very difficult to treat. It is not something that can be cured, and sending an impaired individual to prison, or a traditional 28-day inpatient program, followed by discharge back to the same situation from whence they came, with little or no aftercare, does a disservice to the addict as well as to society. Often the costs of such a meager program cannot be covered by addicts in treatment and they are discharged prematurely, only to chronically relapse and require further treatment. Who ultimately pays the price for these failed treatments? Who pays directly for the costs associated with repeated relapse? Who pays the opportunity costs associated with the loss of a productive member of society? What about the costs of caring for this individual when he or she is not in treatment and unable to care for him or herself? What about the costs of treating the injuries, either self-inflicted or inflicted on others by the impaired individual? What about the cost of crime associated with addiction?

Society generally does not place the same value on the treatment of addictive disorders that it does on the treatment of other serious medical conditions such as diabetes, cancer, and heart disease. In the United States, even the very best insurance programs frequently cover only half of the costs of the initial addiction treatment and place unrealistic limits on the amount of aftercare available to patients.[3, 4] This is both shortsighted and wrong. If we expect the addict to recover, we have to treat the disease properly, and this takes both time and money.

It is a long and arduous road to recovery that many are unwilling or unable to take without significant support. It is expensive and inconvenient, and in today's climate of immediate gratification the period of time required for proper treatment can seem like a lifetime. Unfortunately for the addict who receives inadequate treatment, the cost can actually be a lifetime.

Establishing national standards for treatment and policies that ensure that any individual addicted to opioids will be referred to a program that has a proven record of successfully rehabilitating individuals with opioid use disorder will, in the long run, prove to be cost-effective and, as well, protect the public. Current models of successful treatment suggest that programs with longer inpatient stays followed by intensive outpatient treatment over the course of years are most effective. Programs for addicted healthcare professionals mandated by state medical societies have success rates twice that of what is available to the general public. Under the current system, access to inpatient programs for initial treatment is limited to those who can pay for the services. Under a more cohesive system based on national standards, patients diagnosed with opioid use disorder would be referred directly to a locally available national center of excellence, with the experience and funding to provide effective treatment in the proper environment for this population. While this may sound expensive, and yes it will be, we believe that the total cost of treatment will ultimately be less than continuing to fund a losing war against the supply side.

We propose changes to the construct of the existing treatment pedagogy, which is heavily weighted on initial treatment, and recommend a shift to extend

[3] Harrison and Asche (1999).   [4] Malivert et al. (2012).

the length of treatment. After successfully completing an initial inpatient program, an individual with opioid use disorder typically returns to his or her home with little or no follow-up care.[5] The use of extended treatment and monitoring programs, which involve regular urine or hair testing to confirm abstinence, have been shown to increase the chance for success in impaired professional programs[6][7] and should be available to the general public as well. It is important to recognize the necessity to develop a policy that protects all involved parties. An addicted individual presents a clear and present danger to themselves and possibly to society in general. We can no longer focus only on the individual and measure success or failure based solely on the results of one person's treatment. We are all in this together and by using a team approach to deal with the opioid epidemic, any member of the team has the potential to significantly increase our chances for success. It's not just the physician who is treating the addicted patient, it's also every single member of the patient's family, friends, and acquaintances who can make an impact, and in the end all of us will benefit from a comprehensive policy change that values addressing the demand side instead of the supply side.

By the summer of 2010, there was continued pressure being applied by lobbying groups representing many states' psychiatric associations to encourage the adaptation of legislation that removes the focus on past addiction and substance abuse in favor of addressing the issue of current addiction and misuse. What is in question is the issue of self-incrimination on applications for professional licenses and other governmental programs, for which a history of drug misuse may prevent the applicant from obtaining benefits. Since the phrasing of questions designed to elicit information regarding past or current use of illegal drugs is different from state to state, lobbyists proposed legislation to create a national standard and specifically determine what type of information must be reported in all applications for federal benefits. In response to this need for policy clarification, individuals in favor of greater regulation pointed to the many problems with the current polies in place, and advocated for change. Meanwhile, the anti-drug education campaigns begun in the 1970s continued to push forward.

The Partnership for a Drug-Free America

During the mid-1980s, a group of advertising professionals in New York City created a marketing campaign with a nonprofit trade association known as the American Association of Advertising Agencies, which was designed to

---

[5] Oudejans et al. (2012).   [6] Bryson (2012).   [7] DuPont et al. (2009a).

target teenage drug use. At the time, the country was in the throes of the crack cocaine epidemic, and dramatic stories such as the one highlighted above by KPIX in San Francisco commonly led the evening news. The country was concerned and highly motivated to reduce the perceived increase in drug use across the board, starting with the youngest members of the population. Officially formed in 1985, the Partnership for a Drug-Free America (formerly known as the PDFA, currently the Partnership to End Addiction) produced a staggering number of anti-drug public service announcements (PSAs), using television, radio, print, and now internet-based media segments to broadcast anti-drug sentiments over the past three decades. Designed to engage the viewer in the same way that commercial advertising does, these well-produced, and highly funded, campaigns were intended to sell the idea that drugs are bad for you. The Partnership was primarily known for their iconic "This is Your Brain on Drugs" campaign, in which the viewer is shown an egg (your brain), followed by a frying pan (the drugs), into which their "brain" is cracked and fried, and finally ending the commercial by asking "Any questions?" Bold, direct, and simple messages produced by the Partnership quickly became part of the cultural milieu, inevitably creating spoofs or what we would now call memes attempting to capitalize on their viral success. "This is your brain on ... " (replace 'drugs' with any sport, game, academic, or recreational activity) tee shirts became commonplace. If they had a "This is Your Brain on Comic Books" back in the 1980s, at least one of us might have worn it to school.

The "Marijuana Changes Nothing" campaign creatively capitalized on the popular notion at the time that regular marijuana use was associated with inactivity and failure to progress through the socially expected steps of becoming an adult. Targeted at adolescents and spurred, in part, by the 1980 NIDA report on marijuana use, which showed a "25 percent increase in the total of those between ages 12 and 17 who had ever used marijuana and a nearly 30 percent increase in the number of that age group who were currently using marijuana" over the five prior years,[8] the campaign subtly implied that "nothing" happens when you smoke marijuana. The video segment opens on a pair of friends, both guys in their early thirties hanging out at home during the middle of the day, watching television and sharing a (marijuana cigarette) joint.[9] As an anti-marijuana commercial comes on the television, in the background one of the guys gets aggravated: "I'm tired of hearing this, how marijuana can mess you up?" he says, "We've been smoking for fifteen years, and nothing happened to me. I didn't get into other drugs. I didn't start

---

[8] NIDA (1980).   [9] https://youtu.be/eNi9uzURP9I.

stealing, mugging people. It didn't make me do anything. In fact, I'd say I'm exactly the same as when I smoked my first joint." Suddenly from off screen we hear the guy's mother ask if he was going to look for a job today while the voice-over announcer explains that "Marijuana can make nothing happen to you too" over the text "Nothing happens with marijuana." "No, ma," he replies while the two open the window and wave away the marijuana smoke so his mom doesn't smell it. The message is clear, a play on the idea that marijuana is a safe drug with few, if any, negative implications, and nothing (good or bad) happens to people who use it.

Creative and compelling advertisements such as this attempted to pivot away from the traditional pedagogical methods of telling and instead used the visual medium of television to show what happens with chronic drug use; yet, despite this change in direction, drug use continued to increase. It wasn't long before advertisements for inpatient rehabilitation facilities began to appear alongside these anti-drug PSAs, promising a cure for alcohol, marijuana, and cocaine dependance. In a classic commercial from 1987, "Schick Hospitals" promises a cure in 10 short days with only two 2-day follow-up visits.[10] According to the actors in the commercial, with Schick "the week after next you'll be a sober man." While these claims may be questionable, their appearance on daytime television marked the growing cultural recognition that America did indeed have a drug problem. Sadly, this approach to drug education, especially when aimed at adolescents, may not have had the intended effect. "When you advertise against it, you may also be inadvertently advertising for it," says Michael Ludwig, professor of health education at Hofstra University.[11] We've all been teenagers and most of us remember how we certainly knew, back then, more than any of the generations who came before us ever did, and, while this type of advertising may have reinforced the beliefs of those who were not going to use drugs in the first place, they may actually have encouraged some of the curious to taste the forbidden fruit.

Drug Abuse Resistance Education

Maybe if we educate kids before they're teenagers, they'll actually listen to us? By the late 1960s, the United States was facing a wave of opioid addiction, misuse, and overdose deaths spurred on by what some believed was a misunderstanding of the implicit danger associated with using these drugs improperly. Groups like the Acid Rescue Squad in St. Louis, the Do It Now Foundation in San Francisco, and the Drug Information Center brought drug

---

[10] www.youtube.com/watch?v=Lo17RPvCtrM.   [11] Balonon-Rosen (2019).

education programs into elementary, middle, and high school classrooms as well as to college campuses across the United States. The idea behind this type of education was to provide people with factual information in order to lessen the potential for harm and not to pass judgment on any personal decisions the students would ultimately make. According to drug historian Emily Dufton, author of *Grass Roots: The Rise and Fall and Rise of Marijuana in America*,[12] parents became concerned that "kids weren't being told not to do drugs ... they were being taught how to do them,"[13] As a result, these programs, which in the late 1960s and early 1970s originally focused on education and facts, had by the 1980s changed to a primary abstinence-based educational model.

In order to get a clearer picture of what was going on at the time, the authors interviewed several people of varying ages, roles (parent, student, teacher) and regions, who were alive during the period from 1965 to 1985. Regional differences aside, many remember having some personal experience with either drugs or anti-drug education. "As a child born in 1970, I grew up in the Haight Ashbury (San Francisco, California), which, at the time, was going through the aftermath of the "Summer of Love."[14] Drugs were still everywhere." Said one respondent who requested to remain anonymous:

> *By the fall of 1981, even though I was only 11 years old, I understood this all too well. I had watched my parents and their friends use cocaine, the smell of marijuana smoke at home was deeply embedded into the living room sofa cushions and yes, I had attended a fifth-grade assembly the prior spring where a local police officer explained to us the dangers of drugs. I distinctly remember him urging us almost-middle-school age students to report to him any suspicious, and potentially drug-related, activity our parents might be up to. The problem with this approach, however, was that I didn't recognize this behavior as suspicious. It was, well, normal.*

Early school-based anti-drug educational programs frequently included such urging for students to report illegal drug use and, though not common, parents were occasionally turned in by their children. Almost 30 years later, students are still encouraged to inform officers regarding the use of drugs by their parents, and in 2010 an 11-year-old boy brought his parents marijuana cigarettes to school to give to the police.[15] While the child's parents were arrested,

---

[12] Dufton (2017).   [13] Dufton E (2014).
[14] This was a social phenomenon that happened in the summer of 1967, when up to 100,000 people, mostly young people of hippie dress and behavior, converged in San Francisco's Haight-Ashbury neighborhood.
[15] WBTV 3 (2010).

they were not jailed; however, their two children were removed from their home as a result of the drug charges.

This was just the beginning, and programs like this were popping up all over the United States. In 1983, Los Angeles (California) police chief Daryl Gates and Harry Handler, superintendent of the Los Angeles Unified School District, formed the most successful of these school outreach programs, the Drug Abuse Resistance Education (DARE) program. Designed to provide elementary school children with the skills necessary to resist peer pressure to experiment with drugs, and taught by actual police officers from the community, the DARE program promised to reduce the number of teenagers who would eventually go on to use drugs through a program of primary prevention. Unfortunately, according to Christopher Ingraham, there is little evidence that this program actually results in lower rates of teenage drug use and may actually, in some cases, increase use. In a *Washington Post* article published in July of 2017[16] Ingraham points out that, faced with dramatic funding cuts due to multiple studies that pointed to the program's ineffectiveness, the DARE program had to "change or die," and change is exactly what the program's leadership chose to do. The current mission of the group, which has pivoted away from "anti-drug-based" educational programs, is now working to "teach students good decision-making skills to help them lead safe and healthy lives," a focus which may or may not actually reduce drug use.

So, what actually works? How can drug education evolve into an engaging and effective platform, which accomplishes the intended goal of reducing the number of people who become addicted and overdose each year? Obviously, this is a complicated question, one without a simple answer. If the goal is primary prevention, that is to reach the younger members of our societies before they begin to use opioids, when it comes to advertising, we have to provide them with realistic and positive role models. We cannot use perfect and infallible superheroes, but rather imperfect and fallible characters who stumble and occasionally fall like each of us do, who reach out for and find help, and are able to eventually succeed. These are the characters we identify with, the heroes in the movies and on television and, in many cases, in our families and neighborhoods. A former high school teacher from New Jersey who was interviewed for this book said: "I do remember local police coming into the school to conduct the DARE program, but I was not convinced that they were always reaching the students." During the 1980s she was not only a teacher but also became a mother and, while she did not use recreational drugs herself, she suspected some of her colleagues and friends did, though not

---

[16] Ingraham (2017).

openly. When asked about what she felt would be a more effective way to educate young people about the potential dangers of substance misuse she had the following to say:

> *One of the most effective, memorable, and direct programs was the time a young man who was driving under the influence the night some of his friends were killed in an auto accident served his sentence by speaking to high school audiences about his experience. He spoke so well; I believe he made a lasting impression. He may have even saved some lives that day because the audience really listened to him. They actually heard what he had to say and related to him. As a teacher in the audience, I was deeply moved. Afterwards, I went back to my classroom and spoke with my students about the program. They related that he had given them a lot to think about. He reached them with his honesty and sincerity. He did not preach, he just related his experience, and his words hit home. I never forgot it.*

One early attempt at using a more positive message to discourage drug use was the weeklong "Get High on Yourself"[17] television special, which aired in the fall of 1981 and combined performances and appearances by over 50 sports and entertainment celebrities, musicians, and well-known popular culture icons, each urging teens not to use drugs. One respondent who was in sixth grade at the time remembers the programming well:

> *When this show came on and preempted my regularly scheduled programming. I was not at all pleased. I had no idea what it was about. The following day at school we all talked about it during recess. Of course, we had all seen it but most of us weren't sure what it was supposed to be about. One of my friends said, "I think it's for people who do drugs, like our parents," and then we all went back to what we normally did which, at the time anyway, was not doing drugs.*

Interestingly, the motivation for this massive weeklong public service announcement was Judge Vincent Broderick's admonition to Hollywood producer Robert Evans that he use his "unique talents where others have failed in this horrible thing of drug abuse by children." Evans was arrested and pleaded guilty to a charge that he attempted to purchase cocaine. He received one year probation and, as a result, the program with a more positive message was born. It's unclear how effective "Get High on Yourself" was in reducing teenage drug use, but anti-drug education that emphasizes the negative consequences of drug use has clearly fallen short of the goal. It is time to pivot, once again,

---

[17] Henry (1981).

and provide positive examples of free-thinking realistic people in real-life scenarios, who have to make hard choices but ultimately succeed. But this is only part of the solution.

Primary prevention education aims to prevent opioid misuse before it ever occurs, but this only addresses half of the problem. Secondary prevention aims are designed to reduce the impact of opioid misuse that has already occurred. The goal is to reduce injury, halt or slow its progress, and encourage personal strategies that can be used to prevent further injury or relapse. By implementing these programs, which are designed to return people to their original health and function, educational programs and anti-drug policies can play a significant role in the prevention of long-term problems to both individuals and to society at large. In an article published in the psychiatric *Journal of the American Medical Association (JAMA Psychiatry)*,[18] Tom McLellan of the Treatment Research Institute, National Institute on Alcohol Abuse and Alcoholism director, George Koob, and Dr. Nora Volkow, president of NIDA, argue for a classification system of addiction that recognizes early behavior patterns with significant personal and societal consequences, which occur, often for an extended period of time, earlier in the course of the disease of addiction than what we currently recognize as the treatment stage. According to Dr. Volkow, "Far too often, the expectation is that someone must hit 'rock bottom' before treatment can work. But this is a myth that can have dire consequences. By then the damage is consequential and a much harder road to recovery. Factually, the best time to get help is as soon as possible." Secondary prevention efforts aimed at "pre-addiction" will likely have the same effect that identifying and treating "pre-diabetes" has had, by reducing the morbidity and mortality associated with the disease. Dr. Volkow goes on to say that, "Frequently when a person asks for help early on, society, friends and family, coworkers, and healthcare systems do not recognize it as a serious issue. They may ignore or deny it" and the authors this is something that needs to change. Social media products such as Twitter, TikTok, and YouTube have successfully engaged target populations with so-called "influencers," much in the same way that the Partnership commercialized public service announcements in the 1980s and, as Volkow suggests, the use of "virtual coaches to motivate and sustain a range of healthy behaviors ... might be adapted to address pre-addiction." What is needed now is the integration of this idea of pre-addiction into mainstream healthcare in the same way that pre-diabetes has been integrated, but such integration faces several substantial hurdles. The "lack of a prominent advocacy group demanding

[18] McLellan et al. (2022).

clinical and policy changes, and little reimbursement for interventions with less severe substance use disorder," as Volkow points out, likely portends slow progress in this direction. Nonetheless, as we have seen from the diabetes example, secondary prevention can work, given a comprehensive and sustained effort, and hopefully these suggested educational interventions will be taken up by advocates for the early treatment of substance misuse disorder before it becomes substance use disorder.

References and Further Reading

Balonon-Rosen P (2019). From cringeworthy to scary: A history of anti-drug PSAs. www.marketplace.org/2019/03/26/advertisings-war-drugs-also-failed.

Bryson EO (2012). *Addicted Healers: 5 Key Signs your Healthcare Professional May Be Drug Impaired*. Summit, NJ: New Horizon Press.

Dufton E (2014). The acid rescue squad: Drug education and prevention in the 1960s and '70s. https://pointshistory.com/2014/05/09/the-acid-rescue-squad-drug-education-and-prevention-in-the-1960s-and-70s.

Dufton E (2017). *Grass Roots: The Rise and Fall and Rise of Marijuana in America*. Toledo, OH: Discover Books.

DuPont RL, McLellan AT, White WL, Merlo LJ, Gold MS (2009a). Setting the standard for recovery: Physicians' health programs. *Journal of Substance Abuse Treatment* 36(2): 159–171.

DuPont RL, McLellan AT, Carr G, Gendel M, Skipper GE (2009b). How are addicted physicians treated? A national survey of physician health programs. *Journal of Substance Abuse Treatment* 37(1): 1–7.

Harrison PA, Asche SE (1999). Comparison of substance abuse treatment outcomes for inpatients and outpatients. *Journal of Substance Abuse Treatment* 17(3): 207–220.

Henry WA III (1981). Video: Get high on yourself. *TIME*, September 21.

Ingraham C (2017). A brief history of DARE, the anti-drug program Jeff Sessions wants to revive. *Washington Post*, July 12. www.washingtonpost.com/news/won k/wp/2017/07/12/a-brief-history-of-d-a-r-e-the-anti-drug-program-jeff-sessions-wants-to-revive.

Malivert M, Fatséas M, Denis C, Langlois E, Auriacombe M (2012). Effectiveness of therapeutic communities: A systematic review. *European Addiction Research* 18 (1): 1–11.

McLellan AT, Skipper GS, Campbell M, DuPont RL (2008). Five-year outcomes in a cohort study of physicians treated for substance use disorders in the United States. *British Medical Journal* 337: a2038.

McLellan AT, Koob GF, Volkow ND (2022). Preaddiction: A missing concept for treating substance use disorders. *JAMA Psychiatry* 79(8): 749–751.

Monroe T, Pearson F, Kenaga H (2008). Procedures for handling cases of substance abuse among nurses: A comparison of disciplinary and alternative programs. *Journal of Addictions Nursing* 19: 156–161.

NIDA (1980). Marijuana research findings: 1980. NIDA Research Monograph. https://archives.nida.nih.gov/sites/default/files/monograph31.pdf.

Oudejans SC, Schippers GM, Spits ME, Stollenga M, van den Brink W (2012). Five years of ROM in substance abuse treatment centres in the Netherlands. *Tijdschrift voor Psychiatrie* 54(2): 185–190.

PBS Frontline (2000). Interview with Dr. Robert DuPont. www.pbs.org/wgbh/pages/frontline/shows/drugs/interviews/dupont.html.

Talbott GD, Gallegos KV, Wilson PO, Porter TL (1987). The Medical Association of Georgia's Impaired Physicians Program Review of the first 1,000 physicians: Analysis of specialty. *JAMA* 257: 2927–30.

WBTV 3 (2010). Elementary student brings pot to school to turn in his parents. www.wbtv.com/story/13330034/couple-facing-drug-charges-after-child-tips-off-cop-at-school/.

Anti-Cocaine public service announcment from 1988: www.youtube.com/watch?v=IzWdTk-2fAY.

Anti-Marijuana public service announcment from 2001: www.youtube.com/watch?v=2lchxh9AOh8.

15 PROACTIVE MEASURES TO PREVENT OPIOID ADDICTION

Our response to the opioid epidemic thus far has primarily been reactive or, in other words, the opioid epidemic was well underway by the time we responded. Reactive medicine is inefficient, costly, and places undue burden on clinicians and healthcare systems that are already stretched thin. But what if we focused more on preventing the problem before it even happens?

This is the primary question studied by experts in the fields of public health and preventive medicine. Prevention interventions can prevent or delay the onset of substance use, the progression from use, to misuse, to opioid use disorder, and/or reduce costs related to substance use. Both the Surgeon General and the United Nations have published reports reviewing evidence and analyzing the associated costs of various prevention programs. Both reports note that the evidence behind many of these programs is sparse but should not discourage further research. As stated in the United Nations International Standards on Drug Use Prevention, "The gaps in the science should make us cautious but not deter us from action … What we do have is an indication of where the right direction lies. By using this knowledge and building on it by means of more evaluation and research, we can foster development of national prevention systems that are based on scientific evidence … ."[1]

Although we are still trying to figure out how best to prevent opioid misuse and opioid use disorder, there are numerous prevention programs under development or already in use. These programs typically differ in at least one of four ways: age of target audience, the setting in which the prevention program occurs, the level of risk of the group targeted, and the focus of action (such as educational, developmental, and so on).[2] When discussing substance misuse, these prevention strategies are typically organized by their target audience using a classification system developed by the Institute of Medicine (IOM), and so this will be used to guide our discussion in the upcoming pages. Using the IOM's system, we can categorize prevention programs in one of three

---

[1] United Nations Office on Drugs and Crime (2018), pp. 4–5.
[2] United Nations Office on Drugs and Crime (2018), p. 41.

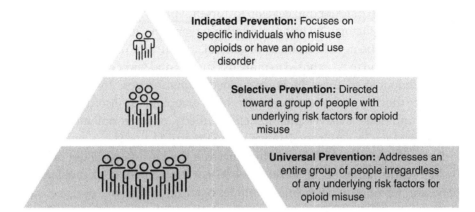

Figure 15.1 Prevention strategy classification pyramid.

groups: universal, selective, or indicated prevention. In its most general sense, universal prevention is directed toward the general population, selective toward those with risk factors for opioid use disorder, and indicated prevention for those who already misuse opioids. It is important to note that most prevention programs to date have been developed for children and adolescents, and the majority focus on the prevention of alcohol misuse. Further research is required to determine if these methods can be effectively adapted for other types of substance misuse.

Types of Prevention

Universal prevention refers to any strategy directed toward an entire group of people without differentiating between people who may be at a higher or lower risk for a certain illness. For example, a public service announcement encouraging adults to exercise daily would be considered a universal strategy to prevent cardiovascular disease. Universal prevention can be further subdivided by identifying the environment in which the intervention is conducted, such as in schools, at home, and within communities. Universal prevention is advantageous as it can be widely implemented and at the same time is unlikely to stigmatize certain individuals. Although universal prevention typically produces modest effects at best, it can also result in economical savings.[3]

Selective prevention targets a specific subset of individuals who are deemed to be at a higher risk for addiction. The goal of selective prevention is to reduce the incidence or severity of the factors associated with opioid misuse and addiction

---

[3] Champion et al. (2021).

(i.e., risk factors) or foster and develop factors that protect an individual from it (i.e., protective factors). By using selective interventions, resources are directed toward those who need it the most. In general, low-income and disadvantaged populations tend to be exposed to more risk factors and fewer protective factors when compared to those in other socioeconomic groups. In addition, the influence that risk and protective factors have on opioid use disorder correlates with certain stages of development such as puberty, or environmental changes and transitions like military deployment or divorce.[4]

Some of the individual factors that increase the risk of opioid use disorder include early initiation of substance use, early and persistent problematic behavior, rebelliousness, positive attitudes regarding substance use, peer substance use, mental illness, and genetic susceptibility to substance use and addiction. Community-based factors such as a high availability of drugs in the community, community normalization of drug use, low socioeconomic status, homelessness, and crime all increase the risk for opioid misuse and addiction. Family conflict, deficiencies in parenting practices, positive parental attitudes toward substance use, and a family history of substance misuse are some of the family-based risk factors, whereas academic failure and lack of commitment to education are also associated with opioid use disorder. In comparison, a variety of protective factors have been identified. These include interpersonal skill competency, self-efficacy, spirituality, resiliency, and active, positive social engagement with teachers, parents, significant others, and the community.[5] As with universal prevention, selective prevention can also be subdivided into school-based, community-based, and family-based strategies.

Finally, indicated prevention (also referred to as "early intervention") focuses its efforts on individuals who are exhibiting earlier signs or symptoms of substance misuse but do not meet the clinical criteria for a substance use disorder. These strategies are tailored to an individual's situation and, similarly to universal and selective prevention, may take place at school, within the family, or in the community.

School-Based Prevention

Most universal and selective prevention strategies occur in the educational setting, as schools possess the infrastructure to effectively provide education while creating an appropriate social and learning environment to minimize

---

[4] United States Department of Health and Human Services (HHS), Office of the Surgeon General (2016), pp. 3–4.
[5] United States Department of Health and Human Services (HHS), Office of the Surgeon General (2016), pp. 3–6.

the risks associated with opioid misuse. These interventions are implemented during an individual's formative years, when there is a chance to positively impact personality development and resiliency while limiting unwanted behaviors. It appears that the most successful school-based programs focus on social competency and life skills, by working to improve decision making and assertiveness. They also provide information about substance use, its associated risks and offer training to help resist negative peer pressure.[6]

Unplugged, Life Skills Training (LST), and the Good Behavior Game (GBG) are three examples of the many school-based prevention strategies that are currently used. Unplugged is a universal, school-based program in Europe that helps 12- to 14-year-old children develop skills related to critical thinking, interpersonal relationships, and empathy. The program also challenges the positive associations with substance while educating the students about the potential harms. Unplugged has been evaluated in Austria, Belgium, Czech Republic, German, Greece, Italy, Spain, and Sweden, and has been deemed to be a "beneficial" program by the EMCDDA's Xchange prevention registry.[7]

LST is another universal prevention program with many similarities to Unplugged. LST has been utilized primarily in the United States and some of Europe, and its three-year curriculum works with students 11 to 14 years of age, in hopes of reducing the long-term risk associated with drugs and alcohol. The program accomplishes this by bolstering factors that limit future opioid misuse (such as problem-solving and social interaction skills), while reducing factors associated with opioid misuse (like favorable attitudes toward substance use) that could impact a student's likelihood of using substances in the future.

The GBG is also conducted in schools. However, unlike Unplugged and LST, the GBG is considered a selective prevention strategy because it is directed toward individuals who exhibit unwanted behaviors, such as aggression or disruptiveness, that are associated with future drug use. At its core, the GBG limits unwanted behaviors through game playing and receiving rewards. Researchers found that when the GBG was implemented in first- and second-grade classrooms, the male students who exhibited high levels of aggression in the classroom were less likely than their peers to use drugs or alcohol as a young adult.[8] By decreasing opioid misuse risk factors, such as problematic childhood behavior, we are also decreasing the likelihood for future opioid misuse.

---

[6] Champion et al. (2021).
[7] The EMCDDA Xchange prevention registry is an online registry of thoroughly evaluated prevention interventions, programmes, and strategies: www.emcdda.europa.eu/best-practice/xchange_en.
[8] Kellam et al. (2011).

Family-Based Prevention

It is well known that certain family traits and dynamics increase the odds that a child will develop a substance use disorder in the future. Therefore, it makes sense to address any family-associated risk factors before this could happen. Family-based prevention programs are not as numerous as for school-based; however, some of these programs are associated with positive outcomes. Strengthening Families Program: for Parents and Youth 10–14 (SFP 10–14) and Strong African American Families (SAAF) are two examples of family-based prevention programs. Both strategies use a combination of educational videos and parenting skills training in hopes of improving the environment in which a child is raised. For the parents, the weekly sessions focus on bonding, setting boundaries, and other important parenting skills. The program also addresses a child's poor school performance and helps strengthen resistance skills toward negative peer pressure. Research thus far has demonstrated that SFP 10–14 leads to improved parenting skills and a reduction of children's problematic behaviors and drug use. In addition, it has been estimated that, for every dollar invested in SFP 10–14, there is a return of US$9.60 in cost-savings.[9] SAAF has been shown to positively impact families, as youth are less likely to start using drugs or develop conduct problems.[10] and mothers are less likely to experience maternal depression.

Community-Based Prevention

Just as family-based prevention focuses on risk factors associated with the family, community-based prevention addresses risk factors within a community. These prevention programs can be tailored to the specific needs of the community. However, the resources required to implement these programs often limits their utility. Communities that Care (CTC) is an evidence-based prevention strategy used to help communities implement programs to improve the health of their children. Using a five-phase strategy, the CTC program helps community members determine the needs of the community and implement activities that address issues like violence. Research has shown that children and adolescents who were part of a CTC community were 33% less likely to smoke cigarettes, 37% less likely to binge drink, and 25% less likely to engage in crime. The positive

---

[9] The Strengthening Families Program (https://strengtheningfamiliesprogram.org) is an evidence-based family skills training program for high-risk and general population families.
[10] Brody et al. (2008).

effects of CTC have economic benefits as well, as every dollar invested in the program results in a return of US$11.14 by way of lower criminal justice and healthcare costs combined with increased earnings and tax revenue.[11]

The Housing First model is an example of a selective community-based prevention strategy directed specifically toward the homeless population within a community. Housing First is based on the belief that people cannot move forward in life without stable living conditions. The program addresses homelessness by moving individuals into housing as quickly as possible and, once housing has been established, these individuals are now able to focus on other things like medical care, mental health, and employment.[12] Housing First works as a prevention strategy for substance opioid misuse by reducing homelessness and poverty, two socioeconomic factors associated with problematic opioid use.

Prescription Opioid Control

Of those individuals who started misusing opioids in the past 20 years, the majority report that their initial source of opioids came from prescriptions, and not necessarily their own. Of those individuals surveyed, over 50% reported that they obtained the opioids from a friend or relative.[13] Until recently, it was common practice for opioids to be prescribed frequently and perhaps carelessly, often in larger quantities than necessary. These larger quantities would sit in medicine cabinets unguarded, easily accessible to others who wished to use them for reasons other than pain. If we can improve the safety of opioid prescribing, we can hopefully prevent opioid misuse and its associated risks. Current prevention strategies target the prescriber, the patient, and the opioids themselves.

One way to limit excessive opioid prescriptions is by focusing on those who prescribe them. For example, some prevention initiatives concentrate on prescriber education, encouraging those who prescribe opioids to do so safely and appropriately. The Center for Disease Control and Prevention (CDC) most recently released the CDC Clinical Practice Guideline for prescribing opioids for pain, to educate physicians and other health providers about best opioid prescribing practices.[14] This document discusses

---

[11] The Center for Communities That Care (www.communitiesthatcare.net) distributes the CTC PLUS system and the Guiding Good Choices parenting program and helps communities learn about and implement CTC PLUS and GGC through personalized training and coaching.
[12] Gaetz (2014).   [13] Lipari and Hughes (2017).   [14] Dowell et al. (2022).

four areas: determining whether or not to prescribe opioids for pain; deciding the best types and dosages of opioids to prescribe; developing an appropriate pain-management treatment plan; and assessing the risks and potential harms associated with opioid use.

As the CDC Guideline states, there are certain individuals who will benefit from opioid therapy, such as those with postsurgical pain or terminal cancer. But there are also individuals who are at risk for opioid misuse, diversion, or overdose, should they receive a prescription for opioids. By accurately identifying these "at risk" individuals prior to initiation of opioid therapy, a process known as "risk stratification," we hope to limit the chances of these unwanted outcomes by only offering opioids to those deemed to be lower risk. Assessing risk in this setting can be performed through a combination of questionnaires, behavioral observations, and a thorough review of someone's medical, psychiatric, and family histories. Tools such as the Opioid Risk Tool (ORT)[15] and the Screener and Opioid Assessment for Patients with Pain – Revised (SOAPP-R)[16] help physicians identify individuals at risk for opioid misuse before they receive opioids, whereas the Current Opioid Misuse Measure (COMM)[17] identifies individuals already receiving a prescription. Behavioral observations that are considered "red flags" include concurrent use of alcohol or other drugs, obtaining opioids from nonmedical sources, and frequently reporting "stolen" or "lost" medication.[18] Other factors associated with prescription opioid misuse can be found in Figure 15.2.

Prescription drug monitoring programs (PDMPs) also encourage appropriate opioid prescribing practices. Each state-specific PDMP collects the prescribing history of every provider and the prescription history of every patient for controlled substances only. One goal of the PDMP is to increase prescribers' awareness about their own personal prescribing practices, by notifying individuals who may be prescribing more than the average provider. If the healthcare provider is prescribing controlled substances, such as opioids, more frequently than their constituents, sending a notification to the prescriber may encourage them to evaluate and adjust their practice accordingly. In addition, the PDMP allows prescribers to review a patient's history of controlled substance prescriptions and, if concerning behaviors are noted, providers will be less willing to prescribe controlled substances to the individual in question.

---

[15] https://nida.nih.gov/sites/default/files/opioidrisktool.pdf.
[16] www.mcstap.com/docs/SOAPP-5.pdf.
[17] www.mdcalc.com/calc/10428/current-opioid-misuse-measure-comm.
[18] Safer Opioid Prescribing HARMS Program (http://harmsprogram.ca).

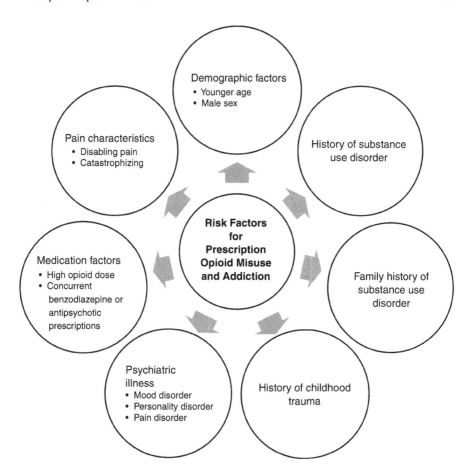

Figure 15.2 Risk factors for prescription opioid misuse or opioid use disorder.

For individuals at a higher risk for opioid misuse or diversion, several "abuse-deterrent" opioids have been developed in recent years. These medications are theoretically more difficult to adulterate or misuse by employing a variety of mechanisms. Some tablets are more difficult to crush (and subsequently inhale through the nose or inject intravenously), whereas others will be destroyed if heated or mixed with a solvent like alcohol (which are steps prior to intravenous injection). Alternatively, some pills have been formulated with the vitamin niacin, which can cause unpleasant side effects if consumed in large doses or inhaled through the nose. Other opioids only become activated in the stomach, so that they must be taken orally (and not injected intravenously) to be effective. However, most individuals who misuse prescription opioids do not adulterate them in any way, and so these new formulations are unlikely to prevent the onset of an opioid use disorder. In addition, these medications are more expensive and frequently not covered by insurance, limiting their utility. It is currently unclear if abuse-deterrent opioids have any impact on the opioid epidemic.[19]

Many argue that by limiting the opioids we are prescribing, we are inadvertently harming the patients with chronic pain who can benefit from them. Although current evidence suggests that long-term opioid therapy is not beneficial and alternative pharmacologic and nonpharmacologic strategies have been shown to be effective for chronic pain, barriers such as high costs, poor insurance coverage, and lack of access prevent people from utilizing them. To ensure that non-opioid treatments are affordable and accessible, policy reform is greatly needed. The Substance Use Disorder Prevention that Promotes Opioid Recovery and Treatment for Patients and Communities Act of 2018[20] (SUPPORT Act) is a bipartisan legislation addressing multiple aspects of the opioid epidemic, including prevention. The SUPPORT Act places requirements on providers to always check the PDMP before prescribing controlled substances and will increase the accessibility and insurance coverage of non-opioid pain management therapies.

The War on Drugs

Just as important as finding effective strategies to prevent opioid misuse is discontinuing those that are found to be ineffective or harmful. Nowadays considered to be a failure by many, the "war on drugs" campaign, which began with the Nixon administration in the 1970s, attempted to reduce the supply of illicit drugs in the United States through incarceration and military intervention. These measures resulted in soaring incarceration rates for nonviolent drug law offenses, from 50,000 in 1980 to more than 400,000 in 1997, with African Americans disproportionately affected.[21] Since its inception, the United States government has spent over 1 trillion dollars to enforce their drug policy.[22] As stated by Professor Christy Thornton of Johns Hopkins University, "Ultimately, more than four decades of the United States-led war on drugs abroad has not only failed to reduce the supply of illicit substances, it has actually made them more dangerous ... [D]rug prices remain steady, purity and potency remain high, drugs remain widely available, and overdoses are skyrocketing."[23]

[19] Salwan et al. (2018).   [20] US Library of Congress (2017–2018).
[21] Drug Policy Alliance (2022).   [22] Lee (2021).   [23] Thornton (2022).

Creating an Effective Prevention Strategy

Needless to say, we cannot develop an effective prevention strategy without learning from those strategies that weren't. In 2018, the United Nations Office on Drugs and Crime identified five requirements necessary for a prevention strategy to be effective.[24] These include:

1. *A supportive policy and legal framework*:
   - Make drugs available for research, while reducing likelihood of diversion.
   - Understand that substance use disorders result from complex interactions between genetics, environment, biological, and psychological factors, and therefore we must treat substance use disorders without punishment.
   - Associate with a national public health strategy to prevent substance use disorders and other diseases.
   - Create national standards using only evidence-based research.
   - Implement programs in schools and workplaces.
2. *Scientific evidence and research*:
   - Choose interventions based on actual circumstances.
   - Rigorously evaluate efficacy and costs associated with policy.
3. *Coordination of the multiple sectors and levels involved (national, subnational, and municipal/local)*:
   - Include stakeholders at all levels, all with well-defined roles and a clear, central authority.
4. *Training of policy makers and practitioners*:
   - Policy makers and practitioners work continuously on skills while educating others.
   - Provide technical assistance to support implementation and quality improvement.
5. *Commitment to providing adequate resources and to sustaining the system in the long term*:
   - Adequately finance policies and interventions.
   - Offer continuous support and resources to policy makers and practitioners.
   - Fund the constant monitoring of policies and adjust when evidence suggests they are needed.

---

[24] United Nations Office on Drugs and Crime (2018).

Does Prevention Make Sense?

The short answer is, "Yes, it does." We are only beginning to understand which preventive strategies for opioid use disorder are effective, but we cannot afford to let the current opioid epidemic maintain its trajectory. Prevention is not only lifesaving but cost-effective as well. For example, the estimated cost of the prevention program LST (discussed earlier in the chapter) is US$105 per participant, whereas the estimated benefits amount to US$1,419. Even more impressive are the economic benefits of the GBG, which costs US$160 per participant and yet contributes over US$10,000 in benefits.[25] Settlement funds obtained from pharmaceutical giants like Purdue should be allocated, in part, for research and implementation of preventive efforts. As attorneys J. Hodge and L. Gostin poignantly state, "Resources cannot erase prior harms but can ameliorate future injuries."[26]

References and Further Reading

Brody GH, Kogan SM, Chen Y, McBride Murry V (2008). Long-term effects of the Strong African American Families Program on youths' conduct problems. *Journal of Adolescent Health* 43: 474–481.

Champion KE, Newton NC, Teeson M (2021). Prevention of substance use disorders. In *Textbook of Substance Use Disorder Treatment*, 6th ed. Washington, DC: APA Publishing, ch. 35.

Dowell D, Ragan KR, Jones CM, Baldwin GT, Chou R (2022). CDC Clinical Practice Guideline for prescribing opioids for pain – United States, 2022. *Morbidity and Mortality Weekly Report* 71: 1–95. www.cdc.gov/mmwr/volumes/71/rr/rr7103a1.htm#B1_down.

Drug Policy Alliance (2022). A history of the Drug War. https://drugpolicy.org/issues/brief-history-drug-war.

Gaetz S (2014). Can housing first work for youth? *European Journal of Homelessness* 8 (2): 159–175.

Hodge JG, Gostin LO (2019). Guiding industry settlements of opioid litigation. *American Journal of Drug and Alcohol Abuse* 45(5): 432–437.

Kellam SG., Mackenzie ACL, Brown CH, et al. (2011). The Good Behavior Game and the future of prevention and treatment. *Addiction Science & Clinical Practice* 6(1): 73–84.

---

[25] Washington State Institute for Public Policy (2019).
[26] United States Department of Health and Human Services, Office of the Surgeon General (2016).

Klimas J, Gorfinkel L, Fairbairn N, et al. (2019). Strategies to identify patient risks of prescription opioid addiction when initiative opioids for pain. *JAMA Network Open* 2(5): e193365.

Lee N (2021). America has spent over a trillion dollars fighting the war on drugs; 50 years later, drug use in the U.S. is climbing again. www.cnbc.com/2021/06/17/the-us-has-spent-over-a-trillion-dollars-fighting-war-on-drugs.html.

Lipari RN, Hughes A (2017). How people obtain the prescription pain relievers they misuse. www.samhsa.gov/data/sites/default/files/report_2686/ShortReport-2686.html.

Livingston CJ, Berenji M, Titus TM, et al. (2022). American College of Preventive Medicine: Addressing the opioid epidemic through a prevention framework. *American Journal of Preventive Medicine* 63(3): 454–465.

Nelson LF, Weitzman ER, Levy S (2021). Prevention of substance use disorders. *Medical Clinics of North America http://harmsprogram.ca/* 106(1): 153–168.

Salwan AJ, Hagemeier NE, Harirforoosh S (2018). Abuse-deterrent opioid formulations: A key ingredient in the recipe to prevent opioid disasters? *Clinical Drug Investigation* 38: 573–577.

SAMHSA (2015). Module 3: primary prevention and the six strategies. www.samhsa.gov/grants/block-grants/sabg/primary-prevention-course.

SAMHSA (2019). *Substance Misuse Prevention for Young Adults*. Rockville, MD: National Mental Health and Substance Use Policy Laboratory. Substance Abuse and Mental Health Services Administration.

Thornton C (2022). The U.S. had led the War on Drugs abroad for decades, and it's been a staggering failure. *New York Times*, September 7. www.nytimes.com/2022/09/07/opinion/colombia-drug-war-us.html

United Nations Office on Drugs and Crime (2018). *International Standards on Drug Use Prevention*, 2nd ed. Vienna; United Nations Office on Drugs and Crime.

United States Department of Health and Human Services (HHS), Office of the Surgeon General (2016). *Facing Addiction in America: The Surgeon General's Report on Alcohol, Drugs, and Health*. Washington, DC: HHS.

US Library of Congress (2017–2018). Substance Use Disorder Prevention that Promotes Opioid Recovery and Treatment for Patients and Communities Act. H.R. 6., 115th Congress (2017–2018). www.congress.gov/bill/115th-congress/house-bill/6.

US Preventive Services Task Force (2020). Screening for unhealthy drug use: US Preventive Services Task Force recommendation statement. *JAMA* 323(22): 2301–2309.

Washington State Institute for Public Policy (2019). Benefit–cost results. www.wsipp.wa.gov/BenefitCost?topicId=9.

16 CAN WE MAKE OPIOID MISUSE LESS DANGEROUS?

As we have seen, chronic opioid misuse puts people at significant risk for contracting blood-borne viral infections such as HIV and hepatitis C through the sharing of injection equipment, as well as hepatitis B and other diseases from unsafe sexual activities performed while under the influence of opioids or as a means to procure funds with which to purchase more opioids. Chronic opioid exposure leads to multiple health problems, caused either by decreased access to preventative care or as a direct result of chronically elevated levels of exogenous opioids. Opiate hyperalgesia or hyperesthesia, for example, is characterized by a dramatically increased sensitivity to painful stimuli or even, in the case of allodynia, a stimulus that is generally not perceived as painful (such as a soft touch) eliciting a strong sensation of pain. People with opioid use disorder often suffer from chronic pain and mental illness and are at significant risk for financial ruin, homelessness, overdose, and death. While it may not be possible to make opioid use completely safe, if we can, we should make it less dangerous. Putting aside the issues directly related to chronic opioid exposure, many of the things that make chronic opioid misuse so dangerous result from impure product manufactured illicitly with little or no quality control or production oversight, which must be procured illegally and is often injected with unsterile equipment in an unsafe and unsupervised environment. All of these factors can and should be addressed as part of a comprehensive strategy to fight the opioid epidemic. By challenging the beliefs that underlie the stigma surrounding opioid use disorder and directly addressing the factors which contribute to the increased morbidity and mortality associated with chronic opioid misuse, we can improve the health and well-being of persons suffering from this disease, reduce the numbers of overdose deaths, and turn the tide of the epidemic. But first, in order to get there, we have to look back to where we came from.

Plant Alkaloids and Animal Behavior

Humans have had a long and sometimes complicated relationship with plants that produce psychoactive substances, and the opium poppy is only one such example. Opioids have been part and parcel of the human experience for millennia, so it is unrealistic to believe that complete cessation of use is a viable option at this point, but is it possible to make their use less dangerous? To do this it is first important to understand what these chemicals actually are and why some humans become addicted to these substances while others do not. Plant alkaloids, such as morphine and codeine, are small organic molecules, often containing nitrogen in a ring structure. These compounds are secondary metabolites, the leftovers that are produced by plants as they generate energy for growth and reproduction, via metabolism of chemicals absorbed through their root systems. Though technically a waste product, these metabolites are still useful and are primarily involved in the plant's defense against herbivores and pathogens. Plant alkaloids make the plant unpalatable for herbivores while also creating a hostile environment for invasive diseases. While these chemicals do not always kill the invading organism or herbivore wishing to make a meal out of the plant, they do have a profound effect on the subsequent behavior exhibited by organisms that have come in contact with them.

All different types of plants have evolved these elaborate defense mechanisms over millions of years, and the compounds that we are familiar with today existed long before we, or any other mammals for that matter, appeared on the face of the earth. Why then would plants that produce these types of alkaloids have evolved to do so without selection pressure from interaction with humans? Clearly, we are not the intended target of their defenses and, according to some researchers, humans are, in actuality, simply "collateral damage"[1] in a battle that has fiercely raged for eons. It may seem strange that the opioid epidemic we are currently battling has its roots in an ancient conflict between plants and nonhuman organisms, but it is clear that plants have the ability to significantly alter and, in some cases, control the behavior of animals.

M. Night Shyamalan's 2008 thriller *The Happening* is a film based on the premise that plants, faced with increasing physiological and environmental pressure, develop the ability to escalate their innate defense mechanisms and begin to alter human behavior on a global scale, in an attempt to protect themselves from the creatures destroying their environment. Avoiding a critical review of the screenplay or of the final production itself, there is no argument that the concept is based on sound science. While we may not yet be at the point where plants have the ability to drive humans toward mass suicide through aerosolized alkaloids, some plants clearly already have the

---

[1] van Staaden et al. (2018).

ability to drive some humans toward equally significant self-destructive behaviors.

It is unlikely that the plant alkaloids that have evolved for self-defense have the same euphoric effects on the invertebrates or other creatures that routinely feed on them, but these compounds have been shown to consistently alter behavior much in the same way that a human or other primate's behavior is altered when they become addicted to these same agents. While the classic behaviors we associate with addiction in humans, such as compulsive drug-seeking and use despite negative consequences, may appear quite complex, they are more or less the same as the behaviors exhibited by members of other phyla including insects (honeybees, fruit flies, ants), crustaceans (crabs and crayfish), roundworms (*Caenorhabditis elegans*), molluscs (snails), and flatworms (planaria).[2] Crayfish, for example, have been shown to respond to exposure to known psychoactive plant-based compounds in characteristic ways, favoring an environment with a higher concentration of these agents over one with a lower concentration. Additionally, these creatures have exhibited stereotyped and reproducible behaviors when exposed to these plant-derived alkaloids, including initial difficulty with ambulation and inability to right themselves, followed by the development of tolerance to these effects and what appears to be, in the case of stimulants such as cocaine, increased locomotor activity. There is considerable evidence to suggest that the reward associated with self-administration of these substances in humans, the reward that is responsible for the characteristic drug-seeking behavior of addicts, is analogous to the way a herbivore's or pathogen's behavior changes after exposure to plant alkaloids.

So it seems that, at a very basic level, most, if not all, of the creatures that have evolved on this planet have done so with the same predictable response when exposed to these compounds produced by plants. The assumption, then, is that this response is somehow protective otherwise it would not have been selected for during the evolution of the different phyla that exist today. That is to say that creatures with this characteristic response were, historically anyway, no more likely to die than creatures without this predilection, and in fact were more likely to survive, at least long enough to produce viable offspring able to live long enough to do the same. If the characteristic response to plant alkaloids is similar across all animals, and may be protective, it should be possible to make human interaction with opioids less dangerous.

---

[2] Hiragaki et al. (2015).

Medication Treatment for Opioid Use Disorder

Using medications such as methadone, buprenorphine, and naltrexone to treat opioid use disorder is not a new idea, but reframing it in a way that emphasizes that opioid use disorder is a disease, and that it can be treated with medications the same way other diseases are, is a concept that has gained traction within the medical community since the mid-twentieth century. Historically called "opioid substitution therapy" (OST) or "medication assisted treatment" (MAT), the preferable term used to describe the treatment of opioid use disorder with medications is simply "medications for opioid use disorder (MOUD)". Methadone, a synthetic opioid agonist developed in the late 1930s, has been used in the treatment of opioid use disorder since the 1960s. When taken daily, methadone relieves cravings and removes withdrawal symptoms, allowing people with opioid dependence to stop using the more dangerous street heroin (diacetylmorphine), which, as we have seen, is very rarely pure and often contains fentanyl or fentanyl analogs as well as any number of inert ingredients. People who have been prescribed methadone for opioid use disorder are required to obtain their daily dose of medication from dispensing or dosing clinics in accordance with controlled substance laws, a practice that further stigmatizes those receiving treatment. Buprenorphine, a synthetic opioid agonist–antagonist, was developed in the mid-1960s and has been used for the treatment of mild to moderate pain as well as opioid use disorder. As a partial mu opioid receptor agonist, buprenorphine binds to opioid receptors to relieve the sensation of pain; however, it does not activate the receptor to the degree that other opioids such as heroin or morphine do. Buprenorphine has a much greater affinity for these receptors; however, so much so that it can prevent other opioids from binding to them and will also displace opioids from these receptors much in the way naloxone does. It is this property that allows the medication to effectively prevent the symptoms of opioid withdrawal while simultaneously preventing other opioids from having an effect. Buprenorphine also acts as an antagonist, a property that comes from its binding to the kappa opioid receptors. It is thought that this is, at least in part, the reason why buprenorphine can act as a mild antidepressant. Buprenorphine is dispensed directly from authorized providers, avoiding the necessity for people in treatment to regularly visit a dispensary, and once on a stable dose of buprenorphine they may obtain an allotment for self-administration at home.

Because evidence has clearly shown that patients receiving medication treatment for opioid use disorder significantly reduce their use of illicit opioids, even in the absence of counseling, attempts have been made to find suitable alternative medications for people who cannot tolerate the side effects of methadone and buprenorphine or for whom these drugs are not effective. Slow or sustained-release oral morphine has been tried as a substitute for methadone, but according to the World Health Organization (WHO) there is limited evidence, inadequate to endorse any recommendations supporting the practice. Additionally, since heroin is metabolized to morphine in the blood, heroin use while taking sustained-release oral morphine cannot be easily assessed through urine drug testing, making a program of supervised recovery difficult. This is probably more important for situations in which the patient is participating in a diversion program (as discussed in Chapter 12), where documented compliance with the use of only approved (and safer) medications is necessitated by protocol. In actuality, opioids can be dangerous, and the concern should be not which opioid is more socially acceptable, but which opioid is safer, less likely to cause harm, and more likely to reduce behaviors which cause harm.

It was with this philosophy that levo-alpha-acetylmethadol (LAAM) was developed. LAAM is a long-acting opioid agonist, which was approved for use as a maintenance treatment for opioid dependence for people in whom methadone and buprenorphine are not effective. There is significant evidence to support the use of LAAM in this context and it has been shown to be more effective at reducing heroin use in people with opioid use disorder than methadone, but it was withdrawn from the market due to its potentially dangerous effects on the heart, specifically a phenomenon called "QT prolongation." In the cardiac cycle, as seen on the electrocardiogram, the QT segment is the length of time between the QRS wave, which represents the contraction of the heart (you know the squiggle when you see it), and the T wave, which represents the repolarization or resetting of the heart's electrical system in preparation for the next depolarization (heartbeat). When this period is prolonged, the heart can sometimes start the next cycle before it is ready, triggering an excessively fast heart rate, the polymorphic ventricular tachycardia called torsades de pointes (TdP), literally "torsion around points." This arrhythmia can be fatal if it persists, so when prescribing a medication that can potentially prolong the QT segment it makes sense to weigh the risks and benefits of use. The phenomenon of QT prolongation does not occur in a vacuum: other risk factors such as electrolyte imbalances (low potassium or magnesium), female gender, increasing age, structural heart disease, renal disease, etc. increase the chances that a medication known to potentially prolong the QT segment will trigger TdP; so some people are inherently at risk. but regardless of risk factors methadone and buprenorphine are also on the short list of medications generally accepted to have a risk for prolongation. Thus, when making the determination of whether or not an opioid is safe, we must weigh the risk of potential complications such as QT prolongation with the possible benefit of using it as a treatment for opioid use disorder.

Non-opioid medications to be used as treatment for opioid use disorder have also been investigated. The opioid antagonist naltrexone, which, as we have seen, is used to reverse the symptoms of opioid overdose, can preemptively be used to prevent people in recovery from experiencing the effects of opioids if they relapse. This includes both the reinforcing euphoria and also the unintended overdose that commonly occurs after a period of abstinence when tolerance to opioids has waned. Slow-release naltrexone implants and injections provide clinically significant dose-dependent opioid blockade for three to six weeks and work as a "safety net" to reduce harm in early recovery as well as provide a platform to help people remain abstinent. A number of different types of naltrexone implants have been developed that can be inserted subcutaneously using local anesthesia, either after opioid withdrawal or as part of an antagonist withdrawal treatment (as described in Chapter 9). These implants or injections must be replaced or repeated on a regular basis, usually at one- to three-months intervals, and this provides an opportunity for contact between the person in recovery and the treating clinician. For people in supervised recovery programs, naltrexone levels in the blood can be assayed to ensure compliance and, like buprenorphine, this type of treatment provides a psychological component as well. Despite the concern that these medications prevent opioids from working to prevent or treat pain, some people in recovery will refuse to stop taking them prior to elective surgery for fear of relapse. So strong is the desire to return to opioid use, sometimes even years into recovery, that they would rather risk enduring pain than risking relapse. Fortunately, however, we now have many ways to provide pain relief without opioids and in most cases the cessation of these medications prior to elective surgery is no longer necessary.

Because methadone and buprenorphine are both opioids, the potential for misuse of these medications exists, and in some areas of the world buprenorphine is as misused as heroin. As with methadone, intravenous abuse of buprenorphine has been reported in many countries and, because of this, when these medications are used for treatment of opioid use disorder, the risk for diversion from intended use to misuse is a concern. In response, a new formulation of buprenorphine, which combines the medication with naloxone in a 4:1 ratio, was developed to decrease the risk for misuse. When taken sublingually as directed, the absorption of naloxone is minimal and the effects of buprenorphine alone predominate; in other words, only the buprenorphine is absorbed into the body and the naloxone has no effect. When misused and injected, both the buprenorphine and the naloxone enter the body and the naloxone prevents the person from experiencing the euphoria associated with buprenorphine injection, making it less subject to misuse than injection of buprenorphine alone. In addition, the injection of naloxone will precipitate acute opioid withdrawal in opioid dependent persons. Despite this, because the half-life of buprenorphine is much longer than naloxone, people will still adulterate and inject the medication that contains both buprenorphine and naloxone and go through a short period of withdrawal (from the naloxone and partial agonism of buprenorphine) just to get to a longer high from the buprenorphine.

Despite significant evidence that these medications work, methadone treatment, and to some extent even buprenorphine treatment, remain controversial. Sharon Hall, PhD, a professor in residence and vice-chair of psychiatry at the University of California San Francisco, believes this stems from long-held misconceptions and stigma associated with substance use disorder. "People don't like it because it is continued provision of an addicting drug. When people come on methadone maintenance, they may stay on it for several years" but, according to the National Institute on Drug Abuse (NIDA), quoting a paper by Dr. Hall and co-workers, as used in maintenance treatment, methadone and buprenorphine are not heroin/opioid substitutes.[3] In this study the idea was to compare methadone treatment with an experimental treatment involving methadone but with a 180-day tapering so that at the end of the treatment period patients were not using heroin or taking methadone. "The idea was to find a method that was as effective [as methadone treatment] but didn't involve indefinite treatment with an addicting drug." Her group confirmed that "Methadone maintenance is more effective in reducing heroin use among addicts than a 180-day detoxification program that included an array of counseling services." The study also found a significant reduction in behaviors likely to increase risk for transmission of HIV and hepatitis C, such as sharing needles.

According to NIDA director Dr. Nora Volkow, "people addicted to prescription opioid painkillers can be effectively treated in primary care settings using Suboxone [the buprenorphine and naloxone combination medication], however, once the medication [is] discontinued, people [have] a high rate of relapse so, more research is needed to determine how to sustain recovery among people addicted to opioid medications." This highlights the need for a comprehensive approach to the treatment of opioid use disorder, which considers all potential modalities, including some which in the past have been stigmatized.

---

[3] Barnett et al. (2009).

Decriminalization

In an attempt to protect individuals and society at large from the multitude of problems associated with opioid misuse, a vast array of laws have been drafted and implemented worldwide. In many countries these laws are based on religious beliefs, which prohibit the use of mind-altering substances as an affront to whichever god the people in power at the time follow, and often they are selectively targeted at racial minority groups, likely intended to control the population as well as the drug trade. Time and time again we have seen the collateral damage produced by ordinances and regulations that prevent those with substance use disorder from accessing medical and social assistance, often trapping people in a vicious cycle in which opioid misuse constantly brings them in contact with law enforcement agencies ill equipped to provide the help they so desperately need. One solution that has been tried in at least three countries so far is the elimination of laws that make personal drug use illegal. To be fair, the elimination of these laws does not specifically address the supply side issues, and in each case the trafficking of illicit opioids and other drugs remains punishable by law, but individual users are released from, according to Dr. Theresa Tam, Canada's chief public health officer, the "stigma and fear of criminalization" that causes "some people to hide their drug use, use alone, or use in other ways that increase the risk of harm."[4] In these extreme cases of harm reduction the focus is on the end user. If we cannot stem the supply, maybe it is possible to stem the harm that the supply causes.

While decriminalization is being revisited in a few regions in North America, specifically Vancouver (Canada) and Oregon (United States), this is not a new concept. In 2001, the entire country of Portugal decriminalized the use and possession of illicit drugs but specifically kept in place the laws which made production and sales a crime. Supporters of reforming drug laws point to the absence of an increase in drug use or overdose deaths in Portugal after decriminalization as evidence that these policies do not increase drug use and actually allow affected individuals to access support systems without fear of incarceration once personal use is no longer illegal. Critics point out that, prior to decriminalization, Portugal's anti-drug laws were only loosely enforced anyway and that the change in policy only codified into law what society had already come to accept. According to a 2015 paper by Hannah Laqueur, published in the American Bar Foundation's journal, *Law & Social Inquiry*,[5] "In the years before the law's passage, less than 1 percent of those incarcerated for

---

[4] Guardian (2022)   [5] Laqueur (2015).

a drug offense had been convicted of use." Not surprisingly, the change in Portugal's law regarding personal use, though not specifically changing penalties for trafficking, appears to be associated with a significant reduction in drug-trafficker sanctioning. "While the number of arrests for trafficking changed little, the number of individuals convicted and imprisoned for trafficking since 2001 has fallen nearly 50 percent." This is similar to the situation with marijuana legalization in Colorado (United States) in which, prior to legalization, concerns were raised that changing the law would significantly increase access, and therefore increase the number of regular marijuana users. In fact, due to the existence of an established network of "medical cannabis" dispensaries that were, according to Mark Kleiman of New York University's Marron Institute, relaxed to the point that many have referred to the situation as "de facto legalization," most people who wanted to use marijuana regularly were already doing so. This may not be the case with opioids, however, and the effects of decriminalization of heroin in countries where laws are not so relaxed will likely provide more relevant data.

In 2020, Oregon (United States) voters passed by referendum "Measure 110," which is also known as "the Drug Addiction Treatment and Recovery Act."[6] This act decriminalized possession of controlled substances, including opioids such as methadone, oxycodone, and heroin, below a threshold amount. Prior to passage of Measure 110, persons caught with any amount of these substances, even if just for personal use, were charged and often convicted of a misdemeanor, or in the case of more than a gram of heroin, a felony. Now, the legal consequences for possession have been reduced from a Class A misdemeanor to a Class E violation. Under Section 19 of the Measure, a Class E violation is punishable by a US$100 fine and the cited individual has the option of completing a health assessment at an addiction recovery center in lieu of paying the fine.[7]

In 2022, Vancouver (British Columbia, Canada) is embarking on a three-year experiment in decimalization of possession of small amounts of heroin for personal use. Spurred by the epidemic of overdose deaths in the city, government officials believe that eliminating the fear of legal consequences will encourage opioid users to seek help. According to Jim Morris and Rob Gillies of the Associated Press, "The policy approved by federal officials doesn't legalize the substances but Canadians in the province who possess up to 2.5 grams of illicit drugs for personal use will not be arrested or charged."[8] As of January 31, 2023, anyone over the age of 18 who is found in possession of

---

[6] Oregon State Government (2020).   [7] State of Oregon Health Authority (2021).
[8] Morris and Gillies (2022).

heroin for personal use will not be criminally charged. Dr. Bonnie Henry, British Columbia's provincial health officer, regards this change in the law as an "important step forward" but acknowledges that this is only one policy change designed to attack the opioid epidemic. Hopefully, as she says, "this will make a difference." Others, such as Canadian drug policy reform activist Dana Larsen, would like to see a safer drug supply. This is "not going to stop anybody dying of an overdose or drug poisoning. These drugs are still going to be contaminated," and perhaps one of the ways we can make opioid use less dangerous is to treat opioids like alcohol and tobacco, with regulations and purity standards. According to Dr. Alissa Greer, assistant professor at Simon Fraser University, overdose deaths and other unintended consequences of illicit drug use could be reduced if users were able to obtain their drugs from "a regulated supply through various models, whether that's a prescription model, a pharmacy model, or a compassion club model." Regardless of the actual way in which it is done, almost everyone agrees that pharmaceutical grade heroin is safer than what is currently available on the streets today.

Prescription Heroin

There is extensive clinical evidence to confirm that medicines used to treat opioid use disorder work well, eliminate cravings and withdrawal symptoms, allow people to get off heroin and prescription opioids, and help people to avoid relapse. Groups such as the Centers for Disease Control, NIDA, and the WHO[9] all support the use of methadone and buprenorphine in this setting, but what about the people for whom stopping heroin use, even with medical treatment, is not possible? Up to 40% of people don't respond well to either methadone or buprenorphine due to side effects such as bone pain, nausea, headaches, or fatigue, and for a smaller percentage the medications themselves do not reduce cravings, prevent symptoms of withdrawal, or prevent relapse. In 10–15% of these cases the only alternative these people have is to return to heroin use, and in the vast majority of cases this is not a safe or sustainable alternative. One solution that has been shown to be safe and effective is prescription heroin. In a supervised setting, enrolled people are provided with pure, medical grade heroin and sterile equipment for injection. Only a few countries allow heroin to be prescribed by a physician for treatment of heroin addiction, but such use has been shown to reduce the incidence of

---

[9] According to the WHO 2009 guidelines, evidence favoring heroin treatment over methadone comes from studies conducted in people who have failed previous methadone treatments.

overdose and reduce transmission of disease by randomized controlled clinical trials performed in Switzerland, the Netherlands, Spain, Germany, Canada, and England.[10] The authors of this 2015 review, published in the *British Journal of Psychiatry*, conclude that "inclusion of this low-volume, high-intensity treatment can now improve the impact of comprehensive healthcare provision."

It is important to note that the use of prescription heroin is not a first-line treatment for opioid use disorder but one which is reserved for people who have not responded to standard treatments such as with other medication and/or residential rehabilitation. Prescription heroin is not considered a medication treatment for opioid use disorder in the way that treatment with methadone or buprenorphine is but falls into the harm-reduction category of options for addressing the opioid epidemic. Prescribed heroin is self-administered by people in a treatment facility where they are under direct medical supervision by healthcare professionals, trained to intervene should the patient unintentionally overdose. Fortunately, unlike illicit heroin purchased on the street, prescription heroin does not contain fentanyl, or any other adulterants, and overdose is much less likely to occur in this setting. Dr. Scott MacDonald, the head physician of the Providence Crosstown Clinic in Vancouver, British Columbia, where a prescription heroin program such as this has been operating since 2011, reports that not a single patient in their program has overdosed at the clinic. In addition to reducing the chance for overdose death, people are also less likely to catch or transmit infectious diseases associated with intravenous drug use, such as hepatitis C and HIV, are less likely to suffer from other diseases such as endocarditis that are associated with injecting heroin, generally require a lower dose per day than people not provided with medical grade heroin, are less likely to suffer from homelessness or to be involved in criminal activity in order to obtain heroin illegally, and are generally able to enjoy the same type of existence that most people not chronically using heroin are able to.

This type of treatment has existed in the United Kingdom since 1926 but has gained more acceptance worldwide as a viable option since it became established in Switzerland in the 1990s. Since then, more and more countries are looking into prescription heroin as an option in the battle to control the epidemic and mitigate damages. Even in the United States, where there is considerable stigma associated with medications like methadone and buprenorphine, prescription heroin is being considered a viable way to combat the exponential rise in overdose deaths related to fentanyl-laced street heroin. In a clinical setting where people are receiving unadulterated heroin and allowed

---

[10] Strang et al. (2015).

to self-administer under observation, the risk for overdose is extremely low and the chances that someone will survive such an event high. According to a 2017 *Baltimore Sun* editorial by Maryland-based drug policy experts, Bryce Pardo and Peter Reuter, "Heroin-assisted therapy addresses the immediate overdose threat posed by fentanyl – something naloxone attempts to do after the fact. Prescribed heroin use in a clinical and supervised setting ensures that users are not consuming fentanyl, and that staff are on hand should something go wrong."[11]

Can We Increase the Purity of Illicit Opioids?

In Chapter 12, we discussed how needle exchange programs make opioid use less dangerous by reducing the chances for transmission or contraction of blood-borne infections and how ready access to naloxone can save the life of someone overdosing on opioids, but what about making the opioids themselves less dangerous? The main reason so many people are overdosing on illicit opioids is less a problem related to being unable to calculate the desired dose because of inconsistencies in the purity of the product on the street but more a problem related to the addition of fentanyl and fentanyl analogs to these products. Fentanyl, as we have seen, is so much more potent than heroin and other opioids that even people who are chronically exposed to opioids and have developed tolerance to their effects are still at high risk for fatal overdose. This is why ready access to easy-to-use fentanyl test strips, which can detect fentanyl in heroin and other opioids obtained on the street, is an essential component of a comprehensive strategy to make opioid use less dangerous.

Providing your repeat customers with a product that has a good chance of killing them may seem like an odd business model, but the cost of producing illicit fentanyl is so much lower than that of heroin, and the volume so much smaller than an equipotent volume of heroin, (making it easier to transport across the borders) that illicit manufacturers are willing to take the risk. Also, due to its much shorter half-life, fentanyl must be re-dosed more frequently to avoid the symptoms of withdrawal, and therefore more can be sold each day. The market for this product exists primarily because there are few safer alternatives, but would it be possible to use these same market forces to encourage these manufacturers to produce a more pure and safer illicit product? The establishment of heroin-exchange programs, similar to the existing needle exchange programs could, in theory, offer a safe way for people to exchange products identified as containing fentanyl for a more pure, safer product.

---

[11] Baltimore Sun (2017).

Of course, while this would help to reduce the number of overdose deaths and the incidence of endocarditis and other diseases associated with injecting contaminated opioids, it would only put pressure on illicit manufactures if enough customers refused to buy the tainted product in favor of something that does not contain fentanyl; otherwise the program would simply be subsidizing the manufacture of illicit opioids. It also would require the legalization of, or at the very least the decriminalization of recreational opioid use, something that has been shown to reduce crime as well as morbidity and mortality but continues to meet with strong resistance when proposed.

Given the severity of the opioid epidemic it is essential that we consider any and all potential solutions and not dismiss ideas based on biases, implicit or otherwise. If we are going to be successful, we must continue to employ the strategies that have been proven effective while also searching for new and creative ways to reduce harm and keep people safe.

References and Further Reading

Baltimore Sun (2017). Is Md. ready for 'heroin assisted therapy'? *Baltimore Sun,* April 10.

Barnett PG, Sorensen JL, Wong W, Haug NA, Hall SM (2009). Effect of incentives for medication adherence on health care use and costs in methadone patients with HIV. *Drug Alcohol Depend* 100(1–2):115–121.

Guardian (2022). Canada to decriminalize some drugs in British Columbia for three years. *Guardian,* May 31. www.theguardian.com/world/2022/may/31/canada-decriminalize-drugs-british-columbia-overdoses.

Hiragaki S, Suzuki T, Mohamed AAM, Takeda M. (2015). Structures and functions of insect arylalkylamine Nacetyltransferase (iaaNAT): A key enzyme for physiological and behavioral switch in arthropods. *Frontiers in Physiology* 6: 113.

Laqueur H (2015). Uses and abuses of drug decriminalization in Portugal. *Law & Social Inquiry* 40(3): 746–781.

Morris J and Gillies R (2022). Drug criminalization test OKed. *San Francisco Chronicle,* June 2, p. A2.

NIDA (2014). Principles of drug addiction treatment: A research-based guide (third edition). https://archives.nida.nih.gov/publications/principles-drug-addiction-treatment-research-based-guide-third-edition.

Oregon Health Authority (2021). Measure 110 Information for Individuals. www.oregon.gov/OHA/HSD/AMH/Docs/Measure-110-Individual-Fact-Sheet.pdf#:~:text=HEALTH%20SYSTEMS%20DIVISION%20Behavioral%20Health%20Programs%20Measure%20110,of%20getting%20arrested%2C%20people%20will%20get%20a%20citation.

Oregon State Government (2020). Drug Addiction Treatment and Recovery Act (Measure 110). www.oregon.gov/oha/hsd/amh/pages/measure110.aspx.

Oviedo-Joekes E, Brissette S, Marsh DC, et al. (2009). Diacetylmorphine versus methadone for the treatment of opioid addiction. *New England Journal of Medicine* 361(8): 777–786.

Sordo L, Barrio G, Bravo MJ, et al. (2017). Mortality risk during and after opioid substitution treatment: systematic review and meta-analysis of cohort studies. *British Medical Journal* 357: j1550.

Strang J, Teodora Groshkova T, Metrebian N. (2012). *EMCDDA Insights. New Heroin-Assisted Treatment: Recent Evidence and Current Practices of Supervised Injectable Heroin Treatment in Europe and Beyond.* Lisbon: European Monitoring Center for Drugs and Addiction.

Strang J, Groshkova T, Uchtenhagen A, et al. (2015). Heroin on trial: Systematic review and meta-analysis of randomised trials of diamorphine-prescribing as treatment for refractory heroin addiction. *British Journal of Psychiatry* 207 (1): 5–14.

van Staaden MJ, Hall FS, Huber R. T (2018). The deep evolutionary roots of 'addiction'. *Journal of Mental Health and Clinical Psychology* 2(3): 8–13.

APPENDIX: ADDITIONAL CONTENT AND RESOURCES

Resources for Help Dealing with Substance Misuse

988 Suicide Prevention Lifeline: A national network of local crisis centers that provides free and confidential emotional support to people in suicidal crisis or emotional distress 24 hours a day, 7 days a week in the United States. (https://988lifeline.org)

Call a Suicide Hotline: A suicide hotline where you can find advice for yourself or someone else. The website contains an extensive list of countries and their relevant suicide hotline telephone numbers. (www.suicidestop.com/call%5Fa%5Fhotline.html)

Directory of International Mental Health Helplines: This website provides country-specific links for emergency and non-emergency advice for a wide range of mental health issues. (www.helpguide.org/find-help.htm)

Narcotics Anonymous Continuous Zoom Meeting: An international online marathon meeting of Narcotics Anonymous. (www.iommna.com)

Narcotics Anonymous World Services: You can use this website to locate helplines and websites for local groups near you who can assist you in finding a meeting. (www.na.org/meetingsearch)

"Families of people who use drugs: health and social responses": A miniguide published by the European Monitoring Centre for Drugs and Drug Addiction. (www.emcdda.europa.eu/publications/mini-guides/families-health-and-social-responses%5Fen)

Nar-Anon Family Groups: A worldwide 12-step program for friends and relatives of persons with substance use disorder. Contains information about the program as well as a meeting locator tool to help find meeting locations and times worldwide. (www.nar-anon.org)

"A single-question screening test for drug use in primary care": Paper validating the single-question screen for drug use in primary care by Saitz et al. published in the *Journal of the American Medical Association* (United States). (https://jamanetwork.com/journals/jamainternalmedicine/fullarticle/225770)

"Principles of drug addiction treatment: A research-based guide (third edition)": Covers effective treatment for persons with drug addiction, published by the United States National Institute on Drug Abuse (NIDA). (https://nida.nih.gov/sites/default/files/675-principles-of-drug-addiction-treatment-a-research-based-guide-third-edition.pdf)

National Alliance on Mental Illness (United States): A free, nationwide (United States) peer support service providing information, resource referrals, and support to people living with a mental health condition, their family members and caregivers, mental health providers and the public. It is not a crisis helpline and is only open Monday through Friday, 10 a.m.–10 p.m., Eastern Time. (https://nami.org/Home)

Substance Abuse and Mental Health Services Administration (United States): Contains contact information for suicide prevention, acute crisis intervention, substance abuse, and behavioral health treatment programs. (www.samhsa.gov)

NIDA Quick Screen (United States): Tool designed to assist clinicians serving adult patients in screening for drug use. It was adapted from the single-question screen for drug use in primary care by Saitz et al. (*Arch Intern Med* 2010;170(13): 1155–1160). (https://nida.nih.gov/sites/default/files/pdf/nmassist.pdf)

Parent-to-Parent support groups (Canada): Provide support for parents whose children (regardless of age) are struggling with addiction. (www.farcanada.org)

Wellness Together (Canada): Mental health and substance use support for people in Canada and Canadians abroad. (www.wellnesstogether.ca/en-CA)

SHARC (Self Help Addiction Resource Centre) (Australia): Provides telephone and online support, education programs, counselling, peer support groups, residential recovery, consumer representation and workforce training. (www.sharc.org.au)

Alcohol and Drug Foundation (Australia): Provides facts, resources and programs to help prevent alcohol and other drug harm in Australian communities. (https://adf.org.au)

FRANK (United Kingdom): This website is run by Public Health England and offers clear and accessible information and advice about drugs. (https://talktofrank.com)

DAN 24/7 (Wales): Wales Drug and Alcohol Helpline. (https://dan247.org.uk)

Drugs.ie (Ireland): Managed by the Health Services Executive National Social Inclusion Office, this organization offers drug and alcohol information and support. (https://drugs.ie)

Association Addictions France (France): A long-standing national organization that provides information and support. (https://addictions-france.org)
Drugcom.de (Germany): A project of the Federal Center for Health Education, this portal provides professional information and advice to those affected by drug addiction. (www.drugcom.de)

Traditional and Alternative Media Content

"The real costs of the opioid epidemic": Text for the segment on National Public Radio's (NPR, United States) October 24, 2019 broadcast of "All Things Considered," in which the financial costs of the opioid epidemic are discussed. (www.npr.org/sections/health-shots/2019/10/24/773148861/cal culating-the-real-costs-of-the-opioid-epidemic)

"How to stop the deadliest drug overdose crisis in American history": *Vox* article by German Lopez (updated last on December 21, 2017), which discusses strategies for mitigating the damage caused by the opioid epidemic. (www .vox.com/science-and-health/2017/8/1/15746780/opioid-epidemic-end)

"The case for prescription heroin": *Vox* article by German Lopez (updated last on June 12, 2017), which discusses the use of prescription heroin as a harm-reduction strategy for mitigating the damage caused by the opioid epidemic. (www.vox.com/policy-and-politics/2017/6/12/15301458/canada-prescription-heroin-opioid-addiction)

"America's war on drugs has failed. Oregon is showing a way out": *Vox* article by German Lopez (updated last on November 11, 2020), which discusses the decriminalization of drugs by referendum vote in Oregon (United States) (www.vox.com/future-perfect/21552710/oregon-drug-decriminalization-marijuana-legalization)

"Oregon just voted to decriminalize all drugs": *Vox* article by German Lopez (updated last on November 3, 2020), which discusses the specifics of Measure 110, which decriminalized drug possession for personal use. (www.vox.com /2020/11/3/21514828/oregon-drug-decriminalization-measure-110-results)

"Portugal decriminalized drugs in 2001. Barely anything changed": *Vox* article by German Lopez (updated last on June 19, 2015), which discusses the consequences 14 years after national decriminalization of drugs by Portugal in 2001. (www.vox.com/2015/6/19/8812263/portugal-drug-decriminalization)

"Needle exchanges have been proved to work against opioid addiction. They're banned in 15 states": *Vox* article by German Lopez (updated last on June 22, 2018), which discusses the stigma that remains against needle exchange programs in the United States. (www.vox.com/science-and-health/2018/6/22/17493030/needle-exchanges-ban-state-map)

"N.Y. doctor gets 2 years in prison for Insys opioid kickbacks": *Reuters* brief related to the Insys opioid kickback scheme. (www.reuters.com/article/hea lth-insys/in-brief-n-y-doctor-gets-2-years-in-prison-for-insys-opioid-kickbacks-idUSL2N27D1PC)

"N.Y. doctor seeks to avoid prison time for Insys kickbacks": Reuters story related to the Insys opioid kickback scheme. (www.reuters.com/legal/trans actional/ny-doctor-seeks-avoid-prison-time-insys-kickbacks-2021-06-08)

"Manhattan doctor sentenced to more than 17 years in prison": Press release issued by the United States Attorney for the Southern District of New York regarding the Insys opioid kickback scheme detailing the sentencing of Dr. Freedman for bribery and kickback scheme and for distributing oxy-codone and fentanyl for no legitimate medical purpose. (www.justice.gov/usao-sdny/pr/manhattan-doctor-sentenced-more-17-years-prison-bribery-and-kickback-scheme-and)

United States v. Burducea: Timeline of legal events in the prosecution of Dr. Burducea for his involvement in the Insys opioid kickback scheme. (www .courtlistener.com/docket/14915187/united-states-v-burducea)

"Manhattan doctor sentenced to nearly five years in prison for accepting bribes and kickbacks in exchange for prescribing fentanyl drug": Press release issued by the United States Attorney for the Southern District of New York regarding the Insys opioid kickback scheme detailing the sentencing of Dr. Burducea. (www.justice.gov/usao-sdny/pr/manhattan-doctor-sentenced-nearly-five-years-prison-accepting-bribes-and-kickbacks)

Inspirery interview with Alexandru Burducea: Our exclusive interview with Dr. Burducea, March 8, 2019. (https://inspirery.com/alexandru-burducea/)

"The full cost of the opioid crisis: $2.5 Trillion over four years": October 28, 2019 White House (United States) press release discussing the financial cost of the opioid epidemic. (https://trumpwhitehouse.archives.gov/articles/ful l-cost-opioid-crisis-2-5-trillion-four-years)

"Percentage of overdose deaths involving methadone declined between January 2019 and August 2021": NIDA press release regarding an investi-gation into the percentage of overdose deaths involving methadone between January 2019 and August 2021, which indicates that coronavirus (COVID)-era treatment expansion was not associated with harms, and supports take-home treatment for opioid use disorder. (https://nida.nih.gov /news-events/news-releases/2022/07/percentage-of-overdose-deaths-involving-methadone-declined-between-january-2019-august-2021)

"The opioid epidemic is a global problem": *MinnPost* opinion piece by Mark Porubcansky entitled "The opioid epidemic is a global problem. And it's getting worse." (www.minnpost.com/foreign-concept/2018/05/opioid-epidemic-global-problem-and-its-getting-worse)

"Justice Department announces global resolution of criminal and civil investigations with Purdue Pharma and members of the Sackler family": United States Department of Justice press release regarding the global resolution of criminal and civil investigations with opioid manufacturer Purdue Pharma and civil settlement with members of the Sackler family. (www.justice.gov/opa/pr/justice-department-announces-global-resolution-criminal-and-civil-investigations-opioid)

"Executions in Saudi Arabia and Iran": 2016 *Guardian* article discussing the practice of executing persons involved with drug trafficking. (www.theguardian.com/news/datablog/2016/jan/04/executions-in-saudi-arabia-iran-numbers-china)

"Breaking bad in the Middle East and North Africa – Drugs, militants, and human rights": 2016 Brookings Institute blog post discussing the increasing problem of drugs in the MENA region. (www.brookings.edu/blog/markaz/2016/03/22/breaking-bad-in-the-middle-east-and-north-africa-drugs-militants-and-human-rights)

Strategies for Harm Reduction

CDC opioid prescribing guideline resources: United States Center for Disease Control and Prevention's (CDC) opioid prescribing guidelines for chronic pain. (www.cdc.gov/opioids/healthcare-professionals/prescribing/index.html)

CDC HIV and injection drug use: CDC educational page on HIV and injection drug use. This page explains why injection drug use puts you at risk for catching HIV and how you can reduce this risk. (www.cdc.gov/hiv/basics/hiv-transmission/injection-drug-use.html?CDC_AA_refVal=https%3A%2F%2Fwww.cdc.gov%2Fhiv%2Frisk%2Fidu.html)

"Painkiller abuse treated by sustained buprenorphine/naloxone": November 8, 2011 press release from the United States National Institutes of Health (NIH) describing an investigation into the effectiveness of adding naloxone to buprenorphine treatment for opioid addiction. (www.nih.gov/news-events/news-releases/painkiller-abuse-treated-sustained-buprenorphine-naloxone)

"Methadone maintenance found to be more effective in treating heroin addiction than 180 day detoxification": March 7, 2000 press release published by the University of California, San Francisco, which discussed the study by Sharon Hall in which she compared the effectiveness of methadone maintenance therapy to methadone maintenance taper, where patients are initially placed on methadone and then slowly tapered off. (www.ucsf.edu/news/2000/03/97477/methadone-maintenance-found-be-more-effective-treating-heroin-addiction-180-day)

"New heroin-assisted treatment": European Monitoring Centre for Drugs and Drug Addiction (EMCDDA) *INSIGHTS* publication in 2012 on heroin-assisted treatment entitled "Recent evidence and current practices of supervised injectable heroin treatment in Europe and beyond." (www.emcdda.europa.eu/publications/insights/heroin-assisted-treatment_en)

"Mortality risk during and after opioid substitution treatment": 2017 *British Medical Journal* systematic review article on opioid substitution treatment. (www.bmj.com/content/357/bmj.j1550)

"Medications to treat opioid use disorder research report": NIDA explains medications treatment for opioid use disorder. (https://nida.nih.gov/publications/research-reports/medications-to-treat-opioid-addiction/overview)

"Guidelines for the psychosocially assisted pharmacological treatment of opioid dependence": A World Health Organization (WHO) publication, which reviews the use of medicines such as methadone, buprenorphine, naltrexone, and clonidine in combination with psychosocial support in the treatment of people dependent on heroin or other opioids. (www.who.int/publications/i/item/9789241547543)

"Heroin on trial": Paper published in the *British Journal of Psychiatry* on the use of supervised injectable heroin as an intensive treatment for entrenched heroin users who have not responded to standard treatments such as oral methadone maintenance treatment or residential rehabilitation. (www.cambridge.org/core/journals/the-british-journal-of-psychiatry/article/heroin-on-trial-systematic-review-and-metaanalysis-of-randomised-trials-of-diamorphineprescribing-as-treatment-for-refractory-heroin-addiction/A3C4F1D0F709099E47472B42507FF97C)

"Global patterns of opioid use and dependence: Population harms, interventions, and future action": NIH report that summarizes evidence for medicinal uses of opioids; harms related to the extra-medical use and dependence upon these drugs, and for a wide range of interventions to

address the harms related to extra-medical opioid use worldwide. (www
.ncbi.nlm.nih.gov/pmc/articles/PMC7068135/pdf/nihms-1065183.pdf)

"Opioid overdose prevention": United States Department of Health and
Human Services (HHS) information on how to prevent opioid overdoses.
(www.hhs.gov/surgeongeneral/reports-and-publications/addiction-and-
substance-misuse/opioid-overdose-prevention-resources/index.html)

"Cost-effectiveness of treatments for opioid use disorder": Article published in
the *Journal of the American Medical Association*, investigating the cost-
effectiveness of treatments for opioid use disorder. (https://jamanetwork
.com/journals/jamapsychiatry/article-abstract/2778020)

Harm Reduction International: Formerly known as International Harm Reduction
Association, a nongovernmental organization in Special Consultative Status
with the United Nations Economic and Social Council, working to support
implementation of harm-reduction strategies. (https://hri.global)

Lectures and Presentations

"Three part solution to the opioid epidemic": Slide set from Dr. Mark
Rosenberg's lecture on the three part solution to the opioid epidemic
(https://knockoutday.drugfreenj.org/wp-content/uploads/2021/05/
kooad_5_20_rosenberg.pdf)

"One year later: The opioid epidemic during COVID": Slide set for Dr. Andrew
Kolodny's lecture on the opioid epidemic during COVID. (https://knockout
day.drugfreenj.org/wp-content/uploads/2021/04/kooad_4_22_kolodny
.pdf)

"The opioid epidemic and the impact on New Jersey families": Slide set for
the February 24, 2022 lecture on the opioid epidemic's impact on families.
https://knockoutday.drugfreenj.org/wp-content/uploads/2022/02/KOO
AD_2_24_webinar.pdf

"The opioid epidemic and the impact of race": Slide set for the December 9,
2021 lecture on the opioid epidemic and the impact of race. (https://knock
outday.drugfreenj.org/wp-content/uploads/2021/12/KOOAD_12_9_webin
ar.pdf)

Knock Out Opioid Abuse Day Webinars: Archived lectures sponsored by "Knock
Out Opioid Abuse Day" (https://knockoutday.drugfreenj.org/webinars)

"The perfect storm: COVID-19's impact on addiction over the past year": Slide
set for the March 18, 2021 panel discussion on COVID-19's impact on
addiction (https://knockoutday.drugfreenj.org/wp-content/uploads/2021/
03/KOOAD_3_18_webinar.pdf)

Rutgers Interdisciplinary Opioid Trainers (RIOT) presentation: Slide set for the December 19, 2019 Rutgers University (New Jersey, United States) RIOT presentation on addressing the opioid epidemic: A primer on opioid addiction, overdose, management and medication assisted treatment. (https://knockoutopioidabuse.drugfreenj.org/wp-content/uploads/2020/10/RIOT_Community_Presentation_print.pdf)

"Where we stand & how we move forward": Slide set for Dr. Andrew Kolodny's October 6, 2022 lecture. (https://knockoutday.drugfreenj.org/wp-content/uploads/2022/10/KOOAD_10_6_webinar.pdf)

Organizational Reports

2022 European drug report: EMCDDA report, which discusses the latest data about trends in drug use and the market, emerging new hazardous drugs and which substances are posing the greatest health threats. (www.emcdda.europa.eu/publications/edr/trends-developments/2022_en)

"The history of the poppy and of opium and their expansion in antiquity in the eastern Mediterranean area": Paper published by the United Nations Office on Drugs and Crime (UNDOC). (www.unodc.org/unodc/en/data-and-analysis/bulletin/bulletin_1967-01-01_3_page004.html)

"The economic costs of the opioid epidemic": September 04, 2019 report by Kaitlyn Hoevelmann of the St. Louis Federal Reserve Bank (United States) on the the economic costs of the opioid epidemic. (www.stlouisfed.org/open-vault/2019/september/economic-costs-opioid-epidemic#:~:text=One%20indirect%20cost%20of%20the,indirect%20cost%20is%20future%20productivity).

"Opioids and the labor market": March 1, 2019 White Paper from the Federal Reserve Bank of Cleveland (WP 1807 R) on opioids and the labor market. (www.clevelandfed.org/publications/working-paper/2019/wp-1807r-opioids-and-labor-market)

"The high price of the opioid crisis": August 2021 Pew Charitable Trusts report on the high price of the opioid crisis. (www.pewtrusts.org/en/research-and-analysis/data-visualizations/2021/the-high-price-of-the-opioid-crisis-2021)

"Financial impact of the opioid epidemic on the US economy": October 16, 2019 American Hospital Association (United States) report on the cost of the opioid epidemic between 2015 and 2018. (www.aha.org/news/headline/2019-10-16-report-opioid-crisis-cost-us-economy-631b-2015-2018)

"Economic and social consequences of drug abuse and illegal trafficking":
1996 United Nations report on the economic and social consequences of
drug abuse and illegal trafficking. (www.unodc.org/pdf/technical_ser
ies_1998-01-01_1.pdf)

"Report on people who inject drugs in the South-East Asia region": WHO
Regional Office for South-East Asia 2010 report on people who inject drugs
in the South-East Asia region. (https://apps.who.int/iris/handle/10665/206
320?locale-attribute=pt&)

"WHO 2020 report from the expert committee on drug dependence": WHO
2020 technical report from the Expert Committee on Drug Dependence.
(https://apps.who.int/iris/bitstream/handle/10665/331486/97892400018
48-eng.pdf)

"The practices and context of pharmacotherapy of opioid dependence in
South-East Asia and Western Pacific regions": WHO 2002 report on the
practices and context of pharmacotherapy of opioid dependence in South-
East Asia and Western Pacific regions. (www.who.int/publications/i/item/
the-practices-and-context-of-pharmacotherapy-of-opioid-dependence-in-
south-east-asia-and-western-pacific-regions)

"OAS report on drug use in the Americas 2019": The Organization of American
States (OAS) 2019 report on drug use in the Americas. (www.cicad.oas.org
/main/pubs/Report%20on%20Drug%20Use%20in%20the%20Americas%
202019.pdf)

"ATLAS on substance use: Resources for the prevention and treatment of
substance use disorders": WHO 2010 report on resources for the prevention
and treatment of substance use disorders. (https://apps.who.int/iris/bit
stream/handle/10665/44455/9789241500616_eng.pdf?sequence=1)

"More imprisonment does not reduce state drug problems": March 8, 2018 Pew
Charitable Trusts report on the relationship between prison terms and drug
misuse. (www.pewtrusts.org/en/research-and-analysis/issue-briefs/2018/0
3/more-imprisonment-does-not-reduce-state-drug-problems)

"The Federal prison population buildup: Overview, policy changes, issues and
options": April 15, 2014 report by Nathan James describing the effect of
anti-drug policies during the war on drugs which resulted in significantly
increasing the federal prison population in the United States. (https://i
a601308.us.archive.org/7/items/R42937TheFederalPrisonPopulationBuild
upOverviewPolicyChangesIssuesandOptions-crs/R42937%20The%20Feder
al%20Prison%20Population%20Buildup_%20Overview%2C%20Policy%2
0Changes%2C%20Issues%2C%20and%20Options.pdf)

"Drug laws in West Africa": November 2017 briefing paper published by the
West Africa Commission on Drugs (WACD) and the International Drug

Policy Consortium (IDPC). (https://idpc.net/publications/2017/11/drug-laws-in-west-africa-a-review-and-summary)

"The evolution of illicit drug markets and drug policy in Africa": ENACT-sponsored continental report on transnational organized crime and the drug trade in Africa, June 2019. (https://globalinitiative.net/wp-content/uploads/2019/07/2019-06-30-continental-report-3-3.pdf)

"Drug control policies in Eastern Europe and Central Asia": 2021 *Economist* report on drug control policies in Eastern Europe and Central Asia. (https://impact.economist.com/perspectives/perspectives/sites/default/files/eiu_aph_investing_hiv_launch.pdf)

"Monitoring the future": NIDA 2020 report. This yearly survey of high school students in the United States investigates adolescent drug use trends. (https://nida.nih.gov/research-topics/trends-statistics/monitoring-future)

National Center for Health Statistics Data Visualization Gallery: CDC dashboard which presents drug poisoning deaths at the national, state, and county levels. US and state trends in age-adjusted death rates are depicted for drug poisoning by selected demographic characteristics, and a series of heat maps of model-based county estimates for drug poisoning mortality. (www.cdc.gov/nchs/data-visualization/drug-poisoning-mortality)

"UNODC world drug report 2022": Report that discusses worldwide changing trends and developing concerns. (www.unodc.org/res/wdr2022/MS/WDR22_Booklet_1.pdf)

The Opioid Epidemic in Specific Populations

"The drug war at 100": Blog post discussing the last century of the war on drugs by Stanford Law School Professor George Fisher. (https://law.stanford.edu/2014/12/19/the-drug-war-at-100)

"World opioid and substance use epidemic: A Latin American perspective": Paper on the Latin American experience with the global opioid epidemic. (https://prcp.psychiatryonline.org/doi/epub/10.1176/appi.prcp.20180009)

"Socio-economic Impact on opioid addiction susceptibility": Article on the socio-economic impact on opioid addiction susceptibility. (https://edelweispublications.com/articles/22/220/Socio-Economic-Impact-On-Opioid-Addiction-Susceptibility)

"The ripple effect: Estimates of the opioid epidemic's impact on children": United Hospital Fund November 2019 report on national and state estimates of the US opioid epidemic's impact on children in the United States. (https://uhfnyc

.org/media/filer_public/6e/80/6e80760f-d579-46a3-998d-1aa816ab06f6/uh
f_ripple_effect_national_and_state_estimates_chartbook.pdf)

"Global patterns of opioid use and dependence: Population harms, interventions, and future action": 2019 Publication on global patterns of opioid use and dependence. (www.ncbi.nlm.nih.gov/pmc/articles/PMC7068135/pdf/nihms-1065183.pdf)

"Drug use and HIV in Asia": 2007 WHO's participant manual for the course on drug use and HIV in Asia. (https://apps.who.int/iris/bitstream/handle/106 65/206034/B1485.pdf?sequence=1)

Substance abuse (Africa): WHO Regional Office for Africa page on substance abuse. (www.afro.who.int/health-topics/substance-abuse)

Substance abuse (Eastern Mediterranean): WHO Regional Office for Eastern Mediterranean page on substance abuse. (www.emro.who.int/health-topics /substance-abuse/feed/rss.html)

"The opioid epidemic in Africa and its impact": Article published on the opioid epidemic in Africa. (www.ncbi.nlm.nih.gov/pmc/articles/PMC7269163)

Miscellaneous Related Topics

Insys Kickback Scheme Indictment: (72-page indictment handed down by the United States in the Southern District of New York regarding physician participation in the Insys opioid kickback scheme. (www.justice.gov/usao-sdny/press-release/file/1044111/download)

United States v. Burducea forfeiture order: Text of the preliminary order of forfeiture money judgment against one of the conspirators involved in the Insys opioid kickback scheme. (www.leagle.com/decision/infdco20200818660)

Burducea consent order: Consent order revoking Dr. Burducea's New Jersey (United States) medical license. (www.nj.gov/oag/newsreleases20/Burduce a-Consent-Order.pdf)

"Economic and social consequences of drug abuse and illegal trafficking": 1996 United Nations report on the economic and social consequences of drug abuse and illegal trafficking. (www.unodc.org/pdf/technical_ser ies_1998-01-01_1.pdf)

Xchange Prevention Registry: Database of prevention interventions. (www .emcdda.europa.eu/best-practice/xchange_en)

Substance Use Disorder Prevention that Promotes Opioid Recovery and Treatment for Patients and Communities Act. Passed by Congress in 2018, this bill addresses strategies to prevent opioid misuse and increase availability of treatment. (www.congress.gov/bill/115th-congress/house-bill/6)

INDEX